SEEKING CHANGES

The Economic Development in Contemporary China

SEEKING CHANGES

The Economic Development in Contemporary China

Yanhui Zhou
Central Compilation and Translation Bureau

World Scientific

中央编译出版社
CCTP
Central Compilation & Translation Press

Published by

World Scientific Publishing Co. Pte. Ltd.

5 Toh Tuck Link, Singapore 596224

USA office: 27 Warren Street, Suite 401-402, Hackensack, NJ 07601

UK office: 57 Shelton Street, Covent Garden, London WC2H 9HE

and

Central Compilation and Translation Press
Room 302B, Part B Hongru Building
#B-5 Chegongzhuang Street Xicheng District
Beijing 100044, China

Library of Congress Cataloging-in-Publication Data
Names: Zhou, Yanhui, editor.
Title: Seeking changes : the economic development in contemporary China / Zhou Yanhui.
Description: New Jersey : World Scientific Publishing Co., [2016]
Identifiers: LCCN 2015034672 | ISBN 9789814651974
Subjects: LCSH: Economic development--China. | China--Economic policy--2000– |
China--Economic conditions--2000– | China--Foreign economic relations.
Classification: LCC HC427.95 .S355 2016 | DDC 338.951--dc23
LC record available at http://lccn.loc.gov/2015034672

British Library Cataloguing-in-Publication Data
A catalogue record for this book is available from the British Library.

This edition is jointly published by World Scientific Publishing Co. Pte. Ltd. and Central Compilation and Translation Press. This edition is distributed worldwide by World Scientific Publishing Co. Pte. Ltd., except China.

Typeset by Central Compilation and Translation Press

Printed in China

Preface

The reform and opening-up does not only change the process of Chinese history, but also change the process of world history greatly. Today, what is indisputable is that the rise of China has become one of the most important factors affecting the pattern of the world.

The world has seen the results of China's economic reform, and also wants to know the process of China's reform.

Since the reform and opening-up, maintaining a sustained and rapid economic development has been the focus of the Chinese government's work. And this issue is also of concern to the theoretical circles of the world. In recent years, more and more western scholars have studied and discussed the issue from different aspects. Just like the old Chinese saying "A bystander is always clear-minded." It may be more comprehensive and objective to see China's economic reform from another view.

This book is a collection of representative research by foreign scholars on the economic development of China. Its topics cover the road of China's economic development, the mode of the country's economic growth, the issue of poverty, environmental and food supply safety, energy, etc. This book analyzes the problems China is now facing and will possibly encounter in the future, and suggests how China can continue down a healthy track of economic and sustainable development. This book provides significant perspectives on China's continued reform of its economic system.

Contents

The Myth Behind China's Miracle

George J. Gilboy[1]

■ The Phantom Menace

China's sudden rise as a global trading power has been greeted with a curious mixture of both admiration and fear. Irrational exuberance about the country's economic future has prompted investors to gobble up shares of Chinese firms with little understanding of how these companies actually operate. Meanwhile, overestimates of China's achievements and potential are fueling fears that the country will inevitably tilt global trade and technology balances in its favor, ultimately becoming an economic, technological, and military threat to the United States. These reactions, however, are equally mistaken: they overlook both important weaknesses in China's economic "miracle" and the strategic benefits the United States is reaping from the particular way in which China has joined the global

[1] George J. Gilboy is a senior manager at a major multinational firm in Beijing, where he has been working since 1995, and a research affiliate at the Center for International Studies at the Massachusetts Institute of Technology.

economy. Such misjudgments could drive Washington to adopt protectionist policies that would reverse recent improvements in U.S.-China relations, further alienate Washington from its allies, and diminish U.S. influence in Asia.

In fact, the United States and China are developing precisely the type of economic relationship that U.S. strategy has long sought to create. China now has a stake in the liberal, rules-based global economic system that the United States worked to establish over the past half-century. Beijing has opened its economy to foreign direct investment (FDI), welcomed large-scale imports, and joined the World Trade Organization (WTO), spurring prosperity and liberalization within China and across the region.

China's own choices along the road to global economic integration have reinforced trends that favor the continued industrial and technological preeminence of the United States and other advanced industrialized democracies. In its forced march to the market, Beijing has let political and social reforms lag behind, with at least two critical—and unexpected—consequences. First, to forestall the rise of a politically independent private sector, the Chinese government has implemented economic reforms that strongly favor state-owned enterprises (SOES), granting them preferential access to capital, technology, and markets. But reforms have also favored foreign investment, which has allowed foreign firms to claim the lion's share of China's industrial exports and secure strong positions in its domestic markets. As a result, Chinese industry is left with inefficient but still powerful SOES, increasingly dominant foreign firms, and a private sector as yet unable to compete with either on equal terms.

Second, the business risks inherent in China's unreformed political system have bred a response among many Chinese managers—an "industrial strategic culture"—that encourages them to seek short-term profits, local autonomy, and excessive diversification. With a few exceptions, Chinese firms focus on developing privileged relations with officials in the Chinese Communist Party (CCP) hierarchy, spurn horizontal association and broad networking with each other, and forgo investment in long-term technology development and diffusion. Chinese firms continue to rely heavily on imported foreign technology and components—severely limiting the country's ability to wield technological or trading power for unilateral gains.

China, in other words, has joined the global economy on terms that reinforce its dependence on foreign technology and investment and restrict its ability to become an industrial and technological threat to advanced industrialized democracies. China's best hope for overcoming its technological and economic weaknesses lies in a renewed focus on domestic political reform. Thus, rather than lapse into shortsighted trade protectionism that could undermine current favorable trends, Washington should pursue a policy of "strategic engagement." Not simply engagement for its own sake, strategic engagement would explicitly acknowledge the advantages of U.S. technological, economic, and military leadership and seek to reinforce them, in exchange for increased prosperity and more security for China—the more so now that China has a compelling economic interest in domestic political reform.

■ Open and Opening

Recent debates about U.S.-China trade overlook the fact that the U.S. economic relationship with China is largely favorable and that it is conducted largely on U.S. terms. In particular, the focus on China's currency as a source of unfair trade advantage is misplaced, as economists Jonathan Anderson of UBS and Nicholas Lardy and Morris Goldstein of the Institute for International Economics have shown. Even a moderate appreciation of the Yuan would make little difference to most U.S. firms and workers. Meanwhile, the currency issue obscures the significant economic and strategic benefits the United States now enjoys in its relations with China.

According to Morgan Stanley, low-cost Chinese imports (mainly textiles, shoes, toys, and household goods) have saved U.S. consumers (mostly middle- and low-income families) about $100 billion dollars since China's reforms began in 1978. (Cheaper baby clothes from China helped

U.S. families with children save about $400 million between 1998 and 2003.) U.S. industrial firms such as Boeing, Ford, General Motors, IBM, Intel, and Motorola also save hundreds of millions of dollars each year by buying parts from lower-cost countries such as China, increasing their global competitiveness and allowing them to undertake new high-value activities in the United States. In an effort to save 30 percent on its total global sourcing costs, Ford imported about $500 million in parts from China in 2003. General Motors has cut the cost of car radios by 40 percent by building them from Chinese parts. And although global sourcing can cause painful employment adjustments, the process can also benefit U.S. workers and companies. A recent independent study sponsored by the Information Technology Association of America found that outsourcing to countries such as China and India created a net 90,000 new U.S. jobs in information technology in 2003 and estimated that outsourcing will create a net 317,000 new U.S. jobs by 2008.

China is not just an exporter; it imports more than any other state in northeastern Asia. Although it had a $124 billion trade surplus with the United States in 2003, it had significant trade deficits with many other countries and areas: $15 billion with Japan, $23 billion with South Korea, $40 billion with Taiwan region, and $16 billion with the members of the Association of Southeast Asian Nations (ASEAN). Most significantly, China is a large and growing market for domestically consumed imports (ordinary trade that excludes imported goods that are processed and reexported). Chinese imports for domestic consumption rose to $187 billion in 2003, from $40 billion in the mid-1990s. Discounting the processing and reexport trade, China ran a $5 billion trade deficit in 2003, compared to a $20 billion surplus just five years earlier. In industries it classifies as "high tech," including electronic goods, components, and manufacturing equipment, China has averaged a $12 billion annual deficit for the last decade.

Unlike other U.S. trading partners in Asia, such as Japan and South Korea, which spurned U.S. imports and investment for decades, China is also a large, open market for U.S. products. Although total U.S. exports have stagnated in recent years, U.S. exports to China have tripled in the last decade. They increased by 28 percent in 2003 alone (whereas overall U.S. exports went up by only 5 percent). In particular, China has become a staple market for advanced U.S. technology products. According to U.S. government data, U.S. aerospace exports to China were valued at more than $2 billion in 2003—about 5 percent of total U.S. aerospace exports and nearly as much as comparable exports to Germany. U.S. firms exported $500 million of advanced manufacturing equipment to China in 2003, more than they exported to France. And U.S. chip makers exported $2.4 billion of semiconductors to China in 2003, the same amount they exported to Japan.

Furthermore, China allows foreign firms to invest in its domestic market on a scale unprecedented in Asia. Since it launched reforms in 1978, China has taken in $500 billion in FDI, ten times the total stock of FDI Japan accumulated between 1945 and 2000. According to China's Ministry of Commerce, U.S. firms have invested more than $40 billion in more than 40,000 projects in China. Given its openness to FDI, China cannot maintain its domestic market as a protected bastion for domestic firms, something both Japan and South Korea did during their periods of rapid growth. Instead, it has allowed U.S. and other foreign firms to develop new markets for their goods and services, especially high-value-added products such as aircraft, software, industrial design, advanced machinery, and components such as semiconductors and integrated circuits.

Thanks to this appetite for imports, powerful domestic coalitions, particularly China's growing ranks of urban consumers and its most competitive firms, will continue to favor trade openness. Chinese consumers pride themselves on driving foreign-brand cars and using mobile phones and computers with circuits that were designed and manufactured abroad. Many Chinese firms resist protectionism, because they need to import critical components for their domestic operations and fear retaliation against their exports. For example, in the 1990s, China's machine tool and aircraft industries failed to secure effective state protection in the face of opposition from domestic firms that preferred imports, and they suffered significant decline as a result.

As an open economy and a large importing country, China could be an ally of the United States in many areas of global trade and finance. Already, Beijing has displayed a willingness to play by WTO rules. It has charged Japan and South Korea with unfair trade practices—markets the United States has also long sought to crack open. China initiated 10 antidumping investigations in 2002 on products with import value of more than $7 billion, and another 20 investigations in 2003. China is now a leading promoter of regional trade and investment regimes, including a free trade zone with ASEAN and a bilateral free trade agreement with Australia, one of the United States' closest allies in the Pacific region. Already, Beijing's proposals on regional economic cooperation seem far more relevant to most Asian nations than do Washington's.

The final benefit the United States enjoys from China's global economic integration is in the long-term, patient battle to promote liberalism in Asia. Foreign trade and development have spurred advancements in Chinese commercial law, greater regulatory consultation with Chinese consumers, slimmed-down bureaucracies, and adherence to international safety and environmental standards. Although it is still limited, the people's freedom to debate economic and social issues has increased, especially in the robust financial media. This process of liberalization is incomplete and uneven, but it is in the interest of both China and the United States to see it continue.

■ Outside in

Despite these benefits, business and political leaders in the United States now fear that China's growing share of world exports, especially of high technology and industrial goods, signals the rise of yet another mercantilist economic superpower in northeastern Asia. But these concerns are unwarranted, for three reasons. First, China's high-tech and industrial exports are dominated by foreign firms, not Chinese firms. Second, Chinese industrial firms are deeply dependent on designs, critical components, and manufacturing equipment they import from the United States and other advanced industrialized democracies. Third, Chinese firms are taking few effective steps to absorb the technology they import and diffuse it throughout the local economy, making it unlikely that they will rapidly emerge as global industrial competitors.

A close look at the breakdown of China's exports by type of producing firm puts China's economic rise in perspective. Foreign-funded enterprises (FFES) accounted for 55 percent of China's exports in 2003. In this respect, China diverges from the typical Asian success story. According to Huang Yasheng of the Massachusetts Institute of Technology, FFES accounted for only 20 percent of Taiwan region's manufactured exports in the mid-1970s and only 25 percent of South Korea's manufactured exports between 1974 and 1978. In Thailand, the FEES' share dropped from 18 percent in the 1970s to 6 percent by the mid-1980s.

The dominance of foreign firms in China is even more apparent in advanced industrial exports. While exports of industrial machinery grew twenty-fold in real terms over the last decade (to $83 billion in 2003), the share of those exports produced by FFES grew from 35 percent to 79 percent. Exports of computer equipment shot from $716 million in 1993 to $41 billion in 2003, with the FFES' share rising from 74 percent to 92 percent. Likewise, China's electronics and telecom exports have grown sevenfold since 1993 (to $89 billion in 2003), with the FFES' share of those exports growing from 45 percent to 74 percent over the same period. This pattern repeats itself in almost every advanced industrial sector in China.

The data highlight another trend that reinforces China's dependence on foreign investment and the growing gap between FFES and domestic Chinese companies. In the 1990s, Beijing permitted a new FDI trend to develop: a shift away from joint ventures and toward wholly owned foreign enterprises (WOFES). Today, WOFES account for 65 percent of new FDI in China, and they dominate high-tech exports.

But they are much less inclined to transfer technology to Chinese firms than are joint ventures. Unlike joint ventures, they are not contractually required to share knowledge with local partners. And they have strong incentives to protect their technology from both domestic and other foreign firms, in order to capture a greater share of China's domestic markets. As a result, according to the most recent Chinese government statistics for high-tech industries (pharmaceuticals, aircraft and aerospace, electronics, telecommunications, computers, and medical equipment), FFES increased their total share of high-tech exports from 74 percent to 85 percent between 1998 and 2002. But perhaps more significant, in the same period, they increased their share of total domestic high-tech sales from 32 percent to 45 percent, while the share of that market held by China's most competitive industrial firms, SOES, fell from 47 percent to 42 percent.

Finally, the data reveal that China's private firms are not yet significant global players. Despite more than two decades of economic reform, China's leading domestic industrial and technology companies are still primarily SOES. Although they remain inefficient and dependent on government-subsidized loans, they account for the bulk of advanced industrial production in China, boast the country's best research and development (R&D) capability, and spend the most resources to develop and import technology. Their preferential access to markets and resources has blocked the rise of private industrial firms. Likewise, collective firms owned by provincial and local governments have failed to emerge as major players in China's advanced industrial and technology sectors.

■ Particular and Exceptional

One of the key reasons that state, collective, and private firms in China lag behind FFES is that they have failed to invest in the type of long-term technological capabilities that their Japanese, South Korean, and Taiwanese predecessors built during the 1970s and 1980s.

Developing technology is a difficult and uncertain process. Neither large capital investments nor a significant stock of existing science and engineering capability can guarantee success. To create commercially viable products and services, firms must monitor and access new forms of knowledge, understand evolving market trends, and respond rapidly to changing customer demand. Firms that can develop strong links to research institutions, financiers, partners, suppliers, and customers have an advantage in acquiring, modifying, and then commercializing new technology. Such horizontal networks are essential conduits for knowledge, capital, products, and talent.

Yet China's unreformed political system suppresses such independent social organization and horizontal networking and instead reinforces vertical relationships. China remains a fragmented federal system, its fractious regions unified by a single political party. The CCP controls all aspects of organized life, including industry associations, leaving few avenues for firms to work together for legitimate common interests. This structure drives business leaders to focus on building relationships through CCP officials and the bureaucracy. Although market reforms have brought more rules to the Chinese economy, without institutional checks and balances or direct supervision, CCP officials still exercise wide discretion in defining and implementing those rules, especially at the local level. They can, and often do, manipulate economic policies to pursue particular local goals. Some engage in this "particularism" because they are corrupt, others because they directly own or operate firms. Most, however, do it because the political elite encourages them to: understand that local economic growth promotes social and political order, the CCP tolerates, and even rewards, officials who use any means to produce local investment and employment. But this often results in fragmented national industries and wasteful overlapping investment.

Chinese business leaders in both public and private firms recognize that an economy dominated by particularism is a risky business environment. Markets are fragmented; rules constantly shift under manipulation by government officials; and political obstacles prevent firms from associating, sharing risk, and taking collective action. To cope with these uncertainties, Chinese business has developed a distinctive industrial strategic culture over the past two decades—a set of values or guidelines about what strategies "work" in this environment. First, in response to the "particular" application of policy, Chinese firms routinely focus on obtaining "exceptional" treatment from key officials: special access to markets or resources, exemptions from rules and regulations, or protection against predation by other officials. Second, to maximize these exceptional benefits, as well as to avoid entanglements with other firms and their patrons, many Chinese companies shun collaboration within their industry, especially if such collaboration crosses regional or bureaucratic boundaries. Third, they generally favor short-term gains over long-term investments. Finally, Chinese firms tend to engage in excessive diversification in order to mitigate the potential damage of fratricidal price competition created by excess production capacity and overlapping investments.

■ Nodes Without Roads

This industrial strategic culture is rational and effective given the current structure of politics and business environment in China. (These features echo patterns of interaction between authoritarian officialdom and merchant enterprise that were established in China's first period of industrialization in the Qing dynasty 150 years ago.) But China's industrial strategic culture weakens the competitiveness of Chinese firms and it may have damaging economic repercussions down the road. Most Chinese industrial firms focus on short-term gains and, despite increasing operational efficiency, sales revenues, and profits, have not increased their commitment to developing new technologies. Their total spending on R&D as a percentage of sales revenue has remained below one percent for more than a decade. R&D intensity (R&D expenditure as a percentage of value added) at China's industrial firms is only about one percent, seven times less than the average in countries of the Organization for Economic Cooperation and Development (OECD).

Focusing on short-term returns has also guided China's imports of industrial technology. Chinese firms tend to import technology by purchasing foreign manufacturing equipment, often in complete sets such as assembly lines. Throughout the 1980s and 1990s, hardware accounted for more than 50 percent of China's technology imports, whereas licensing, "know-how" services, and consulting accounted for about 9 percent, 5 percent, and 3 percent, respectively.

Although China has recently begun importing more "soft technology"—mainly in the form of licenses for the use of imported equipment—the knowledge embodied in it must be absorbed and mastered (or, in technology parlance, "indigenized") before it can become an effective basis for domestic innovation. Chinese firms remain weak in this regard. Over the last decade, large and medium-sized Chinese industrial firms have spent less than 10 percent of the total cost of imported equipment on indigenizing technology. Indigenization spending at state firms in the sectors in which China is most often cited as a rising power (telecom equipment, electronics, and industrial machinery) is also low (at 8 percent, 6 percent, and 2 percent of the cost of imported equipment, respectively). This is far lower than the average for industrial firms in OECD countries, which amounts to about one-third of total technology import spending. The practice of Chinese firms also stands in contrast to spending patterns in Asian countries such as South Korea and Japan in the 1970s and 1980s, when they were trying to catch up with the West. Industrial firms in those countries spent between two and three times the purchase price of foreign equipment on absorbing and indigenizing the technology embodied in the hardware.

Chinese firms have also failed to develop strong domestic technology supply networks. In 2002, Chinese firms devoted less than one percent of their total science and technology budgets (which include technology imports, renovation of existing equipment, and R&D) to purchasing domestic technology. China's best firms are among the least connected to domestic suppliers: for every $100 that state-owned electronics and telecom firms spend on technology imports, they spend only $1.20 on similar domestic goods. Thus Chinese technology suppliers do not enjoy a strong "demand pull" from the best domestic firms to stimulate their own innovative capabilities; they are relegated primarily to serving rural enterprises and less competitive state-owned enterprises. And because FFES use their investments in China as technology "snakeheads" (a Chinese term for portals), through which they bring product designs, advanced manufacturing equipment, and high-value components from foreign firms or their China subsidiaries, they too are poorly linked to Chinese domestic technology markets.

Industrial collaboration and horizontal networking are also rare, prompting Chinese firms to run their R&D projects in relative isolation. In the most recent national R&D census in 2000, Chinese industrial firms reported that they spent 93 percent of their $2.7 billion total R&D outlay in-house, but only 2 percent on collaborative activities with universities and less than 1 percent on projects with other domestic firms. China's research institutes are increasingly insular, too, especially since market reforms have forced them to commercialize their operations. In 2000, only 38 of China's 292 national industrial research institutes devoted more than one-third of total activities to collaborative projects, even though these institutes are specifically tasked with diffusing technology. Instead, many are becoming competitors of the firms they are supposed to serve. A 2003 World Bank report found that many Chinese engineering research centers have been mass-producing and marketing the products of their research for their own financial gain, rather than diffusing these technologies through patents.

Failed collaborations have also plagued China's attempts to commercialize domestic innovations. Julong Technologies, the firm that developed China's first digital telecom switching equipment, is no longer a major telecom-equipment player due to conflicts among its research, production, and marketing arms, which came under the influence of competing political officials. China's homegrown mobile telephone standard, TD-SCDMA, has received central government support, but thus far none of China's major telecommunications operators have agreed to commit to it, preferring a foreign standard, WCDMA, instead.

Given the political perils of challenging competitors and their local patrons, few Chinese firms develop alliances with or invest in companies in other provinces. One recent survey of 800 companies that have conducted domestic mergers and acquisitions found that 86 percent of them invested in firms within their own city and 91 percent invested in firms within their own province. Strong local political ties tend to isolate a region from the rest of the economy, which helps explain why Chinese firms are often small and the country's industries fragmented. For example, a recent study performed for the State Council (China's cabinet) revealed that Chinese managers regard the country's two most politically powerful technology and industrial hubs, Beijing and Shanghai, as leading centers of local protectionism in China. Among the industries most affected by such protectionism were pharmaceuticals, electrical machinery, electronics goods, and transport equipment. SOES and private firms suffered the most, FFES the least—which suggests that the burden of particularism falls most heavily on Chinese firms.

To avoid the difficulties of developing interregional supply chains while securing short-term profits, Chinese firms tend to engage in excessive diversification—also with damaging results. Many of China's most famous firms have made unsuccessful forays into ancillary businesses: Haier (from household appliances into computers, mobile phones, and televisions), Fangzheng (from computers into tea, steel, software, and financial services), and Shougang (from steel into banking, auto assembly, and semiconductors). Huawei, China's best technology firm and maker of network equipment, has recently made a questionable entry into the mobile-handset market, where sales prices and margins have fallen dramatically for the last five years and 37 licensed vendors produced excess inventories of 20 million phones in 2003.

Together, China's institutions and the industrial choices of local firms have restricted the ability of Chinese firms to develop new products and services. The share of total sales revenues accounted for by new products at Chinese industrial firms was flat, at about 10 percent, throughout the 1990s. (In contrast, new products account for 35 percent to 40 percent of sales revenue for industrial firms in OECD countries. Chinese firms lag behind firms in other developing countries as well: in 2000, for example, new products accounted for about 40 percent of total sales revenues in Brazil's electrical machinery industry.) And because of overlapping investments, fragmentation, and the weakness of industry associations, even those firms in China that make new products often find themselves engaged in vicious price competition, which prevents them from reaping high returns from their innovations.

Rather than thinking of China as yet another Asian technological and economic "giant," it may be more useful to regard it, like Brazil or India, as a "normal" emerging industrial power. Thanks to the interaction of political structure and industrial culture, China's twenty first-century technological and economic landscape looks like a pattern of "nodes without roads"—a few poorly connected centers of technological success. Burdened by these peculiarities, China has yet to lay the domestic institutional foundations for becoming a technological and economic superpower. Without structural political reforms, its ability to indigenize, develop, and diffuse technology will remain limited. And most of its industrial firms will struggle to realize exiguous margins at the lower reaches of global industrial production chains.

■ Strategic Engagement

Given these limits on China's potential to threaten the global balance of economic power, the United States should resist the false promise of protectionism, whether in the form adopted by the Bush administration (rhetorical jabs at the Chinese currency peg) or that recommended by the AFL-CIO labor federation (calls for tariff protection in the guise of better rights for Chinese workers).

Rather, recognizing both the challenges and the opportunities presented by China's industrial landscape, Washington should pursue a policy of strategic engagement with Beijing. The purpose of this policy would be to bolster U.S. technological, economic, and political leadership, while helping China become more prosperous, stable, and integrated into global economic networks. Pursuing it will require simultaneously strengthening the basis for U.S. technological and manufacturing mastery in the United States and promoting U.S. exports, investment, and liberal values abroad.

The United States should revitalize manufacturing at home, for example. Tax cuts are no panacea; the United States needs focused policies to strengthen R&D, reduce legal and health care costs, and improve education. Innovation is critical to growth, but R&D spending in the United States has declined in relative terms from 60 percent of world R&D in the 1960s to 30 percent today. Meanwhile, although U.S. manufacturing productivity has risen by 27 percent in the last five years, health care premiums have risen by

34 percent and litigation costs by about 33 percent, according to the National Association of Manufacturers.

To maintain its lead abroad, the United States should push its products into the portal opened by its investment "snakeheads" in developing markets. It currently lags behind competitors in doing so: while Japan and the EU exported \$79 billion and \$49 billion in goods to China in 2003, the United States exported only \$37 billion. Both the U.S. government and U.S. industry must do more to help small and medium-sized U.S. firms reach out to China's markets.

The United States must accept that China is a work in progress and cannot yet meet all of the standards common in advanced industrialized economies. But focused bilateral sanctions, WTO complaints, and multilateral diplomacy should be vigorously pursued if China undertakes unfair trade practices that challenge core U.S. interests. The United States should prioritize carefully, however, focusing on the issues that pose the greatest threats and present the greatest opportunities. These include China's recent attempts to impose technical standards on foreign firms in China, such as for DVD players, wireless communications, and mobile telephones, or to tax imported goods such as integrated circuits (a policy tantamount to a domestic subsidy and prohibited by WTO rules). Washington should also urge Beijing to curb investments in excess manufacturing capacity, as they could threaten key industries such as automobiles and semiconductors.

Continued engagement of this kind will help the United States consolidate the benefits it already reaps from the current relationship, ensure China's continued prosperity and stability, and encourage China to play by global rules. Working with its allies to further incorporate China's economy in international trade and industrial networks, the United States can reinforce the technological leadership of the advanced industrialized democracies, while diminishing the scope for Chinese technological and economic mercantilism.

The paradox of China's technological and economic power is that China must implement structural political reforms, not simply freer markets or greater investment, before it can unlock its potential as a global competitor.

But if it were to undertake such reforms, it would likely discover even greater common interests with the United States and other industrialized democracies. Pursuing strategic engagement is thus a way for the United States to hedge its bets: to preserve its competitive edge while encouraging China to continue developing its economy and liberalizing its politics. Chinese political reform is in the long-term interest of both Beijing and Washington. Unfortunately, the burden of a long history of fragmentation and authoritarian rule weighs heavily against China's successfully completing this final modernization.

China at the Crossroads

Peter Nolan[1]

■ Introduction

Since the late 1970s, China has enjoyed one of the most remarkable periods of economic growth ever seen. However, the country faces deep economic, political and social challenges. These include the vast extent of poverty and rapidly growing inequality; the challenge for Chinese businesses from the global business revolution; a deeply degraded natural environment; declining capabilities of the state; a comprehensive challenge in international relations; widespread corruption; and extreme dangers in engaging closely with the global financial system. The Chinese leadership is trying to deal simultaneously with the challenges of globalisation, transition and development. No country has ever faced such a set of challenges. There are no textbooks to guide China along this path. The responsibilities for the leadership are massive, because the price of failure is so huge. The possibility of social and political disintegration is real. Every effort of policy has to be directed towards

---

1 Peter Nolan is the Sinyi Professor of Chinese Management at the University of Cambridge and Chair of the university's Development Studies Committee.

avoiding this potentially catastrophic outcome. In their search for a way forward, China's leaders are looking to the lessons from the country's own past, as well as to those from other countries, in order to find a way to build a socially just, stable, cohesive and prosperous society. This effort is of vital importance, not only for China, but also for the whole world.

■ Challenges to China's Economic and Political Stability: Poverty and Inequality

Behind almost every aspect of China's development process in the early 21st century lies the harsh reality of the "Lewis model" of economic development with unlimited supplies of labour (Lewis, 1954). China has a huge population of almost 1.3 billion, increasing by around 15–16 million people each year (SSB, ZTN, 2002). Almost 70 percent of the Chinese population still lives in the countryside. There are as many 150 million "surplus" farm workers. Rural incomes stagnated from the mid-1990s to the early 2000s, and may even have declined. Rural income distribution has become much more unequal: the Gini coefficient of rural income distribution rose from 0.21 in 1978 to 0.40 in 1998. There was a massive decline in absolute poverty in the early years of China's rural reforms post-Mao (Nolan, 1988). However, Chinese official data show that there are approximately 580 million rural dwellers (73 percent of rural households) with less than US $360 per year (SSB, ZTN, 2002, p.343).[1]

The great extent of rural underemployment provides intense incentives for rural-urban migration, and intense downward pressure on non-farm wages in unskilled and low-skilled occupations. There are as many as 150 million rural migrants working in the urban areas. They are predominantly unskilled labour, earning US $1–2 per day. Alongside the poor rural migrants, as many as 40–50 million workers have lost their jobs due to reform in state-owned enterprises.

---

1 The World Bank estimates that in 1995 there were 716 million people (58 percent of the population) who had less than US $2 per day, and around 280 million who lived on less than US $1 per day (World Bank, 2001, p. 236)

Alongside these disadvantaged social groups, a new urban "middle class" is fast emerging. Large amounts of FDI by multinational firms is producing clusters of modern businesses and residential areas, isolated and protected from the surrounding mass of poor people. Chinese privatisation has been characterised by widespread insider dealing and corruption, most notably in the ubiquitous triangular relationship between the local Communist Party, the banks and the allocation of publicly owned land for "development". The official Gini coefficient of the urban distribution of income rose from 0.25 in 1992 to 0.34 in 2001 (SSB, ZTN, 1993 and 2002). However, these data exclude most rural migrants and foreign employees, and underestimate the highest incomes segments among the native Chinese urban population. If all these factors are considered, then China's urban income distribution is among the most unequal in the world. The early years of the 21st century witnessed a level of strikes and protests that has not been seen in China since the 1920s.

The global business revolution

Since the 1980s, China has implemented industrial policies intended to nurture a group of globally competitive large firms. On a fundamental basis, these industrial policies have failed. China is becoming the workshop for the world, rather than the "workshop of the world". Over sixty percent of its industrial exports are from foreign invested enterprises. A substantial fraction of the remainder of the country's exports consists of industrial products that are either OEM manufactures, or low value-added, low technology, non-branded goods for global giant firms (e.g. garments, footwear, furniture, toys). While the world's giant firms are rapidly building their research and development bases in China, employing relatively cheap, highly-skilled Chinese researchers, indigenous Chinese firms spend negligible amounts on research and development. There is not a single Chinese firm in the world's top 700 firms by research and development expenditure (DTI, 2003). China does not have a single one of the world's top 100 brands. Its leading firms are almost unknown outside the country. Among the fourteen Chinese firms in the Fortune 500, none has become a truly globally competitive company that could compete without government protection.[1] All of these firms are state-owned and subject to systematic state interference in their operation.

On the domestic front, China's industrial policy encountered numerous problems. These included policy inconsistency; misguided pursuit of "enterprise autonomy" rather than the multi-plant large firm; an impoverished mass of consumers within the protected domestic market; institutional barriers to cross-regional mergers and acquisitions; pursuit of greater firm size through diversified operations, leading to an "illusion of scale"; persistent intervention in enterprise decisions by Party and Government officials; and huge "legacy costs" deriving from the large numbers employed in the former SOEs.

On the international front, China's large firms face severe challenges. China's attempt to build large globally competitive firms has coincided with a revolutionary epoch in world business history, with a unique intensity of merger and acquisition. An unprecedented degree of industrial concentration has been established. A veritable "law" has come into play. Within the high value-added, high technology, and/or strongly branded market segments, a handful of giant firms, the "systems integrators", occupy more than one-half of the global market (Nolan, 2001a; 2001b). The process of concentration ripples across the value chain. Leading firms in each sector select the most capable suppliers, in a form of "industrial planning", adopting "aligned partners" who can work with them across the world. A "cascade effect" produces intense pressures upon first tier suppliers, forcing them to develop leading global positions, achieved through expanded research and development, and investment in global production networks. The result is a fast-developing process of concentration at a global level in numerous industries that supply the systems integrators.

The full flowering of capitalism's tendency towards industrial concentration presents a comprehensive challenge for large firms in developing countries. At the dawn of the 21st century, intense industrial concentration among both

---

[1] Baosteel is a possible exception.

systems integrators and their supply chain, brought about through pressure from the "cascade effect", presents a comprehensive challenge for both Chinese firms and policy-makers. Not only do they face immense difficulties in catching up with the leading systems integrators, the visible part of the "iceberg", but they also face immense difficulties in catching up with the powerful firms that now dominate almost every segment of the supply chain, the invisible part of the "iceberg" that lies hidden from view.

In September 2004, almost three years after China joined the WTO, Li Rongrong, Head of the State-owned Assets and Administration Commission (SASAC) acknowledged: "There is still a huge gap between China's large enterprises and the world's leading multinational companies, whether one looks at the comparison in terms of their number, scale or efficiency, or from the angle of strength of profits and innovative capability, or internationalization" (*People's Daily* website). Successful late-comer industrialising countries, from the USA in the late nineteenth century to South Korea in the late twentieth century, each produced a group of globally competitive firms. China is the first successful latecomer not to have done so. It has become the sixth largest economy (the second largest in PPP terms) (World Bank, 2004) without having a group of internationally competitive large firms. This is highly significant in the history of economic development.

The environment

China's environmental issues reflect the intense pressure of a huge and growing population upon China's already fragile natural environment, with the impact hugely reinforced by high-speed industrial growth. Recent Chinese provincial-level studies of "Green National Product" estimate that "real output growth" falls to negligible levels when destruction of the natural environment is taken into account. The area affected by serious soil erosion has increased to include around 38 percent of the entire country (UNDP, 2000, p.70). The area of desert is increasing at the rate of around 2,500 km^2 per year, equivalent to the area of a medium-sized country. In the past four decades, almost one-half of China's forests have been destroyed, so that China now has one of the sparsest forest covers in the world. There is "rampant water pollution", and a serious and worsening shortage of fresh water. China's emission of organic water pollutants is as large as that of the USA, India, Russia and Japan combined (World Bank, 2004, Table 3.6).

China explosive industrial growth has led to high-speed expansion of energy-intensive industries. By the mid-1990s, China had overtaken the USA as the world's biggest coal producer, accounting for almost thirty percent of global output. Coal provides a low-cost way to meet a large fraction of China's booming energy demands. China is the world's second largest producer of carbon dioxide, standing at 50 percent of the level of the USA, but its per capita emissions are still a mere 11 percent of those of the USA (World Bank, 2004, Table 3.8). If China follows the U.S. path, allowing complete dominance for the automobile, then the prospects for the world are terrifying. If China were to sustain its current growth path and at some point catch up with today's USA level of per capita income, and were to use similar technologies, China's emission of carbon dioxide would be one-fifth greater than those of the entire world today.

The capability and role of the state

The professional capability of the Chinese state has greatly increased since the early 1980s. However, it needs comprehensive reinvigoration that goes far beyond improved technical competence. It needs to expand its scope substantially in order to undertake activities that the market is unable to provide and to re-establish its ethical foundations. Reinvigorating a state apparatus that has atrophied may present greater challenges than constructing from scratch a strong, effective apparatus to serve development needs.

Government

China is a vast, poor country with urgent development needs, which can only be met by state action. The Chinese state attempted to increase its fiscal strength after the mid-1990s, with a series of important reforms. However, central government revenue still accounts for only around seven percent of GDP (World Bank, 2004, Table 4.11). The share of central government revenue in GDP is not only below that of other large developing countries, but also below even that of Russia.[1] The state's reduced fiscal strength has forced it to look for drastically increased contributions from fees paid by people when they use health and education services. By the end of the 1990s, budgetary allocations covered just 46 percent of actual expenditures on education (World Bank, 2002, p.85). A wide variety of other sources of funding have been mobilised to finance education, including surcharges, fees collected from students, revenues from school-run enterprises, work study programmes, donations and gifts. Between the late 1980s and mid-1990s, there was "a substantial deterioration in the educational status of the poor" (World Bank, 2002, p.42).

Over the past five decades, China has built an impressive rural health system, and overall health achievements are impressive, with a life expectancy of 70 and an infant mortality rate of 31 per 1000 live births. At the peak of the rural people's communes before 1976, around 85 percent of villages had a co-operative medical system, albeit often rudimentary. When the agricultural collectives were disbanded in the early 1980s, the financial basis for risk-sharing was largely eliminated. Over 90 percent of the rural population were without any coverage from risk-pooling welfare schemes (World Bank, 2002, p.116). In 1999, the government budget funded just eleven percent of total health expenditure, while 59 percent came from out-of-pocket payments (World Bank, 2002, p.43). These changes have resulted in a system that provides highly unequal access to health services. China ranks 61st out of 191 countries in overall quality of health, but 188th in terms of fairness in financial contribution (World Bank, 2002, p.iv).

Party

Communist Party leadership is the foundation of China's modernisation. The Party is deeply intertwined with every aspect of socio-economic life. In the late 1980s and early 1990s, Deng Xiaoping warned repeatedly of the dangers

[1] In 2001, the share of central government revenue in GDP stood at 7.2 percent in China, 13.0 percent in India, 14.8 percent in Mexico, 15.6 percent in Pakistan, 21.2 percent in Indonesia, and 26.8 percent in the Russian Federation (World Bank, 2004, Table 4.11).

of China collapsing into chaos. In his 2001 speech to celebrate the 80th anniversary of the founding of the Chinese Communist Party, Jiang Zemin stated: "The Party must address the two major historic subjects of enhancing the Party's ability of exercising state power and art of leadership, and resisting corruption and warding off risks... We must be strict in Party discipline. We should have a deeper understanding of the loss of political power by some Communist Parties in the world that had long been ruling parties and learn a lesson from them."

In recent years, the level at which Party members were tried and sentenced for corruption (including even execution in some cases) has risen to include many in high positions. These include a former deputy governor and former mayor of Shijiazhuang, Hebei's largest city; the mayor of one of China's largest cities, Shenyang; a former vice-minister of public security; a former chief of military intelligence; and a deputy chairman of the National People's Congress. Official reports to the National People's Congress in early 2003 declared that in the previous five years, the war against graft had been substantially stepped up, with a total of almost 13,000 prosecutions of government officials (SCMP, 11 March 2003). The reason that so many cases of corruption have come to light is that China's leadership is aware of the threat that it poses, and is trying to do something about it.

International relations

In 1999, the USA's military budget stood at US $253 billion, compared with just US $135 billion for NATO Europe (IISS, 1999, p.37). In the wake of September 11, the USA announced that the military budget would rise to US $379 billion by 2006, while there are no plans to increase real military expenditure by NATO Europe countries (FT 18 February 2002). Europe trails far behind the world's military superpower.

The USA fears that China's rise will transform fundamentally the balance of world economic and military power. President Bush warned China: "In pursuing advanced military capabilities that can threaten its neighbors in the Asia Pacific region, China is following an outdated path that, in the end, will hamper its own pursuit of greatness. It is time to reaffirm the essential role of American military strength. We must build and maintain our defences beyond challenge... Our forces will be strong enough to dissuade potential adversaries from pursuing a military build-up in hopes of surpassing, or equalling, the power of the U.S." (quoted in FT 21 September 2002). Following September 11, the consensus among the inner core of Bush administration shifted to the view that "in the long-term the U.S. would only find security in a world in which U.S. values were widely held and spread" (FT 6 March 2003). There is a powerful set of U.S. interests that believes serious conflict with China is unavoidable. Henry Kissinger cautioned that the U.S. foreign policy hawks see China "as a morally flawed inevitable adversary".

However, the final shape of the USA's view of how best to "engage" with China is unclear. In the 1980s, the prime goal of American foreign policy was the overthrow of the "evil empire" in the Soviet Union. This goal was pursued through acceleration of the arms race and numerous channels of influence upon Soviet policy-makers. U.S. policies played a significant role in the collapse of Soviet communism and the disintegration of the USSR. "Regime change" resulted in state disintegration, with disastrous consequences for the economy and for the welfare of most Russians. The Soviet economy had only negligible linkages to the U.S. economy. The USSR accounted for a tiny fraction of American exports and there was no investment in Russia by U.S. multinationals. Soviet exports to the USA were trivial in scale. The collapse of the Soviet economy had a negligible impact on the U.S. economy other than the short-term fall in military expenditure.

The Chinese and U.S. economies have become deeply intertwined. U.S. consumers benefit from the explosive growth of low-priced Chinese exports. U.S. companies and shareholders benefit from China's absorption of booming American investments and from access to the low-cost manufacturing supply-chain in China. U.S. primary product producers (including food, oil and mining companies) benefit from exports to China, both directly from the USA and, increasingly, from production bases in other countries. The U.S. government benefits from Chinese government purchase of its debt, which, ultimately, helps to underpin the growth of U.S. personal consumption. "System disintegration" in China, such as the U.S. helped bring about in the USSR, Afghanistan and Iraq, would be a disaster for China, but would also have severe economic consequences for the USA. One can only guess at the military consequences. From this perspective it is in the interests of U.S. business and the mass of U.S. citizens, not to speak of the rest of the world, to support the efforts of China's Communist Party leadership to sustain the country's "peaceful rise".

Financial institutions

The Asian Financial Crisis provided a shocking insight into the fragility of the country's financial institutions. China appeared to escape any effects of the crisis, due to the fact that the renminbi was not fully convertible. In fact, the crisis had a deep impact through the medium of Hong Kong and the massive debts accumulated there by Mainland "trust and investment" and "red chip" companies. The most visible of these were GITIC (Guangdong Trust and Investment Company) and GDE (Guangdong Enterprises) which included five floated "red chip" companies. During the Asian Financial Crisis, GITIC went into bankruptcy while GDE was insolvent and comprehensively restructured. Prior to the crisis, they each had been regarded as model institutions by international lenders. GITIC's bankruptcy and GDE's restructuring allowed the outside world to look closely inside large Chinese companies for the first time. The investigations revealed comprehensive failure in corporate governance, including disastrous lending practices: a large fraction of their loans were made to firms and institutions that were unable or unwilling to repay their debts. A substantial part of their "investments" were highly speculative, including heavy participation in the property boom in Guangdong Province and Hong Kong. Investigations into Guangnan, one of GDE's "red chip" companies, concluded that it was basically a "criminal company": 35 people from Guangnan were either arrested or had warrants for their arrest issued in Hong Kong. Guangnan was a Hong Kong-listed company, a "red chip", Hong Kong's environment of high quality rules on corporate governance; over forty percent of its shares were owned by public investors; its accounts were audited by a famous international accountancy firm; it had two independent directors, both prominent Hong Kong businessmen.

In the late 1990s, especially after the Asian Financial Crisis, the central government began a massive attempt to "clean up" the country's financial institutions. The cases of GITIC and GDE demonstrate how long and complex will be the process of changing China's financial institutions into well-governed, modern financial institutions. The clean up revealed shocking evidence about the state of corporate governance in China's main banks. In early 2002, it was revealed that the five bank officials at the BOC branch in Kaiping city (Guangdong) had stolen the equivalent of nearly US $500 million. The problems penetrated to the apex of the country's banking system, Zhu Xiaohua, Li Fuxiang and Wang Xuebing were members of Premier Zhu Rongji's team of four "can-do-commanders". From 1993 to 1996, Zhu Xiaohua was deputy governor of the People's Bank of China and then head of China's foreign exchange reserves. In 1996 he was appointed head of China Everbright Bank. In 1999, he was arrested, and subsequently sentenced to fifteen years imprisonment. Li Fuxiang was formerly the head of the Bank of China's foreign exchange dealings in New York, and subsequently was placed in charge of the national foreign exchange reserves. In May 2000 he committed suicide. Wang Xuebing, formerly head of the China Construction Bank and then of the Bank of China, was arrested in 2002 and subsequently sentenced to twelve years imprisonment.

Under the terms of the WTO Agreement, China's financial firms will face escalating international competition. Since the 1980s the world's leading financial firms have been through a period of unprecedented merger and acquisition. The period saw the emergence of super-large financial services firms, such as Citigroup, JP Morgan Chase, and HSBC. They have rapidly acquired dominant positions in Latin America and Eastern Europe. When Citigroup acquired Banamex, Mexico's "national champion" in financial services, the Financial Times commented: "The acquisition of Bannamex underscored the rapacious appetite of Citigroup for assets in the developing world." Citigroup itself said: "China is top of our radar screen." If China's indigenous large financial firms cannot achieve their own self-reform, then the global giants are likely to assume an increasing role in the commanding heights of China's financial sector. Citigroup argues that the big four banks in China should be "torn apart into small units in order to avoid the financial crisis", which would make it far easier for the global giants to "rout the enemy one by one".

Conclusion

China faces wide-ranging challenges that threaten the entire social, economic and political system. Due to the number and intensity of the challenges that China faces, there is a high possibility that at some point a "fire" will break out. It is highly likely that it will be connected with the financial system. During the Asian Financial Crisis, China came close to a major financial crisis. The country survived only by adopting bold and effective policies. If China were to face a financial crisis of the dimensions that have regularly attacked developing countries since the 1980s, it would be difficult to maintain overall system stability. The relationship of political instability with financial crisis is long-standing: "Since the commencement of the eighteenth century there has been no serious revolution in Europe which has not been preceded by a commercial and financial crisis" (Marx, 1853, p.9).

China's political economy has reached a crossroad. Which direction will it take?

Primitive capitalist accumulation?

Many people believe that China has no choice but to follow the harsh logic of "primitive" capitalist accumulation, as outlined in Marx's Capital, Vol. 1 (Marx, 1887). They argue that China will become a "normal" capitalist economy. Indeed, it is already well-advanced on this path, with the state-owned sector already occupying under one-half of national output. They consider that the brutal nature of the accumulation process during the "Lewis" phase of industrialisation, with its foundation in "economic development with unlimited supplies of labour" at a constant real, subsistence wage, demands an authoritarian political structure, with political power confined to the minority ruling class.

In Britain during the take-off into capitalist industrialisation after the mid-eighteenth century, it took around one hundred years before the rural reserve army of labour was absorbed into the modern sector. This provided strong downward pressure on urban wage rates, with no significant trend improvement in unskilled workers' real wages between 1750 and the 1820s at the earliest. There was a prolonged phase of capital accumulation during which there was a widening of income disparities and no diminution of absolute poverty. Capitalist accumulation was accompanied by harsh measures of social control to maintain political order. In the late eighteenth and early nineteenth century the predominant political philosophy in Britain considered that the wide divergence of interests between socio-economic groups made it impossible to obtain a democratically worked-out compromise consistent with economic growth (Hirschman, 1977). China's emerging "global middle class" today is nervous about the consequences of extending political rights to the country's sea of poor people.

Advocates of the "primitive capitalist accumulation" approach in China draw comfort from the wider lessons of the history of early capitalist industrialisation. Democratic institutions were introduced in almost all cases only after the harsh phase of early capitalist accumulation had been accomplished (Therborn, 1977, pp.33-4). The examples of Japan in the Meijii Period (1868–1912), as well as Taiwan region and Korea in recent times are invoked to provide support for the necessity of China passing through a prolonged phase of "primitive capitalist accumulation" during the prolonged "Lewis Phase" of development. In each case there was an initial phase of harsh political rule, with rapid absorption of rural surplus labour into the urban workforce at a constant real wage. Once the supply of rural surplus labour dried up, real wages for unskilled urban workers started to grow. It was at this point that demands for political democratisation began to develop.[1]

It will be several decades before China's rural surplus labour supply is

---

[1] See (Nolan, 1995; Chang, 2002) for summaries of the evidence on this point.

exhausted, assuming that the rest of the world has sufficient demand, and sufficient employment flexibility, to absorb the manufactured exports needed to absorb this vast sea of China's rural workers. If the main rationale for political authoritarianism were the existence of a "Lewis-type" process of capital accumulation, then China would face the prospect of a long period under such a structure. It is questionable whether this structure would be stable over such a long period, given the prospects for growing inequality in the midst of accelerated integration of China into the global economy. In the event that such a structure did survive, it would constitute a prolonged and oppressive form of late industrialisation.

Democracy and the free market?

Many people believe that the fundamental condition for continued successful Chinese development is a drastic downgrade of the state. A major reason that they advocated China joining the WTO was to help achieve this purpose. Many influential international scholars and policy makers believe that the Chinese Communist Party should give up its monopoly control of political power. At the end of the 1980s in China, a consensus among international opinions was developed which affirmed that the overthrow of the Chinese Communist Party would lead to a great improvement in welfare for the Chinese people. No idea was more pervasive in the early years of "transition" in the former USSR and Eastern Europe than that which argued that the state should be destroyed before it could be reconstructed. In recent years U.S. government advisors on China policy have promoted the desirability of "regime change" in China.

The blunt reality is that the overthrow of the Chinese Communist Party would plunge the country into social and political chaos. China has experienced long periods of system disintegration. The "dynastic cycle" was so devastating when it entered a downward path at the end of each dynasty, that the theme of avoidance of "great turmoil" was the focus of Chinese political thought from the earliest times right through to the present day. At the core of the Chinese reform programme after the death of Chairman Mao was a belief in the need to prevent China's political economy from disintegrating and the country descending into "big turbulence", which would "deprive the Chinese people of all hope". It is possible that the entire Chinese system of political economy could disintegrate, notwithstanding US $500 billion-worth of FDI.

The USSR was a highly sophisticated country, with great human and technological resources. It had huge potential for high-speed advancement in economic performance and living standards if appropriate policies had been adopted (Nolan, 1995). In fact, it has been "de-developed" in a way never witnessed before in peacetime. China is still a poor country. Comparable "de-development" for China would cause immense suffering. It was unimaginable to most people that there could be system meltdown either in the USSR, in Yugoslavia, once a sophisticated European state, in Argentina, the IMF's favourite pupil in Latin America, or in Indonesia, the exemplar of the "East Asian Model". Yet such a comprehensive system meltdown occurred, with disastrous consequences for the people of those countries. The central task of Chinese political economy is to learn from those experiences and avoid such an outcome.

A widespread view among those who wish for "regime change" in China is the belief that China can "follow the American path". American foreign policy is based on the premise that the whole world, including China should, and will, follow this "natural" path of development. Intense external pressure is exerted already through innumerable channels upon Chinese internal ideology to promote this view of the desirable future political economic structure for China. Such views will become ever more influential as the U.S.-dominated global mass media is allowed to penetrate the Mainland in accordance with the WTO Agreement. President Bush's national security strategy document of September 2002 is entitled "How the U.S. will lead 'freedom's triumph'". It states: "Freedom is the non-negotiable demand of human dignity; the birthright of every person—in every civilisation… Today, humanity holds in its hands the opportunity to further freedom's triumph over all [its] foes. The U.S. welcomes our responsibility to lead in this great mission." It commits the USA to "defend liberty and justice because these principles are right and true for all people everywhere". It commits the USA to "stand firmly for the non-negotiable demands of human dignity: the rule of law; limits on the absolute power of the state; free speech; freedom of worship; equal justice; respect for women; religious and ethnic tolerance; and respect for private property".

In fact, the interpretation of the word "freedom" has been the object of intense debate in the USA (Foner, 1998). At the heart of this struggle is the battle over the role of the state. Was the U.S. state to serve purely as the guardian of individual liberties or "negative freedom", or was the state to serve the as the instrument for the achievement of "positive freedom" of all citizens to enable them to be fulfilled human beings?

Struggles over the interpretation of "freedom" have existed in America since the eighteenth century.

By the late nineteenth century the idea that "freedom" essentially meant freedom of contract became the bedrock of "liberal" thinking. The true realm of freedom meant "the liberty to buy and sell, and mend and make, where and how we please, without interference from the state" (Foner, 1998, p.120). The period saw the rise of Social Darwinism, which strongly opposed any form of state interference with the "natural" workings of society. Labour laws were seen as a form of slavery, which interfered with the individual's rights to dispose freely of their property.

In the 1890s, alongside intensifying class struggle, powerful critiques of free market fundamentalism emerged, opposing the idea that meaningful "freedom" could exist in circumstances of extreme inequality, such as that in the USA. The American Economics Association was established in 1885 with the express purpose of combating Social Darwinism and "laissez-faire orthodoxy". Its founder AEA, Richard T. Ely, wrote: "We regard the state as an educational and ethical agency whose positive assistance is one of the indispensible conditions of human progress" (quoted in Foner, 1998, p.130).[1] Many younger economists believed that the private property had

---

[1] It is an extreme irony that one hundred years later, the AEA should have become the vehicle for conveying the most stultifying form of orthodoxy, which eliminated from the subject of "economics" anything other than formal mathematical modelling, largely based on free market models, leaving the subject far removed from the open-minded analysis of the real world from which AEA originally derived its inspiration.

become a "means of depriving others of their freedom", and that "poverty posed a far graver danger to the republic than an activist state" (Foner, 1998, p.130). During the Progressive Era leading up to the First World War, T.H. Green, the British philosopher made a profound impact with his lecture in the USA in which he argued that freedom was a "positive concept".[1] The Great Depression had a major impact on the struggle over the interpretation of "freedom". In 1933, Franklin D. Roosevelt proclaimed: "For too many Americans, life is no longer free; liberty no longer real; men can no longer follow the pursuit of happiness" (quoted in Foner, 1998, p.196). Under his guidance, the Democratic Party led the country towards large-scale state intervention to reconstruct the economy and provide comprehensive social security. These ideas remained as the mainstream of U.S. political thought long into the post-war world.

In the 1950s, a group of conservative thinkers set out to "reclaim the idea of freedom". For them, freedom meant de-centralised political power, limited government, and a free market economy. The immediate intellectual origins of the movement can be traced back to the publication of Hayek's book *The Road to Serfdom* (Hayek, 1944), which became a clarion call for conservatives to reclaim the word "freedom" from the socialists. The dominant view in the USA came to equate "freedom" with individual choice in the market place with minimal interference from the state. The idea gained force that the U.S. should lead the world towards a universal free market. The collapse of the USSR deeply reinforced Americans' confidence in the free market.

The idea that the free market is a moral concept stands at the centre of political discourse in the USA at the start of the 21st century. President Bush's Security Strategy declaration of September 2002 states: "The concept of 'free trade' arose as a moral principle even before it became a pillar of economics. If you can make something that others value, you should be able to sell it to them. If others make something that you value you should be

---

1 Green's ideas on "positive freedom" far precede similar notions propounded by such late twentieth century philosophers as Isiah Berlin (Berlin, 1969) or A.K. Sen (e.g. Dreze and Sen, 1989).

able to buy it. This is real freedom, the freedom for a person—or nation—to make a living" (Bush, 21 September 2002). In the wake of September 11, the U.S. government is even more firmly convinced of its historic function to spread the moral principle of the free market across the whole world: "The great struggles of the 20th century between liberty and totalitarianism ended with a decisive victory for the forces of freedom—and a single sustainable model for national success: freedom, democracy and free enterprise. Today, the U.S. enjoys a position of unparalleled military strength, and great economic and political influence... We seek to create a balance of power that favours human freedom... The U.S. will use this opportunity to spread the benefits of freedom across the globe... We will make freedom and the development of democratic institutions key themes in our bilateral relations" (Bush, 21 September 2002).

Which American tradition should China turn to: that which argues for a powerful role for the state to ensure positive freedom for all citizens, or "free market fundamentalism", whose current intellectual and political ascendancy may turn out to be a relatively brief intermission in the long sweep of U.S. history?

Backwards to Maoism?

Chairman Mao led the Chinese Communist Party in an attempt drastically to attack social inequality. This amounted to nothing less than an attempt to transform people's work motivation, to overcome the classic "principal-agent" problem, by liberating human productive energies from the link with material reward. "Serve the people" was the foundation of Maoist ideology. Chairman Mao hoped to build a non-capitalist, humane society, which provided the opportunity for the whole population to fulfill their human potential. It was a philosophy that was powerfully driven by the intention to restrict drastically the population's "negative" freedom to act in accordance with their individual wishes free of external restriction, while providing the maximum equality of opportunity for citizens to achieve their "positive freedom": "In a socialist society, it is necessary to acknowledge the differences in the rewards for labour, but the differences ought not to be too great. We must actively create the conditions for communist society's stage, 'from each according to their abilities, to each according to their needs', and should constantly strive to lessen the three great differences and increasingly extirpate the influence of bourgeois right" (Comrades, 1974, p.597).

From the mid-1950s, through to the mid-1970s, China's GNP growth rate was faster than that of most developing countries. In normal times, the mass of the people enjoyed a high degree of livelihood security. Life expectancy at birth rose from 36 years pre-1949 to 71 years in 1981 (Nolan, 1995, p.49). These achievements were applauded by numerous Western scholars as evidence that redistributive policies could enable low income countries to achieve high levels of "basic needs" long before average per capita incomes had risen to high levels.[1]

However, China paid a high price for the attempt to suppress market forces completely, to cut the country off from the global economy and society, to drastically constrain the dimensions of inequality, to eliminate material incentives, and to radically limit cultural freedom, and for wild, nation-wide mass movements: "The decade of the Cultural Revolution brought catastrophe upon us and caused profound suffering… Had it not been for 'Left' interference, the reversals of 1958, significant progress would certainly have been achieved in our industrial and agricultural production and in science and education, and the people's standard of living would certainly improved to a fair extent" (Deng Xiaoping, 1980, p.234).

Diversity of thought was crushed. Large numbers of people were imprisoned for their political views. Freedom of cultural expression was dramatically narrowed, causing large-scale damage to people's welfare. The intense political struggles to limit social differentiation caused immense suffering to innumerable participants. Although growth rates were high, they were achieved in a highly inefficient way, with slow technical progress, a long-run fall in capital productivity, and stagnation in average per capita incomes. Apart from improvements in consumption of a narrow range of consumer durables, per capita consumption of most other items either

1 See, especially, the numerous writings of A.K. Sen on this topic.

stagnated or declined. The proportion of the population in absolute poverty remained at around 30 percent in the mid-1970s, totally around 270 million people, compared with around 190 million in 1957 (Nolan, 1995, p.50). The utopian attempt to leap into a communist society during the Great Leap Forward resulted in a colossal man-made disaster. The collapse in farm output caused the biggest famine of the twentieth century, with as many as 30 million "excess deaths".

The Maoist development path is not one to which many Chinese people would wish to return. China cannot go back. It needs to steer a course between the pursuit of extreme individual "negative" freedom and extreme collective "positive" freedom.

Use the past to serve the present?

In their search for a way forward, China's leaders can engage with international experience, but, above all can turn to the country's own past for a source of inspiration. This rich history can provide intellectual nourishment for persisting with the approach of "groping for a way forward", "seeking truth from facts" devising policies in a pragmatic, experimental, non-ideological fashion to solve concrete problems.

China's long-run economic dynamism

Needham (1954–) demonstrated that China made great technical advances before the West. This led scholars to ask why China failed to experience an "Industrial Revolution", despite having made much early technical progress. Most scholars used to believe (and some still do) that the "totalitarian" traditional Chinese state crushed the development of the market (e.g. Balazs, 1964; Huang, 1990; Wittfogel, 1957; Lin, 1996). A corollary of this perspective is that China should "learn from the past" by reducing even further the state's economic role in order to sustain China's growth.

Recent research by Chinese economic historians has shown that the traditional Chinese economy was far more dynamic over the long-term than had formerly been thought.[1] Economic historians are increasingly investigating why the Chinese economy made such sustained progress over more than 1000 years. This necessitates probing deeply into China's traditional political economy, especially the relationship of state and market. Key aspects of China's traditional system of political economy form an inspiration for understanding the possible solutions to the challenges facing China today. They provide a source of confidence to resist the intense pressures to adopt free market economics as the solution to these challenges.

The foundation of Chinese civilisation was, and still is, agriculture. For almost 1000 years up until the mid-twentieth century Chinese rice-based agriculture responded positively to sustained population growth and absorbed productively the huge long-term increase in farm labour force (Perkins, 1968). From the tenth to the thirteenth century, China set out along the path of the "Second Industrial Revolution" well before Europe (Needham, 1954–). A steady stream of significant technical advances was made thereafter through until the nineteenth century (Xu and Wu, 2000). China's technological achievements were stimulated by long-term growth of both domestic and international trade. For long periods, the Chinese state united the vast territory of China into a single integrated market and international trade operated free of government controls.

The textile industry was the most important in traditional China. Towards the end of the Ming dynasty (1368–1644), cotton replaced hemp and silk as the principal fabric for daily wear. Cloth spinning and weaving became the largest handicraft industry, of which around one-half was for sale on the market. By the early Qing (1644–1911), in the late seventeenth and early eighteenth century, there were numerous large-scale businesses, including mining, iron manufacture, salt-making, porcelain and shipbuilding (Xu and Wu, 2000, pp.250-298). Imperial China had a high level of urbanisation for a pre-industrial society. In the nineteenth century there were estimated to have been a total of 35,000 "standard" and "intermediate" market towns (Skinner, 1997b). Above this dense local trading structure

---

1 See especially (Li, 1986; 1998; 2000; Xu and Wu, 2000).

were a further 2,300 "central market towns", 932 "cities" and 26 huge "metropolitan trading systems", which in turn formed eight great economic systems. China possessed cities of a size and level of sophistication that far exceeded those of contemporary Europe until late in the latter's development.

In 1750, China's share of global manufacturing output stood at around 33 percent, compared with 25 percent in India/Pakistan and just 18 percent in the "West" (Bairoch, 1982). In 1800, China's per capita GNP was US $228 (at 1960 prices) compared with US $150–200 for England and France (Bairoch, 1981). As late as 1798, Malthus declared China was the richest country in the world (Dawson, 1964, p.7). In his description of McCartney mission to China in 1793, Sir George Staunton said: "In respect to its natural and artificial productions, the policy and uniformity of its government, the language, manners, and opinions of the people, the moral maxims, and civil institutions, and the general economy and tranquility of the state, it is the grandest collective object that can be presented for human contemplation or research" (quoted in Dawson, 1964, p.7).

State and market in Chinese development

The bureaucracy

The traditional Chinese state combined a hereditary emperor with a large professional civil service, selected by competitive examination. In addition, there was a much larger number of members of the local "gentry" who dealt with many interests of their local communities for which the official government had no time (Michael, 1964, p.60). The bureaucracy's ideology was conveyed through the examination system, for which Confucianism was the foundation, forming the key to the system's long-term stability and cohesion. The over-riding values were those of "the primacy of order and stability, of co-operative human harmony, of accepting one's place in the social hierarchy, of social integration" (Feuerwerker, 1976, p.15). The sole test of a good ruler is "whether he succeeds in promoting the welfare of the common people... This is the most basic principle in Confucianism and has remained unchanged throughout the ages" (Lau, 1979, pp.32, 37). In order to serve the interests of the mass of the people, the bureaucracy must gain the trust of the masses: "Only after he has gained the trust of the common people does the gentleman work them hard, for otherwise they would feel ill-used" (Confucius, 1979, p.154). It is disastrous if the bureaucracy becomes corrupt and loses its moral foundation: "Those in authority have lost the Way and the common people have for long been rootless" (Confucius, 1979, p.155).

Merchants performed an essential function in expanding the division of labour, facilitated through trade, but were excluded from political power and the ideology underpinning that structure. They were at the bottom of the bureaucracy's official ranking of social strata, behind the scholars, farmers and artisans. There was no official representation of their interests in either the local or the central government. However, this did not mean that trade itself was regarded as undesirable. The successful merchant's wealth "had always drawn covetous awe if not respect" (Faure, 2001). If merchants wished their families to enter the ruling bureaucratic class, their children needed to go through the laborious and highly competitive examination system, which resulted in their thorough absorption of the ideology of the ruling scholar-bureaucrat elite.

Law

During the long periods in which it functioned relatively effectively, the Chinese state provided a framework of law and order and protection for property rights within which long-term economic development took place. Chinese merchants never developed the independence from the state that occurred in increasingly autonomous towns in late medieval Europe (Balazs, 1964). However, in periods when the central government functioned well, the cities provided a secure environment in which to conduct business and in which their property rights were protected by the state. The huge quantities of merchandise would not have been traded without security that the corresponding contracts were legally enforceable, or that robbery of the merchants' property was illegal. Research on late Imperial Hankow has shown that before 1850 there were all manner of written commercial agreements, including shipping orders, bills of lading, promissory notes and contracts of sale, all of which were routinely circulated and enforceable in the city (Rowe, 1984). Local officials in late imperial Hankow played a key role in ensuring debt repayment.

The army

The most important function of the imperial state was to provide long periods of relative peace and stability over the vast territory under its rule. For long periods China was distinguished from the rest of the world by the fact that the central authorities were able to establish peaceful conditions over vast territories. Even in the midst of long dynasties, such as the Ming, China had the world's largest army (Huang, 1981, p.160). The presence of so many troops also provided a source of security for economic activities during the long periods in which they were under effective control from the civilian authorities. They provided merchants with the confidence to undertake trade that far exceeded that in other parts of the world until modern times. The normally peaceful environment over wide areas provided a powerful incentive to those with capital to undertake long-term investments. It also enabled the entire territory of China to form a single unified free trade area. The degree of state interference in trade was small, in normal times confined mainly to taxation of small number of key items. Estimates for the eighteenth century show that only around seven percent of national income went into the central government budget, of which the vast bulk, 74 percent came from the land tax and just 14 percent came from the domestic and international customs revenue (Nolan, 1993, p.17). Therefore, long before any other comparable region of the world, China was able to enjoy for a long period the powerful "Smithian" stimulus of specialisation, the division of labour, the rapid spread of best practice techniques, and powerful incentives to accumulate capital.

Money

In the traditional Chinese economy exchange was almost always a monetary transaction (King, 1965, p.42). During the Yuan dynasty, the Mongol rulers were the first economy in the world to have paper money. Marco Polo was amazed that "all the people's and populations who are subject to the Great Khan's rule are perfectly willing to accept these papers in payment, since wherever they go they pay in the same currency, whether for goods or for pearls or precious stones or gold or silver. With these pieces of paper they can buy anything and pay for anything" (Marco Polo, 1958, p.148). For over two thousand years, the Chinese government was aware of the importance of money to a sound economy. One of its ongoing struggles was to ensure that the money supply was not debased and that the quantity of money corresponded to current economic needs. The central government tried persistently to maintain central control over the amount and nature of currency in circulation. Detailed accounts from the early Qing dynasty show the way in which the central government closely monitored the money supply, frequently changing the specified weight and composition of coins in response to changing economic conditions, and attempting to maintain a constant exchange rate between copper cash and silver coinage (King, 1965, pp.133-143).

Water control

The most important single function of the state in traditional China was water control, both for drainage and irrigation, as well as for transport. Large water control projects were almost exclusively public, organised either directly by the central government, or by lower levels of the bureaucracy. Water control activities carried a grave moral imperative for government officials, with a similar responsibility as national defence: "Building embankments on the Yellow River is like constructing defenses on the frontier, and to keep watch on the dike is like maintaining vigilance on the frontier" (a high official of the Ming dynasty, quoted in (Chi, 1936, p.73)). The central administration had important functions in inter-district water projects or projects with large expenses. In the Ming and Qing dynasties, maintenance of the embankment of the Yellow River was in the charge of a special official who ranked high in the bureaucratic hierarchy. The Grand Canal was by far the greatest transport infrastructure achievement of the traditional Chinese state. It played a significant part in providing a transport system linking the productive south with the political north, engaging the attention of the best minds of China for more than ten centuries. It demanded countless millions of lives and a large portion of the wealth of the country for its improvement and maintenance.

Local government officials had an important role in water control. For almost any local water works beyond the capacity of the peasants of a single village, the magistrate intervened with the delegation of the duty of mobilizing forced labour, supervising the construction of local works, and regulating the use of water by rival villages. There was a heavy moral burden upon local officials to ensure that the innumerable local water control activities were provided at an adequate level. The ideal magistrate "is an official close to the people, and flood and drought should be of as much concern to him as pain or sickness of his person" (Ku Shih-lien, an early Qing dynasty scholar and official, quoted in (Chi, 1936, p.72)). The ideal magistrate should make extensive visits to the countryside during the slack season: "He should survey the topography of the region, ask about conditions of drainage, and investigate sluices and locks…All these affect the conditions of the public treasury and the welfare of the people and must be carefully considered by the magistrate" (Ku Shih-lien, quoted in (Chi, 1936, p.72)).

Famine relief

Famine relief in the Chinese empire included famine investigation, providing relief funds, supplying relief grain, controlling prices, strengthening and rebuilding production (Will, 1990).[1] Many of the measures to fight famine demonstrated subtle strategies by the State in providing relief to the poor and the capability of the State in using the market to combat famine problems. Many of the measures adopted anticipate the analysis of famine made by modern writers such as A.K. Sen. The "detailed and formalised procedures for combating famine" were permitted by "the sophistication,

---

[1] Will (1990) provides a meticulous account of famine relief in late Imperial China.

centralisation, and stability of the (Chinese) bureaucratic system" (Will, 1990, p.4).

The local gentry had a prominent part in fighting famine and distributing relief. Collective action at the local level was "to the advantage of both the bureaucrats and the holders of local power, headed by the great landowners and the gentry, that appropriate measures be taken to prevent the ruin of the economy and social disorder, and this was certainly a powerful factor for cohesion within the global power system" (Will, 1990, p.5). Official famine prevention measures had been formulated as early as the Song period. Many of the recommended procedures—surveys of the disaster and its victims, the regular distribution of grain, public soup kitchens, and so forth—had been practised for centuries, albeit on a smaller scale, by the local notables and landlords in cooperation with the bureaucracy (Will, 1990, p.74).

Commodity price stabilisation

From early in Chinese history, the Chinese state sought for ways to stabilise basic commodity prices, with deep awareness of the damaging effects of speculation upon ordinary people's livelihood. As early as the Warring States Period (475–221 BC), the government tried to keep fluctuations in the grain price within a certain range (Hu Jichuang, 1984, p.17). Marco Polo described the provision of grain in the Yuan Dynasty (1271–1368). When harvests were plentiful and the price of crops was cheap, the Great Khan accumulated vast quantities of grain and stored them in huge granaries. When crops failed he drew on these stocks, "releasing enough for all...throughout all parts of his empire" (Marco Polo, 1974, p.157). Will's (1990) meticulous account shows the way in which in eighteenth century China the bureaucracy intervened in the rice market to protect the livelihood of the masses from price fluctuations and speculation. The government established a vast network of "ever-normal granaries" across the country in order to stabilise grain prices. In addition to maintaining emergency reserves, the purpose of the "ever-normal granaries" was "to cushion the impact of seasonal price fluctuations by buying up grain immediately after the harvest, when prices were low, and reselling it at a low price during the lean period before the new harvest came in". The "ever-normal granaries" spring sales and autumn purchases were supposed to even out prices by compensating for the weakness of the private sector or by competing with it when it tended to take advantage of and speculate on seasonal and/or regional price differentials.

Conclusion

The traditional Chinese state strongly encouraged the market, but did not allow commerce, financial interests and speculation to dominate politics and society. It stepped in where markets failed, not only in respect to immediate growth issues, but also in relation to the wider issues of social stability and cohesion. Behind the edifice of authoritarian Imperial rule was a pervasive morality based on the necessity that all strata of society observe their duties in order to sustain social cohesion, to achieve social and political stability and to achieve environmental sustainability. When these functions operated effectively, there was "great harmony", a prosperous economy and a stable society. When they operated poorly, there was "great turmoil", economic retrogression and social disorder.

■ Conclusion

If by the "Third Way", we mean a creative symbiotic inter-relationship between state and market, then we can say that China practised its own "Third Way" for two thousand years. This was the foundation of its hugely impressive long-run economic and social development. The Chinese "Third Way" was a complete philosophy that combined concrete ways of both stimulating and controlling the market, with a deeply thought out system of morality for rulers, bureaucrats and ordinary people. When the system worked well, the philosophical foundation was supplemented by non-ideological state actions to try to solve practical problems that the market could not solve. Confucianism produced a deeply developed concept of "duty" which was the foundation of social prosperity and collective action. The fact that the system went through regular cycles when these principles were poorly observed, rulers and bureaucrats were corrupt and the economy and society foundered, should not blind us to the underlying coherence and lasting benefit from this integrated system.

In recent decades Europe has been groping its own way towards a "Third Way". However, Europe is already industrialised, with a dominant middle class. It is militarily strong, and contains a mass of powerful, globally competitive firms. China today is groping for its own Third Way in totally different circumstances. It is painfully weak militarily compared with the USA. The vast mass of the population are poor farmers or unskilled migrants, and it is still locked into the "Lewis phase" of "economic development with unlimited supplies of labour". The "global middle class" constitutes a small fraction of the population. The economy is increasingly "dependent", with the modern sector increasingly dominated by international capital, forming complete productions systems within China, and accounting for over one-half of the country's export earnings. China faces intense pressure to liberalise comprehensively its financial system as the price for participation in the international economy. China's leaders are trying to construct a civilised society in this uniquely challenging setting.

China cannot close itself off from the main trend in international economics and politics. It cannot turn round and go back to the Maoist period. However, system survival necessitates that it uses the market as the servant of the development process, not the master, as if the market possesses an intrinsic moral value, which the current U.S. leadership and proponents of the unfettered free market believe to be the case. In this effort China's leaders can make common cause with powerful streams in international thought that have gone against the current mainstream.[1] They have at certain periods been highly influential both in the West, including even in the USA, and in the Far East outside the Chinese mainland.

Can free market fundamentalism prevent a "China Financial Crisis"? Can it solve the problem of the rapid rise in social inequality within China?

---

1 See, for example, Nolan's (2004) analysis of the relevance of Adam Smith s Theory of Moral Sentiments to China's current situation, and its close relationship to key ethical concepts in the Chinese Confucian tradition.

Can it solve the problems of the Chinese farm economy? Can it enable China's large firms to compete on the global level playing field? Can it help China to deal with the massive international relations challenge? Can it solve the Chinese environmental crisis? Can it provide China with an ethical foundation for building a socially cohesive society? Anglo-Saxon free market fundamentalism, which reached its modern apogee in the 1990s, offers no hope for sustainable global development, at the level either of ecology, society, or international relations. China's numerous deep socio-economic challenges each requires creative, non-ideological state intervention with the market, to solve the innumerable practical problems that the market alone cannot solve.

If China is able to marry the "snake" of the global market economy with the "hedgehog" of China's ancient history, as well as its recent history, it will offer a way forward for a stable, socially cohesive society within the country. If it fails in this attempt, the Chinese entire system of political economy may collapse. This would be devastating, not only for China, but for the whole global political economy. At the very least, China may be condemned to a long period of harsh social control to contain the surging tensions of the country's high-speed growth. During the Asian Financial Crisis, China had to take a "choice of no choice" to survive by "cutting the trees to save the forest" (i.e. making GITIC bankrupt). If it wishes the system to survive today it must also take the "choice of no choice" to re-establish an ethical foundation for social cohesiveness, confidently using its own past traditions and the best traditions from outside the country.

If China were to "choose" the path of "state desertion" and free market fundamentalism, it would lead to uncontrollable tensions and social disintegration. Full liberalisation of international financial firm competition inside China and full liberalisation of international financial flows is the most dangerous area through which this disintegration might occur. A crisis in the financial system would fan the flames amidst the "combustible material" in all other sectors of society, into which the long tentacles of the financial system extend. The "choice" to increase and make more effective the role of the state to solve the intensifying socio-economic challenges facing the country can only succeed if the Chinese state today, with the Communist Party at its core, as in periods of greatest prosperity in the past, can radically improve its level of effectiveness, and eliminate rampant corruption. State improvement, not state desertion, is the only rational goal for Chinese system reform. This is the "choice of no choice" for China's system survival.

By taking the "choice of no choice", China's own survival can contribute to global survival and sustainable development, by offering a beacon as an alternative to the US-dominated drive towards global free market fundamentalism. This is the crossroads not only for China, but for the whole world.

References

Bairoch, P. (1982), "International industrialisation levels from 1750 to 1980", Journal of European Economic History, Fall, 269-334.

Bairoch, P. and M. Levy-Leboyer (eds.) (1981), Disparities in economic development since the Industrial Revolution, London, Macmillan.

Balazs, E. (1964), Chinese civilisation and bureaucracy, London, Yale University.

Berlin, I. (1969), Four essays in liberty, Oxford, Oxford University Press.

Chao-ting Chi (1936), Key economic areas in Chinese history, New York, Paragon Reprint.

Comrades from the Shanghai Hutong Shipyards and the Sixth Economic Group of the Shanghai Municipal May Seventh Cadre School, 1974, Two kinds of society, two kinds of wages, in Selden, 1979.

Confucius, The Analects (Lun Yu), translated, with an Introduction by D.C. Lau, Harmondsworth, Penguin Books.

Dawson, R. (ed.) (1964), The legacy of China, Oxford, Oxford University Press.

Dawson, R. (ed.) (1964), "Western conceptions of Chinese civilisation". In: The legacy of China, Oxford, Oxford University Press.

Deng Xiaoping (1994), "The present situation and the tasks before us". Deng Xiaoping wenxuan, Renmin Chubanshe.

Deng Xiaoping (1984), Selected works of Deng Xiaoping, Beijing, Foreign Languages Press.

Department of Trade and Industry (DTI) (2003), The 2003 R&D scoreboard, London, DTI.

Dreze, J. and A.K. Sen (1989), Hunger and public action, Oxford, Clarendon Press. Faure, D. (2001), "Beyond networking: An institutional view of Chinese business", mimeo.

Foner, E. (1998), The story of American freedom, New York, W.W. Norton.

Frank, A.G. (1967), Capitalism and underdevelopment in Latin America, New York, Monthly Review Press.

Hu Jichuang (1984), Chinese economic thought before the seventeenth century, Beijing, Foreign Language Press.

Huang R. (1990), China: A Macro-History, New York, M.E. Sharpe.

International Institute for Strategic Studies (1998), The military balance, London, IISS.
King, F.H. (1965), Money and monetary policy in China, Cambridge, Mass, Harvard University Press.
Lau, D.C. (1979), "Introduction". In: Confucius Says, Hong Kong, Federal Publications.
Lewis, A. (1954), "Economic development with unlimited supplies of labour", Manchester School, May.
Li Bozhong (1986), The development of agriculture and industry in Jiangnan, 1644–1850: Trends and prospects, Hangzhou, Zhenjiang Academy of Social Sciences.
Li Bozhong (1998), Agricultural development in Jiangnan, 1620–1850, Basingstoke, Macmillans.
Li Bozhong (2000), The early industrialisation of Jiangnan, 1550–1850 (in Chinese), Shehui Kexue Wenxian Publishing House, Beijing.
Lin Yifu, Cai Fang and Li Zhou (1996), The China miracle, Hong Kong, Chinese University Press.
Marx, K. (1887), Capital, vol.1, New York, International Publishers Edition, 1967.
Needham, J. (1954–), Science and civilisation in China, Cambridge, Cambridge University Press.
Nolan, P. (1993), State and market in the Chinese economy, Macmillan, Basingstoke.
Nolan, P. (1995), China's rise, Russia's fall, Macmillan, Basingstoke.
Nolan, P. (2001a), China and the global business revolution, Basingstoke, Palgrave.
Nolan, P. (2001b), China and the global economy, Basingstoke, Palgrave.
Perkins, D.H. (1968), Agricultural development in China, 1368–1968, Edinburgh, Edinburgh University Press.
Polo, Marco (1974), The travels, The Penguin Books.
Rowe, W.T. (1984), Hankow: Commerce and society in a Chinese city, 1796–1889, Stanford, Stanford University Press.
Selden, M. (1979), The People's Republic of China, New York, Monthly Review Press.
Skinner, G.W. (ed.) (1977a), The city in late Imperial China, Stanford, Stanford University Press.
Skinner, G.W. (1977b), "Regional urbanisation in nineteenth century China", in G.W. Skinner (ed.), 1977.
Smith, Adam (1761), The theory of moral sentiments, revised edition, Indianapolis, Liberty Classics edition (1982).
Smith, Adam (1776), The wealth of nations, Chicago, University of Chicago Press, Cannan edition (1976).
Therborn, G. (1977), "The rule of capital and the rise of democracy", New Left Review, No. 104, May-June.
UNDP (2000), China: Human development report 1999, New York, Oxford University Press.
Will, Pierre-Etienne (1990), Bureaucracy and famine in eighteenth-century China, Standford University Press.
World Bank (2002), China: National development and sub-national finances, Washington, DC, World Bank.
World Bank (2004), World development indicators, Washington, DC, World Bank.
Xu Dixin and Wu Chengming (2000), Chinese capitalism, 1522–1840, edited and annotated by Charles Curwen, Basingstoke, MacMillan's.

Rebalancing Growth in China: A Three-Handed Approach

Olivier Blanchard and Francesco Giavazzi[1]

■ Introduction

On July 21, 2005, China began the process of rebalancing its economy. The new exchange rate rule will, over time, reduce the incentive to invest in the export sector. This is the right move for China since there are increasing signs that the economy has proceeded too far into manufacturing for export markets, to the point that the country's capital stock is misallocated: too much in manufacturing, too little in the domestic service industry—in particular in the provision of health services.

At the same time the government has announced that the national poll tax will be eliminated in all rural provinces and is considering reducing, in those provinces, some local taxes as well. It has also introduced free

[1] Olivier Blanchard is the professor of Economics at the Massachusetts Institute of Technology. Francesco Giavazzi is the professor of Economics in the University of Italy.

elementary education and some free basic health services for all rural households. These policies are also right, for two reasons. First, the prices of agricultural products in China follow international prices very closely: The revaluation will therefore be accompanied by a corresponding fall in the local currency price of foodstuffs and, as a consequence, a fall in rural incomes. Second, a substantial revaluation risks pushing the economy into a recession—or at least a significant slowdown in growth. Using fiscal policy to support domestic demand is clearly appropriate. Doing so by focusing primarily on rural provinces, appears therefore to be the right approach both from a distribution and from a macroeconomic viewpoint.

Our paper is an attempt to define the contours of the right macroeconomic strategy for China. In a nutshell, we believe that the package includes a decrease in savings, with a focus on private savings, an increase in the supply of services, in particular health services, and an appreciation of the RMB. This is why we refer to this strategy as a "three-handed approach": action on the fiscal and budgetary front, accompanied by currency revaluation.

Before describing the optimal policy mix, we start by asking in Section 2 how the Chinese economy got to where it is—what the strategy has been since the beginning of the reforms, and what the main characteristics of the economy are today. In Section 3 we use this assessment to ask what is the desirable path for the future, and which are the main policy tradeoffs implied by such a path. Finally, in Section 4 we put the various pieces together to describe what we believe is a consistent policy package.

■ The Strategy so far

Savings and exports

Partly as a result of deliberate policy choices, partly by historical accident, China's economic strategy since the early 1990's has been characterized by two features: high savings and high capital accumulation, and export-led growth.[1]

[1] A more detailed characterization of China's growth, with a comparison to other rapid growth experiences such as those in Korea and Japan earlier in time, is given in Hausmann (2005).

1) High savings

China's national savings rate, 43 percent of GDP in 2003, is unusually high, no matter which group of countries China is compared to (see Table 1).

Table 1 National savings rate (percent of GDP, 2003)

China	43.2
Low-income countries	20.3
Lower-middle income countries	30.4
Middle income countries	28.3
Upper-middle income countries	23.9

Source: World Development Indicators (2004).

The high national savings rate reflects both high private and high public savings. The fraction of savings invested abroad has been relatively small: In the past 15 years China has always run a current account surplus, but never a very large one: 2 percent of GDP on average since 1990. As a result of high household savings, private consumption has been relatively low: As shown in Table 2, it is now 56 percent of GDP, having lost six percentage points since the early 1990's. This reduction in private consumption has gone entirely into financing domestic investment, which over the same period has gained the same share of GDP, 6 percent.

Table 2 The composition of demand (percent of GDP)

	1991	2003
Consumption	62	56
Private	49	43
Public	13	13
Investment	36	42
Exports	16	31
Imports	14	29

Source: IWEP, Chinese Academy of Social Sciences.

2) High exports and high imports

Openness, measured by the share of trade (exports plus imports) in GDP is 60 percent today (2003): China is about as open as France and Italy, two economies deeply integrated in the European Single Market (for comparison, average trade openness is below 40 percent in Latin America). In less than ten years, China has nearly doubled its degree of openness by raising both exports and imports by an order of magnitude more than the increase in world trade (see Table 3). Much of this trade is related to Chinese processing of imported intermediate goods (processing trade accounts for about one-half of total Chinese trade). One of the major benefits of openness, learning-by-doing, occurs precisely in the area of processing trade.

Table 3 The growth rate of exports and imports (percent per year)

Exports	1980's	1990's	2000–2003
China	5.7	12.4	23.1
World	5.0	6.2	5.8(*)
Imports	**1980's**	**1990's**	**2000–2003**
China	10.2	15.5	23.5
World	4.7	5.8	5.3

(*): 2000–2002.
Source: World Development Indicators (2004).

Overall, this has clearly been a very successful strategy:

1) Per capita income

In just 15 years Chinese GDP per capita (PPP corrected) has increased from being equal to that of India to being now twice as large. Or to take another example, it has gone from 18% of Korean GDP to 29%. These are impressive achievements.

2) Total factor productivity and learning-by-doing

Between 1990 and 2002 labor productivity growth in industry has averaged 12.5 percent per year. These productivity gains are obviously related to the high investment rate, but (as shown in Hu, Jefferson, Xiaojing and Jinchang, 2003) learning-by-doing has contributed to increase total factor productivity.

The estimates of TFP growth computed by various authors and discussed in Wang (2005) range around 3 percent per year since the beginning of the reforms (Table 4). More recently however, as discussed in Hu and Zheng (2004), TFP growth appears to have slowed significantly; we shall return to this below.

Table 4 Total factor productivity growth, various estimates

Author	Period	Annual TFP growth
Wang Mengkui	1978–1985	0.5
	1978–2003	2.4
Li Shantong	1982–1997	1.4
Maddison	1952–1978	−0.8
	1978–1995	2.2
World Bank	1978–1995	3.1
Zheng Jinghai	1979–1984	7.7
	1985–1990	2.2
	1991–1995	3.7
	1995–2001	0.6
Zhu Baoliang	1978–2002	3.0

Source: As reported by IWEP, quoting from Wang, unpublished.

3) No evidence of overheating

With respect to labor, there appears to be no general pressure on wages. With respect to capital, the evidence from prices of machinery and building materials in particular, suggest, if anything, excess supply (Table 5).

Table 5 Price indices (rate of change, 2003)

Ex-factory prices	2.3%
Price deflator, investment in fixed assets	2.2%
Price deflator, machine building industry	−3.0%
Price deflator, building materials industry	−0.4%

Source: IWEP, Chinese Academy of Social Sciences.

Imbalances

Along with growth, a number of social and economic imbalances have emerged however.

Uneven growth across provinces

In the 1970s, per capita income in urban areas was 3 times its level in rural areas: Controls on the price of foodstuffs and limitations to labor mobility were aimed at favoring the cities. The reforms of the 1980s brought that ratio down to 2.2. Since 1990, however, it has risen again and was back to 3.2 in 2003. The same has happened to per capita consumption in urban and rural areas (Table 6). This divergence between urban and rural households is also reflected, not surprisingly, in an increasing divergence in income per capita between provinces (last column of Table 6). The standard deviation of income per capita across provinces has increased by 72 percent between 1998 and 2003.

Growth differences across provinces have been larger than what can be explained by different characteristics, such as geography, or the endowment of human capital. In particular, the policy of awarding fiscal privileges to exporters and investors in selected areas has contributed directly to the widening of income differences. Cities that have been granted the status of special "economic zones" have grown by as much as 5 percent per year faster than the rest (Jones et al., 2003). Spillovers across provinces have also contributed to the widening of income disparities because (as shown in Brun et al., 2002) such spillovers have been positive among coastal provinces, but non-existent between coastal and inland or western regions.

Table 6 Ratio of per capita income and consumption. Urban to rural households, and top 8 to bottom 22 provinces

Year	Income ratio (Urban to rural)	Consumption ratio (Urban to rural)	Income ratio (Between provinces)
1979	2.6	2.9	
1990	2.2	3.0	
1998	2.9	3.4	2.8
2003	3.2	3.6	3.1

Source: IWEP, Chinese Academy of Social Sciences.

Uneven growth across skill levels

We estimate that the skilled-unskilled wage differential has risen from 1.3 to 2.1 in a decade (the details of estimation are given in Box 1). The large migration flows from rural to urban areas and from inland and western provinces to coastal provinces suggest that the countryside has been used mainly as a reservoir of labor. The high supply elasticity of unskilled labor has certainly been a factor in the rise of the skilled-unskilled differential.

Box 1: Estimating skilled-unskilled wage differentials

Denote the average wage in sector *i* in year *t* by wit. Decompose workers in two groups, skilled (high school and more) and unskilled (less than high school), and denote their respective wages by w^s_{it} and w^u_{it}. Let the proportions of skilled and unskilled workers be denoted by α^s_{it} and α^u_{it} respectively. Then, by definition:

$$w_{it}=\alpha^s_{it}w^s_{it}+\alpha^u_{it}w^u_{it}$$

If we assume that the wages of skilled and unskilled workers are the same across sectors, this implies:

$$w_{it}=\alpha^s_{it}w^s_{it}+\alpha^u_{it}w^u_{it}$$

We can then recover w^s_t and w^u_t from cross-sector regressions for each year of the average wage on the proportions of skilled and unskilled workers in that sector for that year. The data are from IWEP, and the regressions are based on 14 sectors. The numbers in the text correspond to the ratio of the first estimated coefficient to the second estimated coefficient, for the years 1994 and 2003 respectively.

How large is this elasticity? Using a survey of residents in the Hubei province, Zhu (2000) finds that the wages of workers who have migrated to the city are twice as high as those of workers who have remained in the countryside. Part of this difference reflects differences in skills. However, even after correcting for differences in skills, the wage of a migrant worker remains higher than that of a farmer (correcting for differences in skills, the ratio falls from 2 to 1.8), suggesting that returns to skills are larger in the city, but also that migrating is costly (one of the main factors here are the legal restrictions on mobility, under the policy known as the Hukou policy). We are thus far from perfect arbitrage between rural and urban jobs. The interesting question, however, is by how much a widening of the wage differential induces higher migration. The same survey indicates that a 10% fall in rural wages—holding wages in the city constant—raises migration flows by approximately 0.5%. Fluctuations in rural incomes are thus an important determinant of the decision to migrate, although the cost of moving prevents perfect arbitrage. As we shall discuss, this is an important fact when asking what are the effects of a revaluation, since a currency revaluation lowers incomes in the countryside.

Uneven growth across sectors

Not surprisingly, given the strategy and the composition of exports (in 2003, 91% of Chinese exports were manufactured goods), the share of manufacturing in GDP is large, quite independently of the group of countries to which China is compared (Table 7). The share of services is correspondingly low. This reflects in particular a low provision of health services with the situation getting worse in the countryside (We shall return to this below). The reported share of retail and wholesale trade is low as well; we are skeptical that this is indeed the case, but we have no data to confirm or challenge it.[1]

Table 7 The composition of output (value added, percent of GDP, 2000)

	Agriculture	Industry	Services
China 1990	27	42	31
China 2003	14	52	33
Other countries (2003)			
Low income countries	25	27	48
Upper-middle income countries	12	41	59
World	4	28	68

Source: World Development Indicators (2004) and IWEP.

[1] The low share of retail and wholesale trade in GDP, compared with countries at a similar stage of development may reflect to some extent from the undervalued exchange rate (more on this below). An undervalued exchange rate is likely to translate in a low price of non-traded goods, such as services, relative to traded goods (manufacturing). Thus, the low share of retail and wholesale trade in GDP may reflect a low price rather than a low quantity of trade services. For the same reason, manufacturing may be overstated, and so may investment volume.

Safety nets have substantially weakened

The high savings rate reflects (as we show below) a high level of individual risk, related to health costs, retirement and the financing of education. The decrease in social insurance has left individuals with the need to self insure—an expensive and very imperfect solution. The decrease in safety nets has become particularly relevant in the area of health, and the transition to a fee-based health care and education system (more on this below) has compounded the effects of widening income inequality.

A misallocation of investment

The savings glut, combined with a bank-centered financial system and privileged access to funds by state firms, has resulted in misallocation of investment. The fall in measured TFP growth (Hu and Zheng (2004) estimate that TFP growth has fallen from 3.7% in 1991–1995 to 0.6% during 1996–2001. The details are given in Box 2) should probably not be interpreted as a decrease in true technological progress, but rather as a reflection of capital misallocation, leading to a marginal productivity of capital close to zero or even negative in parts of manufacturing. Capital productivity is probably still high however for investment in social capital (health, education, ...) especially in rural areas. It is therefore hard to say whether China is investing too much, but it is certainly misallocating at least some of its investment.

Box 2: Can measured TFP growth really be close to zero if growth is so high?

The answer is yes:

Assume that production is given by $Y=F(hL, K, A)$ where h is human capital per worker, L is the number of workers, K is the physical capital stock, A measures technological progress, and the function F has constant returns to scale. Then, under the assumption that factors are paid their marginal product, it follows that the Solow residual, *TFP* growth, is given by:

$$S \equiv \Delta Y/Y - \alpha_N(\Delta h/h + \Delta L/L) - \alpha_K(\Delta K/K)$$

For the period 1995—2001, using the information in Hu and Zheng

(2004) the numbers are as follows:

$$\Delta Y/Y=8.2\%;\ \Delta h/h=28\%;\ \Delta L/L=1.2\%;\ \Delta K/K=12\%$$

So, if we use a share for capital of 0.4 (and by implication a share of labor of 0.6), this implies:

$$S=8.2\%-0.6(2.8\%+1.2\%)+0.4(12\%)=1.0\%$$

Minor changes in assumptions can easily make it smaller. Consider for example the construction of the rate of growth of the capital stock:

$$\Delta K/K=I/Y\cdot(Y/K)-\delta$$

The growth rate of capital used above is based on $I/Y=45\%$, $K/Y=2.5$, and $\delta=0.06$, so $\Delta K/K=12\%$. There is considerable uncertainty about K however, which is constructed using a perpetual inventory method. Assuming a value of $K/Y=2$ gives instead $\Delta K/K=16.5\%$ and, by implication, a small negative Solow residual. (Using a labor share of 0.47 and capital share of 0.53 the *OECD* estimates a growth rate of *TFP* equal to 4% over the period 1979–1985 and 1991–1995. It estimates that the growth rate of *TFP* has decreased further since, reaching −3% in 2003 (*OECD* Economic Survey of China, August 2005).)

The implication of this computation should not be however that there is no technological progress in China. The assumption underlying the computation is that factors are paid their marginal products. If, in fact, capital has been misallocated, then, contrary to this assumption, the marginal productivity of capital in those sectors where there has been excessive investment could be negative. Therefore, the right way to interpret the computation is that, while technological progress is surely present, it is partly offset by capital misallocation.

Growing macroeconomic imbalances

High savings and export-led growth do not imply trade surpluses. Investment can be equal to savings, and imports equal to exports. But, recently, savings have been running ahead of investment; equivalently exports have been running ahead of imports. The trade surplus is widening: US \$30 billion in 2004, and may be running at a yearly rate as high as US \$100 billion in 2005.

This description of the strategy China has followed so far with its successes and drawbacks, suggests a number of directions for reform to which we now turn.

■ Directions of Reform

Large policy swings would be unwise: Notwithstanding the imbalances that have emerged, China's growth story is an extraordinary success, and one should be careful before meddling with success. Corrections of the strategy pursued so far should come more in the form of inflexion than of drastic change. We see three main directions for reform:

1) Improve the ability of individuals to insure against risk. At this stage, Chinese individuals are exposed to high levels of retirement risk, health expenditure risk, and even education risk (the probability that a child is bright and requires an expensive education).
2) Reduce or reallocate investment. Investment appears to be too high in manufacturing, too low in services, especially public services. This suggests in particular higher public investment in health and education, especially aimed at rural provinces where the need is more acute.
3) Allow the RMB to appreciate to reduce the trade surplus. (By implication, allow for a decline in savings relative to investment.)

Each of these three directions is desirable on its own. The question is how best to combine them. A dramatic decrease in savings, by itself, would create overheating. A large appreciation of the RMB would create a recession in the export sector, and perhaps in the economy as a whole.

In some dimensions, the three directions fit well together. The combination of a decrease in savings and an appreciation of the RMB can in principle be combined to allow a decrease in the trade surplus while maintaining internal balance.

In other dimensions, they may conflict. Too large a decrease in private savings, due to the provision of insurance, may lead to a required large appreciation of the RMB to prevent overheating, reducing the export sector too much, and curtailing the process of learning by doing. Too large an appreciation of the RMB may increase the inequality between rural and other provinces.

With this in mind, we proceed in two steps. First, we consider the motivations and the effects of each reform, discussing what it would imply for China's macroeconomic imbalances if it were adopted in isolation. Next we ask how the three reforms can best be combined.

Private savings

A savings rate of 43% is very high. Especially so, when one realizes that, in an economy with overlapping generations, the aggregate savings rate is the net result of savings by the young, and dissavings by the old. This implies that the savings rate of the young must be even higher than 43%. How much higher? The answer depends roughly on the growth rate and the average length of an individual's life. With a growth rate of 8–10 percent per year and a half-life of 30 years, the savings of the young in China dwarf the dissavings of the old. This implies that the savings rate of the young is higher than 43%, but not much higher.

From a macroeconomic viewpoint, is a 43% savings rate "too high"? A useful benchmark is the "golden rule". In the standard neo-classical growth model, the "golden rule" savings rate—the savings rate that maximizes steady state consumption—is equal to the share of capital in GDP: By that standard, 43% is probably too high. But China has certainly not reached its steady state and this can justify a higher savings rate in the transition.

How much of the savings rate can be explained by life cycle considerations and how much by other considerations?[1] It is useful here to start with the breakdown of savings between households, enterprises, and the government. Table 8, from Kuijs (2005), provides this breakdown for China and a few other countries. Enterprise savings account for almost half of China's savings rate, but the outlier in Table 8 is clearly households' savings.

---

1 These issues are also explored by Chamon and Prasad (2005).

Table 8 Sectoral savings (percent of GDP)

	China 2001	China 2003	Japan 2001	Korea 2001	Mexico 2001
Households	16.0	16.6	8.2	4.5	8.0
Enterprises	15.0	18.9	19.4	14.8	10.6
Government	7.5	7.0	−2.2	11.7	2.2
National savings	38.5	42.5	25.5	31.0	20.8

Source: Kuijs, 2005.

Why are household savings so high? Modigliani and Cao (2004) conclude that it is largely consistent with the life-cycle model (which emphasizes savings for retirement), once one takes into account the high growth rate and the one-child policy in China. High growth increases the savings of the young relative to the dissavings of the old, leading to a higher net savings rate. And the one-child policy, they argue, can account for most of the rest: A child is often an effective substitute for life cycle savings. Consequently, when strict birth control measures came into effect in the 1970s (the one-child policy) the accumulation of life cycle (tangible) assets gained in importance as a substitute for children and savings increased. While life cycle savings are surely very relevant, there is however plenty of evidence suggesting that at least part of the high savings rate reflects "precautionary" savings, the result of a number of distortions that force Chinese individuals to self-insure through asset accumulation:[1]

With the decline of state-owned enterprises, the public retirement system has largely broken down (triggering reform projects, not yet implemented. See Diamond (2004)). Much of the risk of retirement—in particular the risk related to the expected length of life—is now borne by individuals.[2]

Beginning in the early 1990s, the provision of health care services and of education has increasingly been based on a system of fees (Table 9). Rural

---

1 In a poll cited by Hongbin (2005), Chinese individuals gave the following key motivations for saving: kids' education (35%), retirement (32%), medical care (10%), home purchase (7%), children's wedding expenditures (6%).

2 The point here is that not only do people save for retirement, but they save a lot more than they could because they cannot insure against risks associated with uncertainty about life expectancy.

households appear to bear a larger share of the cost of health services than urban households (Table 10), possibly because enterprises in the city provide workers with some form of health insurance. The hypothesis that the risks born by individuals are particularly severe in the countryside is indeed consistent with the evolution of the savings rate in urban and rural areas (Table 11). Safety nets are particularly weak from migrant workers who have moved from rural to urban areas and live with temporary permits (17.7 percent of the urban population according to the 2000 Census (Bian, 2004)). Table 12 shows that their access to social insurance is much more limited than that of urban permanent residents.

Table 9 Who pays for health care and education?

	Health expenditures	Out of pocket % of health spending	School fees % of education spending
1965	4.7	16%	n.a. (0?)
1980	10.9	18%	n.a. (0?)
1991	37.7	50%	2.3%
2001	101.7	61%	12.5% (*)

(*): 1998.
Health expenditures: Recurrent health expenditures, yuan per capita, constant prices.
Source: Kanbur and Zhang (2003).

Table 10 The allocation of health care costs in 1998 (percent of total cost)

	Cities	Countryside
Paid by the state	16.0	1.2
Labor related	22.9	0.5
Semi-labor related	5.8	0.2
Insurance	3.3	1.4
Cooperative	4.2	6.6
Self-paid	44.1	87.4
Other	3.7	2.7

Source: China Health Yearbook 1999 (Ministry of Health, 1999), p.410, from Kanbur and Zhang (2003).

Table 11 Household savings rates in urban and rural areas (percent of disposable income)

	Urban households	Rural households
1993	18.1	16.5
2003	23.1	25.9

Source: IWEP.

Table 12 Access to social benefits of temporary and permanent urban residents: Five major cities, 2000 (percent of all individuals in the group)

	Migrants	Local residents
Health insurance	12.4	67.7
Pension program	10.2	74.4
Unemployment benefits	0.8	33.3
Workplace injury insurance	14.3	25.3
Maternity leave	31.0	71.1

Source: Gao et al., 2002.

Other factors appear to contribute to the high private savings rate, also having to do with poor financial markets:

Savings for housing. A mortgage market exists and is rapidly expanding, but remains small. One obstacle is the poor definition of property rights. For example, banks can seize a property if the borrower defaults, but are then limited in their ability to sell it.

Savings to start firms. When the growth rate is 10% there is a good probability of running into a good business idea. If that happens, the only way to transform the idea into an investment is through one's own funds. Banks lack a credit culture and bank officers are not used to taking risks: Their first concern is likely to be that, in case the idea does not work and the company defaults, they may be accused of having been bribed.

Providing retirement and health care insurance is clearly desirable. In both cases, self-insurance is an expensive and very imperfect solution to the presence of individual risk. Any measure that allows risks to be pooled across the population will increase welfare. A similar argument holds for the development of a mortgage market, or for lending less on collateral and more on projects.

Insurance can in part be provided by the market. For this to happen, what is needed most is a set of reforms of the legal system. For instance, in the case of mortgages, foreclosure needs to be made easier, otherwise banks will not lend. In the area of health services, private insurance can go some way towards pooling and diversifying risks, but improved access to health services, especially in the countryside, can hardly come entirely from the private sector.

All such measures however have one important macroeconomic implication. They will decrease the private savings rate—equivalently increase consumption. Other things equal, this may lead to overheating, or/and a decrease in capital accumulation. This implication must be kept in mind when thinking about the overall strategy below.

Health services, taxes, and deficits

Among the growth imbalances we listed earlier is the unusually small share of services, among them health services. The evidence is that, in the 1990s, health services have not increased in proportion to income per capita, and that the shortfall has been particularly pronounced in rural provinces. Indexes of health personnel and of hospital beds per capita show an absolute decline in the 1990s in the countryside (Table 13). Infant mortality in the countryside has also deteriorated relative to cities; the ratio, which stood at 1.5 in 1980, has increased to 1.7 in 1990, and 2.1 in 1995 (Kanbur and Zhang, 2003).

Table 13 Health care in the cities and in the countryside

	% Change in hospital beds per 1000 people		% Change in health care personnel per 1000 people	
	Countryside	Cities	Countryside	Cities
1952–1978	+1.662%	+220%	+72%	+176%
1978–1990	−2%	+24%	+16%	+22%
1990–1998	−23%	+5%	−9%	0%
1998–2003	n.a.	n.a.	n.a.	n.a.

Source: Comprehensive Statistical Data and Materials on 50 Years of New China (China State Statistical Bureau, 2000), from Kanbur and Zhang (2003).

There are likely three factors behind inadequate health services:

We focused on the first earlier: The lack of health insurance leads people both to self insure through savings—the effect we focused on—but also to buy less health care.

The second is income distribution. With the shift to a fee-based system, health care has become too expensive for many to afford (this is conceptually different from the lack of insurance.) In a recent survey, 34% of urban respondents and 44% of rural respondents said they did not seek health care when ill because they could not afford it. As we have seen this problem is particularly acute in rural areas and among migrant workers in urban areas.

With the privatization of TVEs and an increased focus on profit rather than social insurance, much of the health care infrastructure has not been maintained. The supply of health care is inadequate, especially in the countryside.

This suggests that reforms aimed at expanding the health service sector must focus both on demand and on supply. On the demand side, we already discussed the introduction of a health insurance system. (The experience of the Vietnam health insurance program, described in World Bank (2001) and studied by Pradhan and Wagstaff (2005), suggests that such a system will improve health while, at the same time, allowing people to save less and consume more.) Distribution considerations suggest that health provision should have a redistributive component. On the supply side, more public spending on health, from building new hospitals and clinics, to increasing the incentives to become doctors and nurses in the countryside, is also needed.

We freely admit to not knowing enough about health care in general, and about health care in China in particular, to make more specific recommendations. We also realize that some of the arguments are relevant for other publicly provided services, such as education; again we leave a discussion of spending on education to people more competent than us. We want however to discuss the fiscal aspects of financing such expenditures, which are clearly of macroeconomic relevance. Take health care. Should increased spending on health provision by the state be financed through debt or through taxes? There are three relevant considerations here.

The first is based on standard principles of public finance. If spending is going to benefit people in the future, it makes sense to finance it through debt rather than through taxes; in this way the stream of taxes (needed to pay the interest on the debt later on) and the stream of benefits can be better aligned. This is the principle underlying the so called "golden rule" of public finance, which implies financing consumption expenditures through taxes, and investment expenditures through debt (this holds even if the investment expenditures have a low financial return, so long as the social return is high enough). These issues have been discussed in the context of the reform of the Growth and Stability Pact in Europe (Blanchard and Giavazzi, 2004); the discussion and the basic conclusion are of more general relevance.

The second is based on the need to achieve internal balance. We can think of fiscal policy, and the choice of taxes versus debt, as trying to avoid overheating and maintain macroeconomic balance. A very relevant example here is the program of electrification of the countryside that China embarked on after the Asian crisis. Electrification, just like health care today, was needed. At the same time, aggregate demand was lower, because of the large depreciations in many Asian countries, that China decided not to match. Financing electrification through deficits was therefore the appropriate policy. The situation may be different this time. We argued earlier that the provision of health insurance may lead to a decrease in private savings, an increase in consumption. If this is the case, the argument for further decreasing savings through public dissavings is weak. Indeed, what may be called for, is a smaller rather than a larger deficit. On the other hand, an appreciation of the RMB may require an increase in demand, and thus a larger deficit. This uncertainty suggests that no hard decision should be made in advance, and that the government should stand ready to finance these expenditures mostly through taxes or mostly through debt depending on the circumstances.

The third argument is based on debt dynamics (see Box 3). When, as in the case of China today, the growth rate is much higher than the interest rate the Chinese government has to pay on its debt, many of the standard worries associated with debt dynamics disappear. If the growth rate were to remain permanently higher than the interest rate, a government could decrease taxes and never have to increase them again: The ratio of debt to GDP would remain positive, but would not explode. If, as is likely, the growth rate will eventually become smaller than the interest rate, the relevant implication is that larger deficits today lead only to a small increase in debt over time, and to a low debt burden in the long run. In other words, larger deficits today may require only a modest eventual increase in taxes in the future. (This is discussed more formally in the box below.) In yet other words, if deficits are justified on macroeconomic grounds, China should not hesitate to use them.

Box 3: Chinese debt dynamics

Debt dynamics are determined by the following relation:

$$d_{t+1}-d_t=(r-g)d_t+x_{t+1}$$

where d is the ratio of debt to GDP, r is the average interest rate on debt, g is the growth rate of GDP, and x is the ratio of the primary deficit (the deficit excluding interest payments) to GDP.

The typical configuration is one in which r is greater than g, so positive debt requires, sooner or later, a primary surplus in order to stabilize debt.

Sometimes however, the configuration is different and r is less than g. This is clearly the case of China today; in 2004, the average real cost of debt service was around 2.5%, and the growth rate was around 9%. Under this configuration, a country can run a primary deficit and still maintain a stable debt ratio. If we take r=2.5% and g=9% for example, the equation above becomes:

$$d_{t+1}=0.935d_t+x_{t+1}$$

If r and g did not change in the future, this would imply that, if China were to run a 2% primary deficit ratio forever (the primary deficit ratio was equal to about 1.7% in 2004), the debt ratio would asymptotically reach 30%—no matter what the initial debt level. (To see this, assume x=2%. Then, check that the debt converges to d=2%/(1−0.935)=30.7%.)

It is unlikely however, both on empirical and theoretical grounds, that China will be able to maintain a growth rate above its interest rate on debt forever. But if we think that it will be able to do it for some time, say another 10 years, a conclusion with a similar flavor obtains. A deficit of 2% for 10 years will only increase the debt to GDP ratio by about 15 percentage points, thus imposing a small burden of the debt in the future.

A similar argument applies to recapitalization of banks by replacing the bad loans they hold on their balance sheets by government bonds. It is generally agreed that making bad loans explicit and replacing them by government bonds in banks' balance sheets, eliminates overhang effects and is therefore desirable. A typical objection however is that this implies a potentially large increase in explicit government debt, and dangerous debt dynamics. It is true that eliminating bank debt overhang this way will lead to an increase in explicit (i.e. financial) government debt today. But the implied increase in debt 10 years out, and so the ultimate burden of the debt, may be small:

The stock of non-performing loans at the end of 2004 was estimated at US $602 billion, or 38% of GDP. Assuming a recovery rate of 20%, recapitalizing the banks would add 30 percentage points to the debt-GDP ratio—up from 25%, the cost estimated by Dornbusch and Giavazzi in 1999. More bad loans are probably in the making. Roubini and Salter (2005) estimate the fraction of current new loans that may end up non performing and come up with a figure close to 15%–25% of GDP. Adding these numbers to the current debt GDP ratio of about 33% implies that the overall financial debt ratio could rise as high as 80%–90% of GDP. Even in that case, and for a given path of the primary deficit at 2%, a debt ratio of 80% today would translate, under our assumptions, in a debt ratio of 55% in ten years ($0.8\times0.93510+0.2\times(1-0.93510)/(1-0.935)$), a much less worrisome number.

The RMB appreciation

On July 22, 2005, China stopped pegging its currency to the U.S. dollar. In the new regime, a managed float, the RMB is allowed to fluctuate inside a small band centered around a dollar parity. Inside the band the exchange rate will fluctuate responding to "supply and demand in the market" and to intervention by the PBC. The crucial element of the new regime is obviously the determination of the central parity.

The central bank says that it will announce the closing price of the U.S. dollar in the inter-bank foreign exchange market after the closing of the market on each working day, and will make it the central parity for the trading against the RMB on the following working day. The closing parity, and thus the central parity the following day, will depend on intervention. In principle, with excess demand for RMB and limited intervention, the currency could hit the top of the band each day. The regime would turn into a crawling peg with a 6% monthly revaluation. The observation that the PBC has not ruled out such an outcome gives an indication of what the final revaluation might be. This possibility by itself will put upward pressure on the RMB: The result is that the accumulation of reserves—required simply to avoid a revaluation in excess of 0.3 percent per day—might be even larger than in the fixed exchange rate regime (the data on reserve accumulation since July suggest that this has not happened so far). Eventually China might find it easier to allow the RMB to float.

How large might the appreciation be in the end? In 2004 the PBC accumulated $200 billion in foreign exchange reserves. One half was related to trade and FDI: $50 billion from the trade surplus and $50 billion from FDI. The remaining $100 billion was largely speculative, in anticipation of revaluation: portfolio investment, remittances and repatriated profits.

Under floating, these one-way speculative flows would disappear. Under pure floating, that is with no further accumulation of reserves on the part of the PBC, the revaluation would need to cancel the sum of the trade surplus and the FDI flows. How large this might be is impossible to tell. The elasticity of exports to the exchange rate is likely to be low; nobody really knows. The most relevant margin may be the loss of competitiveness vis-à-vis countries like China, Pakistan, Egypt, and the Maghreb in particular. In any case a very large appreciation could not be ruled out. Using U.S. elasticities, which are likely to be larger than those relevant for China, an appreciation of at least 30% would be likely.[1] 20–30% is the relative price difference among Chinese goods and similar goods produced

1 Typical estimates for the United States imply that an appreciation of 10% decreases exports by 9% and increases import volumes by 8%. Using these numbers for China, assuming export and import ratios to GDP of 25%, and the need for a change of 5% in the ratio of the current account to GDP implies an appreciation of about 30%.

by some of China's main competitors, for instance other South-East Asian countries or the Maghreb.

To relieve the pressure on the RMB, the PBC could do two things:

First, it could remove capital controls asymmetrically, that is remove them on capital outflows but not on inflows. The bank could let Chinese investors acquire foreign assets, or announce a path for the gradual removal of capital outflows; this does not need to happen right away for it to have an effect on the exchange rate today. The extreme RMB exposure of Chinese investors suggests that portfolio diversification might significantly add to the supply of RMB, limiting the appreciation.

Would the gradual removal of capital controls create problems in the banking system? The concern is that portfolio diversification would reduce deposits at a rate faster than the speed at which banks can liquidate their loan portfolio. This risk is probably limited. The central bank has sterilized the reserve inflow by issuing sterilization bonds, and most of these bonds are held by commercial banks. So, consider the simple case where private Chinese investors diversified by buying all the reserves of the central bank and reduced their deposits with commercial banks by the same amount. In this case the effects on the balance sheet of commercial banks would cancel. On the asset side the banks would lose the equivalent of $700 billion in sterilization bonds, and the same would happen on the liability side, through the fall in deposits.

What if Chinese private investors wanted to acquire more dollar assets than the dollar assets currently held by the PBC? A simple computation is useful here.

The reserves of the PBC are roughly equal to 40% of Chinese GDP. Financial wealth, measured by broad money, is equal to 180% of GDP. If Chinese investors were to hold 25% of their wealth in the form of U.S. assets, they would want to accumulate U.S. assets equal to 45% (180% times 25%) of GDP, so more than the PBC currently holds. In this case a credit squeeze would become a possibility. Even more serious would be the possibility that banks might be unable to recover loans fast enough since the moment they attempted to do so, they would discover that many of these loans can no longer be recovered. Some banks may become bankrupt. This suggests that liberalization of capital outflows, while necessary to relieve the pressure on the RMB, should be gradual. This could for example be done along the lines suggested by Prasad and Rajan (2005), namely the creation of a closed-end mutual fund, available to domestic investors, and invested in foreign assets. Wider liberalization could then take place after the improvement of the banking system, in particular after the creation of a "credit culture" and better screening of loans by banks.

The second way in which the PBC can limit the appreciation, at least for some time, is by continuing to accumulate reserves. There is potentially a good argument for doing so: By limiting the appreciation, reserve accumulation allows for higher exports, and potentially higher learning by doing and productivity growth. The capital loss on the accumulated reserves when the appreciation eventually takes place could in principle be smaller than the output gain from the higher productivity growth; in that case, it makes sense to accumulate further reserves, at least for some time. Whether this condition is satisfied is obviously very difficult to assess. In Box 4, we offer a computation which suggests that, while some reserve accumulation may be justified, the current rate of accumulation is almost certainly too high.

Box 4: Reserve accumulation and learning-by-doing

Suppose that an appreciation of x% would be needed to balance the current account of China.

Suppose that because of capital controls, the exchange rate can be maintained at its current level, but at the cost of reserve accumulation per year equal to z% of GDP.

Suppose that delaying the appreciation for one year implies larger exports, higher learning by doing, and thus higher growth for a year of y%.

Delaying the appreciation for a year therefore has a cost, the cost of the expected capital loss on accumulated reserves, so x% times z% of GDP. It has a benefit, namely the higher level of output now and forever, equal to y% of GDP. (One may instead assume that learning would have come later anyway so that, in the long run, output returns to the same value, whether or not the exchange rate appreciates this year. This would lead to a declining stream of benefits.)

In 2004, reserve accumulation was roughly equal to $200 billion, or 12% of GDP. If we assume that the eventual appreciation will have to be of the order of, say, 30%, this implies a cost of 3.6% of GDP.

As to the benefits, the (very difficult) question is how much more growth can we expect from an undervalued exchange rate. (Unpublished) work by Hausmann and Rodrik give us a useful hint. Using panel data on countries and time, they first compute a measure of undervaluation of the exchange rate for each country and each year as the residual of a regression of the real exchange rate on the level of income per capita and the population of the country. (They find the Chinese exchange rate to be undervalued by roughly 30%.) They then show that, among emerging countries, undervaluation has typically been associated with fast growth. To formalize this idea, and again using data on countries and time, they estimate the coefficient on the real exchange rate residual in a panel data regression of the growth rate on this residual and a number of other controls. The coefficient they obtain implies that a 1% undervaluation is associated with a 0.015% increase in growth.[1] If we interpret the relation as a causal relation from undervaluation to growth, a 30% undervaluation, as may be the case in China, implies higher growth of GDP of 0.45%.

Thus, under these assumptions, reserve accumulation equal to 3.6% of GDP for a year implies a level of output higher by 0.45% forever, or at least for many years. This implies a high social internal rate of return.

So why not continue to do it? Apart from the caveats due to the limits of the computation, and the internal (and international) tensions from an undervalued RMB, which are left out of this computation, the rate of reserve accumulation required to maintain the exchange rate is likely to increase rapidly, as Chinese investors find more and more ways around capital controls. This makes the trade-off less and less appealing as time passes.

Turn now to the macroeconomic effects of an appreciation. They are likely to be twofold (The appendix at the end of the paper discusses both aspects more formally):

---

[1] We are indebted to Ricardo Hausmann for providing us with the results of these regressions.

First, to the extent that the appreciation worsens China's competitiveness, exports will decrease, and so will the export sector. In the absence of other measures, the fall in exports is unlikely to be accompanied by an increase in demand in the rest of the economy. The positive terms-of-trade effect of the revaluation (an argument used by the PBC in explaining the reasons for the new exchange rate regime) is likely to be limited. To maintain internal balance, the revaluation must be accompanied by an increase in internal demand.

This takes us back to our earlier discussion of savings. The reduction in risk and the implied decrease in savings may be justified not only on welfare grounds, as discussed earlier. They may also be justified as the right policy to accompany the revaluation.

Second, the appreciation is likely to worsen inequalities between regions, and between skilled and unskilled workers. The reason is that China is a price taker in world agricultural markets. Given a price in dollars, the appreciation will lower the domestic currency price of agricultural products and thus real income in countryside.[1] Furthermore, through migration, it will put downward pressure on the wage of unskilled workers in the industrial sector: The skilled-unskilled differential will also widen.

The fall in local food prices induced by the appreciation is a transfer from farmers to urban (and rural) consumers. With equal propensities to consume, there will be no effect of the transfer on aggregate demand. Propensities to consume may be different however. If it is higher in the countryside than in the cities, the fall in rural incomes (with an official population count of 800 million in the countryside) will have an independent depressing effect on domestic demand. This reinforces the first argument above.

Even if there is no effect on aggregate demand from the transfer, increasing inequality is undesirable. This takes us back to our discussion

---

1 Two examples from the past: In the inter-war period, when Italy returned to the gold standard revaluing the Lira by 50%, the result was a deep recession in the countryside. Agricultural prices fell notwithstanding the attempt to isolate the Italian market through a tax on imported wheat Similarly—as Keynes vividly described in his Essays on Persuasion—the return to gold in the UK destroyed the coal industry.

of inequalities earlier. The provision of health care, or measures aimed especially at rural provinces such as the elimination of the poll tax, are justified on welfare grounds, whether or not the RMB is revalued. But they are even more justified in the face of the revaluation induced change in income distribution.

Are there other ways to reduce manufacturing exports while avoiding the adverse effect of an appreciation on farm income and inquality? In principle, yes, and these should be explored. For example, the introduction of a pollution tax and a decrease in subsidies to FDI, would limit the extent of currency appreciation needed to reduce the incentive to invest in the export sector. (Some have suggested the use of an export tax, which would potentially limit the fall in agricultural prices. We are skeptical that such an export tax can be implemented without major distortions in China today.)

■ A Tentative Package

Our discussion suggests the following package:

Eliminate some of the imperfections behind the high precautionary savings rate. Measures here range from the design of a more robust retirement system, to the provision of health insurance, to the development of private insurance, to better property rights leading banks to lend less on collateral and more on projects.

These measures will increase welfare directly, but also decrease savings in the process.

Let the RMB appreciate, so as to reallocate activity away from the export sector. The announced gradual removal of controls on capital outflows and of tax breaks on FDI's would limit the upward pressure on the RMB. Eventually, China should consider replacing the exchange rate rule announced in July with a simple clean float, since the new rule is more likely than not to induce an acceleration of capital inflows.

Other tools can help here. A pollution tax, for instance, would reduce the incentive to invest in the export sector without negatively affecting rural incomes. The larger the pollution tax, the smaller the required appreciation for a given reallocation, and the smaller the effect on rural/urban inequality.

Increase the public provision of health and other public services. Do so in such a way that these are especially targeted to the countryside, all the more so since the appreciation will redistribute income from rural to urban areas. During funds' transference from the center to the rural provinces, avoiding the funds' disappearance through corruption is obviously a first order priority.

The three ingredients, however, need to be carefully balanced:

Too much reduction in individual risk would lead to a large drop in savings.

To avoid overheating this would require a large appreciation.

Too large an appreciation would increase inequalities: regional (price of agricultural goods) and skill (the implied wage in export sector). It would also slow down the process of learning by doing in the export sector, reducing TFP growth.

So, how to make sure that the transition does not run into a recession, or into overheating, or into too sharp a reduction in the role of exports? The right instrument is probably fiscal policy, in particular the degree of tax versus debt financing of the new health care expenditure. Given the current growth and interest rate, debt dynamics allow for potentially large primary deficits, at little cost in terms of the ultimate burden of debt.

Could monetary policy help as well? In principle, with capital controls, an increase in interest rates would help slow down domestic demand if needed. But capital controls have large leakages and may not prevent an upward pressure on the exchange rate.

Two final remarks: If successful, such a strategy is likely to reduce the (measured) growth rate of China. This is because productivity growth in services (at least measured productivity growth) is lower than in manufacturing. Lower growth would not however mean lower welfare. Think of the extreme case of a country fully specialized in high-tech manufacturing, but with no health care.

The growth rate would be even higher than it is today; welfare would nevertheless be quite low. Nor does lower output growth imply lower employment growth. If productivity growth is lower by $x\%$, then output growth lower by $x\%$ is compatible with the same employment growth rate as before. The notion of a given "employment elasticity of growth", invariant to the composition of output, used in some analyses of Chinese growth and discussions of the appropriate growth rate for China, makes no sense and should be discarded.

■ Appendix: RMB Appreciation, Reallocation and Income Distribution

In this appendix, we look at the general equilibrium effects of the RMB appreciation. We proceed in two steps. First, we build a standard model of tradables/nontradables. Then, we introduce two Chinese specificities: The importance of the agricultural sector, and labor mobility between agriculture and non agriculture, leading to partial arbitrage between farm income and wages.

■ Non-Tradables/Tradables, Home and Foreign Goods

Think of Chinese consumers/firms as buying three types of goods:

Non-tradables, denoted N, with price P_N in terms of domestic currency;

Home tradables (tradables produced at home, and sold either domestically or abroad as exports), denoted H, with price P_H;

Foreign tradables (tradables produced abroad, sold either abroad or in China as imports), denoted F, with price P_F. Let E be the exchange rate, defined as the price of domestic currency in terms of foreign currency (so an increase in E is an appreciation). Given the world price P_F^*, $P_F=P_F^*/E$.

Internal balance

Write the supply and demand functions for the two goods produced at home, non-tradables and home tradables, as:

$$Y_N(P_N/W)=D_N(X) \tag{1}$$

$$Y_H(P_H/W)=D_H(P_H/P_F,X)+D_H^*(P_H/P_F) \tag{2}$$

The supply of non-tradables is an increasing function of the relevant product wage, P_N/W. The demand for non-tradables is taken to be just a function of real domestic expenditure, X, a convenient simplification for expository purposes.

The supply of home tradables is an increasing function of the relevant product wage, P_H/W. The demand for home tradables is the sum of domestic and foreign demand. Domestic demand is a function of real domestic expenditure, X, and the terms of trade, P_H/P_F. Foreign demand is a function of real foreign expenditure, omitted for simplicity, and the terms of trade.

Assume that the labor force is fixed. Labor market equilibrium gives us another relation between the two product wages:

$$L_N(P_N/W)+L_H(P_H/W)=\bar{L}$$

Together, these equations give us a relation between domestic expenditure and the terms of trade required for internal balance. Consider for example an increase in domestic expenditure, X. This increase leads to an increase in the demand for non-tradables, requiring an increase in the price of non-tradables relative to the wage. From labor market equilibrium, this implies a decrease in the price of home tradables relative to the wage. From equilibrium in the home tradables market, the decrease in supply must be matched by a decrease in demand, and thus an increase in the relative price of home versus foreign tradables, an increase in the terms of trade.

This internal balance relation is drawn as the upward sloping locus in Figure 1. In short, an increase in expenditure requires a shift in production towards nontradables away from home tradables; this is achieved by decreasing demand for home tradables, by making home tradables more expensive relative to foreign tradables, through an increase in the terms of trade.

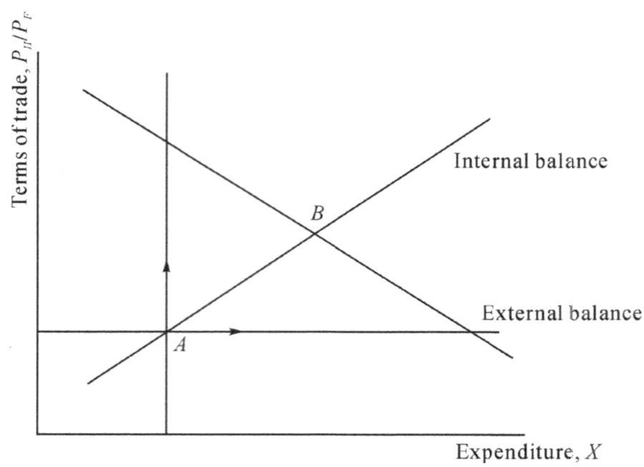

Figure 1

External balance

Assume the domestic demand for foreign tradables to be a function of domestic expenditure, and of the terms of trade:

$$D_F = D_F(P_H/P_F, X)$$

The trade balance, expressed in terms of home goods, is thus given by:

$$TB = D_H^*(P_H/P_F) - (P_F/P_H)D_F(P_H/P_F, X)$$

This equation gives us the relation between domestic expenditure and the terms of trade required for external balance. An increase in domestic expenditure leads to an increase in the demand for foreign tradables. If the trade balance is to remain equal to zero, this increase must be offset by a decrease in the relative price of home tradables, a decrease in the terms of trade (this assumes that the Marshall Lerner condition is satisfied). This external balance relation is drawn as the downward sloping locus in Figure 1.

Adjustment

A country can be at any point in Figure 1, depending on its level of expenditure and terms of trade. Different points correspond to different trade positions and activity levels. China can be thought to be at a point such as A. The economy is roughly at full employment (on the internal balance locus), but China is running a trade surplus (it is below the external balance locus).

Consider measures to decrease savings. By themselves, these will increase domestic expenditure, and shift the economy to the right from point A. They will reduce the trade surplus (the economy is closer to the external balance locus) but they will lead to excess demand in the labor market, and overheating.

Consider instead measures to reduce the trade surplus, such as an appreciation of the RMB, leading to an increase in $P_H/P_F = EP_H/P^*_F$. By itself, the appreciation will increase the terms of trade, moving the economy up from point A. The trade surplus will be reduced, but at the cost of excess supply in the goods market, and the risk of a recession.

The right combination is obvious, a decrease in savings and an appreciation. Together, these can take the economy from A to B, maintaining internal balance while achieving external balance.

So far, the analysis has been standard. We now introduce two aspects more specific to the Chinese economy, which turn out to be important.

■ Agriculture, Income Distribution, and Appreciation

Agricultural prices in China are closely linked to world prices. Using data from 1990 on, the correlation between the price of rice in China (expressed in U.S. dollars) and the price of rice in the United States is 0.66; the corresponding correlation for the price of wheat is 0.57. Put another way (and assuming similar standard deviations for world and Chinese prices), a 10% appreciation of the RMB relative to the dollar implies a fall in agricultural prices on Chinese markets of approximately 6%.

Agricultural prices are in turn the main determinant of rural incomes. Using data from 1991 on, the correlation between the change in wheat prices and the growth rate in rural incomes is 0.64.

With these facts in mind, we introduce a second tradable good, agriculture, with price P_A in terms of domestic currency. Assume that China is a price taker in world agricultural markets, so $P_A = P^*_A/E$: An appreciation leads to a decrease in the domestic currency price of agricultural goods.

Internal balance

Assume that the equations for non-tradable and home tradable goods are unchanged (this is again a simplification, as one might expect the relative price of agricultural goods to affect them).

Solving Eq.(1) for P_N/W gives:

$$P_N/W = f(X), f' > 0 \tag{3}$$

An increase in expenditure implies an increase in the demand for nontradable goods, and thus requires an increase in supply, so an increase in the price—equivalently a decrease in the product wage.

Solving Eq.(2) for P_H/W gives:

$$P_H/W = g(X, P_H/P_F), g'_X > 0, g'_t < 0 \tag{4}$$

where g'_t is the derivative of g with respect to the terms of trade. An increase in expenditure implies an increase in the demand for home tradables, and thus requires an increase in supply, so an increase in the price—equivalently, a decrease in the product wage. An increase in the terms of trade implies a decrease in demand and requires a decrease in supply, so a decrease in the price—equivalently, an increase in the product wage.

Turn now to the labor market. People can work either in the non-tradable sector, in the home tradable sector, or in agriculture. Assume a common labor market and thus a common wage in the non-tradable and tradable non agricultural sectors. And assume that the supply of labor to that labor market is an increasing function of the ratio of the wage to agricultural income, which we shall take to be proportional to the price of agricultural goods:

$$L_N(P_N/W) + L_H(P_H/W) = L(W/P_A)$$

Rewrite W/P_A as:

$$W/P_A = (W/P_H)(P_H/P_F)(P^*_F/P^*_A)$$

and replace in the labor market equilibrium condition to get:

$$L_N(P_N/W)+L_H(P_H/W)=L((W/P_H)(P_H/P_F)(P^*_F/P^*_A))$$

Combine the two equations characterizing goods market equilibrium, Eqs. (3) and (4) with the labor market condition above to get the internal balance relation:

$$L_N(f(X))+L_H(g(X, P_H/P_F))=L((1/g(X, P_H/P_F))(P_H/P_F)(P^*_F/P^*_A))$$

This gives us again a relation between expenditure, X, and the terms of trade P_H/P_F:

An increase in X increases both P_N/W and P_H/W, increasing labor demand. It decreases W/P_H, decreasing labor supply. The result is an excess demand for labor.

An increase in P_H/P_F decreases the demand for home tradables, decreasing P_H/W, and decreasing labor demand. It also leads to an increase in labor supply, both directly and indirectly (through W/P_H). The result is an excess supply of labor.

Internal balance delivers therefore a positive relation between X and P_H/P_F. The slope of the relation is given by:

$$\frac{\mathrm{d}(P_H P_F)}{\mathrm{d}X}=\frac{L'_N f' + L'_H g'_X + (L'/g^2)g'_X}{-L'_H g'_t - (L'/g^2)g'_t + L'/g}>0$$

The internal balance locus is still unambiguously upward sloping. The main difference is that an increase in the terms of trade now leads to a positive labor supply effect: The price of agricultural goods decreases, making it more attractive to work outside agriculture.

To see this, consider the extreme case of perfect labor mobility between agriculture and the rest of the economy, so $L'=\infty$ and W/P_A remains constant. Recall that we can rewrite W/P_A as:

$$W/P_A=(W/P_H)(P_H/P_F)(P^*_F/P^*_A)$$

So constancy of W/P_A implies that the product wage in home tradables vary inversely with the terms of trade. The higher the terms of trade, the lower the product wage:

$$W/P_H = \text{constant} \frac{1}{P_H P_F}$$

Now return to the equilibrium condition for home tradables, Eq. (2). An increase in the terms of trade, P_H/P_F, decreases demand for home tradables as before. But now, we know that it decreases the product wage W/P_H, leading to an increase in supply. So the supply of home tradables now goes up. A (larger than before) increase in domestic expenditure X is needed to maintain market equilibrium; the internal balance locus is upward sloping. Given X, equilibrium in the market for non-tradables determines in turn P_N/W; the increase in X implies a decrease in W/P_N.

So, as we move up the internal demand locus, an important implication is that the wage decreases in terms of P_H and in terms of P_N. As, by assumption (perfect mobility), it does not change in terms of P_A and P_F (P_A and P_F move together with the exchange rate when there is an appreciation), and given that the price of the consumption basket depends on all four prices, the real consumption wage must decrease.

External balance

The derivation of the external balance relation, and the need for both a decrease in X and an increase P_H/P_F to achieve internal and external balance, is basically unchanged (except for the presence of agricultural exports in the trade balance relation).

Implications

The important conclusion from this extension is the following:

Relative to the case we considered in the previous section, an appreciation leads to a shift from agriculture to the other sectors, to a decrease in the real wage, and a decrease in real farm income. In other words, an appreciation worsens income distribution, both across regions (agriculture, non agriculture), and across individuals (the wages of the unskilled workers, who are the relevant group thinking about moving out of agriculture, are likely to decrease).

There may be other implications as well. After proper use of expenditure and appreciation to decrease the trade surplus while maintaining internal balance, both the non tradable sector and the home tradable sectors may actually be larger—at the expense of the agricultural sector. This comes again from the labor supply effect, and the potential migration flow from the countryside.

References

Biàn Yanjie, Zhang Weimin and Liu Yongli (2004), "Social stratification, home ownership and quality of living: Evidence from the 2000 Census", paper presented at the international conference on China's 2000 population and housing census, Beijing, April.

Blanchard, Olivier and Francesco Giavazzi (2004), "Improving the SGP through a proper accounting of public investment", in "Reformer le Pacte de Stabilité et de Croissance" , Conseil d'Analyse Economique, Paris.

Brun, J.-F., J.-L. Combes and M.-F. Renard (2002), "Are there spillover effects between coastal and non coastal regions in China? ", mimeo, Université Blaise Pascal.

Chamon, Marc and Eswar Prasad (2005), "Determinants of household saving in China", mimeo, Research Department, IMF, September.

Diamond, Peter (2004), "Report on social security reform in China", China Economic Research and Advisory Programme, November.

Dornbusch, Rudiger and Francesco Giavazzi (1999), "Heading off China's financial crisis", in "Strengthening the Banking System in China: Issue and Experience", BIS Policy Papers, No. 7.

Fang, Cheng, Zhang Xiaobo and Fan Shenggen (2002), "Emergence of urban poverty and inequality in China: Evidence from household survey", *China Economic Review*, 13, 430-443.

Feldstein, Martin (1973), "The welfare loss of excess health insurance", *Journal of Political Economy*, 81(2), 251-280.

Gao Jun, Qian Juncheng, Bo Eriksson and Erik Blas (2002), "Health equity in transition from planned to market economy in China", *Health Policy Planning*, 17, Suppl. 1, 20-29.

Gruber, Jonathan and Aaron Yelowitz (1999), "Public health insurance and private savings", *Journal of Political Economy*, 107(6), 1249-1274.

Hausmann, Ricardo (2005), "China's growth miracle in perspective", mimeo, Kennedy School of Government, Harvard University, September.

Qu Hongbin (2005), "China's economic insight. Reducing the saving glut", HSBC, June 30.

Hu Albert, Gary Jefferson and Qian Jincheng (2003), "R&D and technology transfer: Firm-level evidence from Chinese industry", William Davidson institute, Working Paper No. 582, June.

Hu An-gang and Zheng Jinghai (2004), "Why China's TFP has dropped", mimeo, Center for China Studies, School of Public Policy and Management, Tsinghua University,

Beijing.

Jones Derek, Cheng Li and Ann Owen (2003), "Growth and regional inequality in China during the reform era", William Davdson Institute, Working paper No. 561.

Kanbur Ravi and Xiaobo Zhang (2003), "Spatial inequality in education and health care in China", International Food Policy Research Institute, Washington, DC.

Kuijs, Louis (2005), "Investment and saving in China", Research working paper No.1, World Bank China Office.

Manning, Willard and M. Susan Marquis (1996), "Health insurance and moral hazard", *Journal of Health Economics*, 15(5), 609-639.

Modigliani, Franco and Shi Larry Cao (2004), "The Chinese savings puzzle and the life cycle analysis", *Journal of Economic Literature*, 42(1), 145-170.

Pradhan, Menno and Adam Wagstaff (2005), "Health insurance impacts on health and nonmedical consumption in a developing country", World Bank Policy Research Working Paper 3563, April.

Prasad, Eswar and Raghu Rajan (2005), "Controlled capital account liberalization: A proposal", IMF Policy Discussion Paper, October.

Rodrik, Dani (2005), "What's so special about China's exports?", mimeo, Harvard University, July.

Roubini, Nouriel and Brad Setser (2005), "China trip report", available at www.stern.nyu.edu /globalmacro/.

World Bank (2001), "Vietnam. Growing healthy: A review of Vietnam's health sector", Hanoi, The World Bank.

Zhang Kevin Honglin and Song Shunfeng (2003), "Rural-urban migration and urbanization in China", *China Economic Review*, 14, 386-400.

Zu Nong (2002), "The impacts of income gaps on migration decisions in China", *China Economic Review*, 13, 213-230.

China: Toward a Consumption-Driven Growth Path

Nicholas R. Lardy[1]

In December 2004 China's top political leadership agreed to fundamentally alter the country's growth strategy. In place of investment and export-led development, they endorsed transitioning to a growth path that relied more on expanding domestic consumption.[2] Since 2004, China's top leadership, most notably Premier Wen Jiabao in his speech to the National People's Congress in the spring of 2006, has reiterated the goal of strengthening

---

1 Nicholas R. Lardy, a senior fellow at the Peterson Institute for International Economics since 2003, was a senior fellow in the Foreign Policy Studies Program at the Brookings Institution from 1995 to 2003. He was the director of the Henry M. Jackson School of International Studies at the University of Washington from 1991 to 1995. From 1997 through the spring of 2000, he was the Frederick Frank Adjunct Professor of International Trade and Finance at the Yale University School of Management. His publications include *China: The Balance Sheet* (Public Affairs, 2006), *Integrating China into the Global Economy* (Brookings Institution Press, 2002), *China's Unfinished Economic Revolution* (Brookings Institution Press, 1998), *China in the World Economy* (Institute for International Economics, 1994), *Foreign Trade and Economic Reform in China, 1978–1990* (Cambridge University Press, 1992), and *Agriculture in China's Modern Economic Development* (Cambridge University Press, 1983).

2 "Central Economic Work Conference convenes in Beijing December 3 to 5", *People's Daily*, December 6, 2004, 1, www.people.com.cn (accessed July 21, 2006).

domestic consumption as a major source of economic growth.[1] This policy brief examines the reasons underlying the leadership decision, the implications of this transition for the United States and the global economy, and the steps that have been taken to embark on the new growth path.

China's announced decision to transition away from growth driven by investment and a growing global trade surplus toward one more dependent on consumption is laudable. It increases the likelihood of China's sustaining its strong growth of recent years, achieving more rapid job creation, improving income distribution or at least slowing the pace of rising income inequality, and reducing its outsized increases in energy consumption of recent years. It also would contribute to a reduction of global economic imbalances.

But to date China's policy initiatives have been too modest to change its underlying growth dynamic. As a result China's external surplus continues to balloon and, short of a U.S. recession, seems likely to expand further in 2007 as well. China also is falling short of meeting several of its key domestic economic objectives.

■ Sources of China's Economic Growth

China has been the fastest growing economy in the world over almost three decades, expanding at 10 percent a year in real terms. As a result, real GDP in 2005 was about 12 times the level of 1978, when Deng Xiaoping launched China on the path of economic reform (National Bureau of Statistics of China 2006a, 24). China is now the world's fourth largest economy and its third largest trader and highly likely, within a year, to move up a notch in each category. Given this stunning long-term success, why would China's leadership even entertain the idea of shifting to a new growth paradigm?

In all economies the expansion of output is the sum of the growth of consumption plus investment plus net exports of goods and services.

---

1 Wen Jiabao (2006), "Report on the work of the government", *People's Daily*, March 14, http://english.people.com.cn (accessed March 14, 2006).

Expanding investment has been a major and increasingly important driver of China's growth. As shown in Figure 1, in the first decade or so of economic reform, investment averaged 36 percent of GDP, relatively high by the standard of developing countries generally but not in comparison with China's East Asian neighbors when their investment shares were at their highest. But since the beginning of the 1990s China's investment rate has trended up. In 1993 and again in both 2004 and 2005 investment as a share of GDP exceeded 42 percent, a level well above the historic experience of China's East Asian neighbors in their high growth periods.[1] Rising investment has been fueled by a rise in the national savings rate, which reached an unprecedented 50 percent of GDP in 2005.[2]

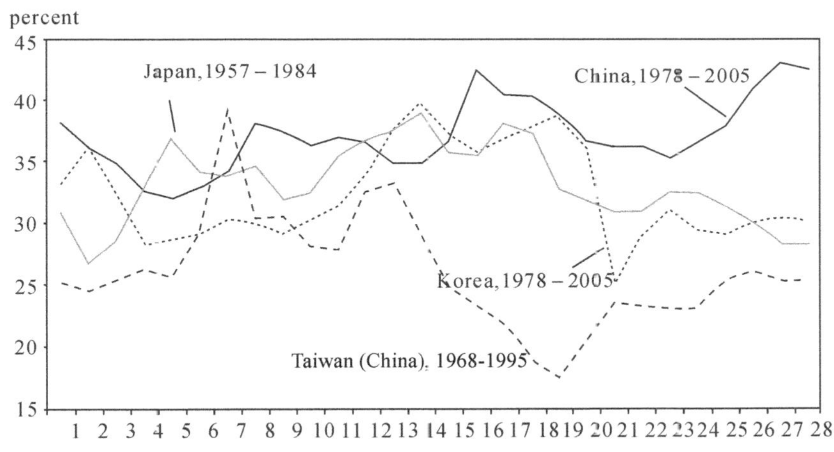

Figure 1 ***Capital formation as percent of GDP***

Note: For each country the time period is when the average rate of capital formation was the highest.
Sources: National Bureau of Statistics of China, China Statistical Yearbook 2006; Council for Economic Planning and Development of Republic of China, Taiwan Statistical Data Book, 1997 and 2006; IMF International Financial Statistics, http://ifs.apdi.net/ (accessed September 27, 2006).

---

1 All of the analysis of the expenditure components of GDP, i.e. consumption, investment, and net exports, is based on the revised GDP expenditure data for 1978 through 2005 released by the National Bureau of Statistics of China (2006b) in late September 2006.

2 By definition, the national savings rate is equal to investment as a share of GDP plus the current account as a percent of GDP. In China, these were 42.6 and 7.0 percent of GDP, respectively, in 2005.

Consumption growth has been rapid in absolute terms throughout the reform period, but over the last decade or so its relative importance as a source of economic growth has diminished substantially compared with that of investment. In the 1980s household consumption averaged slightly more than half of GDP. This share fell to an average of 46 percent in the 1990s. But after 2000 household consumption as a share of GDP fell sharply and by 2005 accounted for only 38 percent of GDP, the lowest share of any major economy in the world.[1] In the United States, household consumption accounted for 70 percent of GDP in the same year. In the United Kingdom, the consumption share was 60 percent. In India it was 61 percent.

As a result of this changing structure of demand, in 2001–2005, increases in capital investment accounted for a little over half of China's economic growth, an unusually high share by international standards (National Bureau of Statistics of China, 2006b, p.70).

In the last few years, the growth of net exports of goods and services has also become, for the first time in almost a decade, a major source of economic growth. Net exports of goods alone, as reported by China's Ministry of Commerce, tripled from $32 billion or 1.7 percent of GDP in 2004 to more than $100 billion or 4.6 percent of GDP in 2005 (National Bureau of Statistics of China, 2006a, p.169).[2] As shown in Figure 2, the net exports of goods and services in 2005 reflected in China's GDP expenditure accounts more than doubled to reach $125 billion and accounted for one-quarter of the growth of the economy. In 2006 I estimate net exports of goods and services will reach $185 billion, and the increase in net exports of goods and services will account for a fifth of China's growth. The contribution of net exports to China's growth has rarely been as high as in 2005–2006.

---

1 The declining share of consumption is due to both a decline in household disposable income as a share of GDP and a decline in consumption as a share of disposable income.

2 The ministry's data, which are released monthly, cover goods only and measure imports inclusive of transportation and insurance charges. Thus the ministry's annual import number differs from the data on trade in goods reported in China's balance of payments in which imports, in accordance with standard conventions, are measured on a free on board (f.o.b) basis.

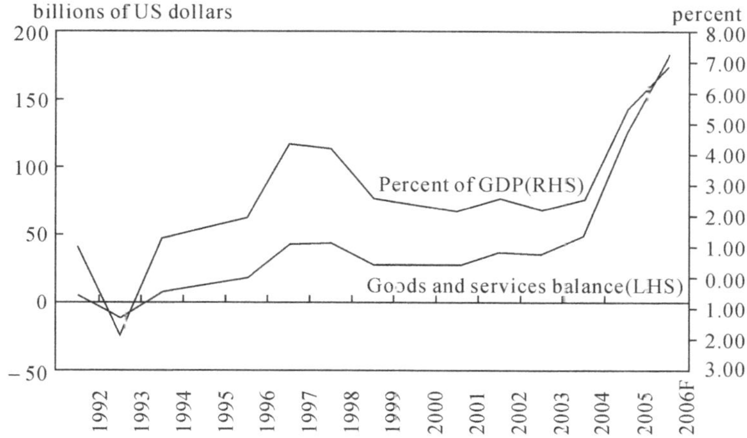

Figure 2 ***Net exports of goods and services, 1992–2006F***

Sources: National Bureau of Statistics of China, China Statistical Yearbook 2006b; International Monetary Fund, International Financial Statistics; author's calculations.

■ Rethinking China's Growth Strategy

The decision of China's leadership at its critical annual Central Economic Work Conference in December 2004 reflected the judgment that China's growth path was not sustainable in the long run. This does not mean the leadership seeks to slow the rate of economic growth markedly. Rather they wish primarily to change the structure of demand and to raise the efficiency of investment. In short, they believe that rapid growth is more likely to prove sustainable if it is generated more by expanding consumption by Chinese households and less by surging investment by Chinese companies and a ballooning global trade surplus.

While the Chinese Communist Party is hardly a transparent decision-making body, it appears that several factors underlay its December 2004 policy choice. First, there was growing evidence that investment-driven growth, or what is sometimes called an extensive pattern of growth, was leading to less efficiency in the use of resources. By most metrics, as investment growth has accelerated, the efficiency of resource use has declined. Multifactor productivity growth, a critical contributor to economic expansion in all economies, averaged almost 4 percent per annum in the first 15 years of economic reform (1978–1993). While still high by international standards, this pace slowed to only 3 percent since 1993 (Kuijs and Wang, 2005, p.2). In short, as the investment share of GDP rose, the contribution of productivity improvements to GDP growth fell. In the words of Martin Wolf (2005), the chief economics commentator for the Financial Times, the surprising thing about the Chinese economy in recent years is not, as so frequently asserted, how fast it is growing but rather, given the stupendous share of output devoted to investment, how slowly it is growing.

The slowing pace of factor productivity growth can be attributed in part to overinvestment and the emergence of excess capacity in a number of important industries. China emerged as the world's largest steel producer in 1996 when its output reached 100 million metric tons, putting it ahead of both the United States and Japan for the first time. The industry has continued to grow at a torrid pace. The National Development and Reform Commission (2006) reported that in 2005 output reached 350 million metric tons, and capacity was even larger at 470 million metric tons. Excess capacity of China's steel industry of 120 million tons exceeded the 112.5 million metric tons of steel output of the world's second largest producer, Japan. Excess capacity will expand further in 2006 since additional capacity of 70 million tons of steel production capacity was under construction but not completed in 2005, while demand growth is softening.[1]

As a result of excess production, steel prices by year-end 2005 were down a quarter compared with a year earlier and by one-third compared with the peak levels of March.[2] This decline in prices has dramatically transformed the profitability of the industry. When China's investment rate soared between 2000 and 2004, the demand for steel rose rapidly, and steel industry profits skyrocketed from less than RMB5 billion ($600 million) in 1999 to RMB127 billion ($15.7 billion) in 2005. But as excess capacity emerged, the growth of profits waned. Profits of steel firms doubled in 2003 and rose a further 80 percent in 2004 but increased by

1 Gong Zhengzheng (2006), "Steel sector to produce slim profits this year", *China Daily*, March 3, 9.

2 Gong Zhengzheng (2006), "Steel profits expected to decline", *China Daily*, January 26, 9.

only 1 percent in 2005. In the first half of 2006, profits in the industry fell by 20 percent compared with the same period in 2005.[1] For the year as a whole, profits are expected to fall by half, according to a Beijing securities firm. But the steel industry invested about RMB650 billion ($80 billion) in the five years 2001–2005, of which less than two-fifths ($30 billion) was financed by after-tax profits. This year a decline of 50 percent or more in industry earnings would impair the ability of some steel firms to service their debt.

The situation is worse in the ferroalloy industry, where capacity utilization in 2005 was only 40 percent. Similar excess capacity has emerged in aluminum, autos, cement, and coke. For example, output of vehicles in 2005 was 6 million units, while capacity was 8.7 million units, with capacity for an additional 2.2 million units under construction. Coke production in 2005 was 230 million tons, but capacity exceeded that by 100 million tons, and the price of coke fell from $450 per ton in 2004 to only $130 per ton in 2005.[2] Excess investment also is evident in high-end property in some cities, where prices are now falling for the first time. Even in electric power, which was in acutely short supply only two years ago, excess capacity is expected to emerge by 2007, as additional capacity of 300 GW now under construction or planned comes on stream.[3]

The second reason underlying the leadership decision to abandon the extensive pattern of economic development is the recognition that it has impeded the growth of personal consumption. Personal consumption in China in 2005 was 30 percent less than the level that would have been achieved if the household consumption share of GDP had remained at the level of 1990 rather than falling by more than ten percentage points. A useful comparison is with India. In 2004 China's per capita GDP was two and a half times that of India. But because household consumption as a share of GDP was so much lower in China, per capita consumption in China exceeded

1 Zheng Lifei (2006), "Soaring industrial profits might prompt investment". *China Daily*, July 21, 9.

2 Wang Ying (2006), "New policies looming for fragmented coke industry", *China Daily*, February 15.

3 Liu Ping (2006), "Overcapacity in 13 industrial sectors", *China Economic News*, May 29, 5–6.

that in India by only two-thirds.[1] The ultimate purpose of economic growth everywhere is improvements in human welfare. By this standard, China is falling far below potential.

Third, and closely related to the slow growth of consumption, China's extensive pattern of development has generated very modest gains in employment. Between 1978 and 1993 employment expanded by 2.5 percent per annum, but between 1993 and 2004, when the investment share of GDP was much higher than in the 1980s, employment growth slowed to only slightly over 1 percent (Kuijs and Wang, 2005). The more capital-intensive pattern of growth that emerged in the 1990s appears to have contributed to a slower pace of job creation for the simple reason that the steel and other industries producing investment goods employ far fewer workers per unit of capital than do light industries producing consumer goods, not to mention the even less favorable comparison with the service sector.

Another reason China's leadership wishes to transition to a more consumption-driven growth path is burgeoning energy consumption and its detrimental effects on the environment. Investment-driven growth has required the output of machinery and equipment, and the inputs to produce them, to grow much more rapidly than the output of consumer goods. Rapid growth of output of investment goods, in turn, increases the demand for energy disproportionately. China's energy elasticity of GDP growth (the number of units of energy required to produce an additional unit of output) averaged a very modest 0.6 in the 1980s and 1990s, leading to a substantial reduction in the amount of energy required to produce each unit of GDP. But this ratio has almost doubled in the past five years (National Bureau of Statistics of China, 2006a, p.147). While this dramatic increase has not yet been properly explained, it is likely that the more capital-intensive growth path has been a significant contributor.

Since two-thirds of China's energy comes from coal, the burgeoning demand for energy generated by capital-intensive growth has increased coal

---

[1] Calculated on the basis of the Indian Ministry of Statistics and Program Implementation, National Account Statistics, available at http://mospi.nic.in; IMF, International Financial Statistics; and National Bureau of Statistics of China (2006a, pp. 34, 36, 171).

consumption by two-thirds since 2000. Coal consumption reached more than 2 billion tons in 2005, almost twice the coal consumption of the United States, even though China's economy is only one-sixth the size of the United States. As a result, China is now the second largest emitter of greenhouse gas and is home to 16 of the 20 cities with the worst air pollution on the globe. As a result of the massive increase in the consumption of coal, the State Environmental Protection Agency (SEPA) reported that, rather than cutting sulfur dioxide emissions in 2000–2005 by 10 percent to 18 million tons as planned, by 2005 emissions rose to 25.5 million tons, 42 percent above the goal.[1]

A fifth factor motivating China's leadership to seek a transition to a more consumption-driven growth pattern is a bit below the radar but nonetheless quite important. Excessive reliance on investment-driven growth in recent years threatens to undo the progress China has made over the past six years in developing a commercially oriented banking system. A critical component of this process has been the injection of almost RMB4 trillion ($500 billion) to cover past loan losses and to raise capital adequacy to meet prudential standards (Ma Guonan 2006). The vast majority of funding has come directly from the government.

Excess investment in some sectors, leading to excess capacity and falling prices, could create a new wave of nonperforming loans that would erode the substantial balance sheet improvements of state-owned banks over the past few years and could push many city commercial banks, which on average are far weaker, into insolvency. The National Development and Reform Commission (2006) in its report to the National People's Congress acknowledged, "adverse effects of surplus production capacity in some industries have begun to emerge. Prices for the products of these industries dropped and inventories grew, corporate profits shrank and losses mounted, and potential financial risk has increased." The steel industry, just discussed, is but one example.

---

1 Shai Oster (2006), "Pollutant takes rising toll in China", *Wall Street Journal*, August 4, http://online.wsj.com (accessed August 4, 2006).

The absence of rising nonperforming loans in the banking system in the past few years is not necessarily a sign that all is well, since China has been in a period of accelerating growth and corporate profits have been rising, albeit at a more modest rate recently in industries like steel. Distress in the banking system is likely to emerge, however, in any slowdown in economic growth over the next few years. But excess capacity is so large in some industries that their ability to service their debt is in question, even in a continuing strong macroeconomic environment.

A final factor underlining the leadership's desire to transition to a more consumption-oriented growth path is that excess reliance on expansion of net exports, i.e., a growing trade surplus, raises the prospect of a protectionist backlash in the United States and other important markets for Chinese exports. China's central bank, the People's Bank of China, was perhaps the first to explicitly acknowledge this factor in its Report on the Implementation of Monetary Policy 2005Q2, in which it candidly stated that an excessive trade surplus "will escalate trade frictions" (People's Bank of China, Monetary Policy Analysis Small Group, 2005, p.28).

In sum, for a variety of reasons China's top political leadership and its leading economic advisory institutions by late 2004 came to the view that sustaining China's long-term rapid growth trajectory required a significant modification of the underlying growth strategy. Failing such a modification they feared that rapid growth could not be sustained.

■ Implications for the Global Economy

China's new growth strategy, if realized, would have positive implications not only for China, but also for the global economy. As shown in Figure 3, China's current account surplus has soared in recent years. In 2006 China decisively surpassed Japan for the first time to become far and away the world's largest global current account surplus country.[1] China now is a

---

[1] In 2005 China's current account surplus was $161 billion, slightly less than Japan's $170 billion. Japan's surplus in the 12 months through July 2006 was $165 billion, suggesting a surplus for the year as a whole about the same as last year's. I estimate China's 2006 current account surplus at $240 billion, based on China's goods trade through August and estimates of the other components of the current account—trade in services, investment income, and transfers.

major contributor to global economic imbalances, along with the United States, which has the world's largest current account deficit. The successful transition to a pattern of growth driven more by domestic consumption demand entails a reduction of the national savings rate. That, in turn, would reduce China's current account surplus. This adjustment should be facilitated by an appreciation of the Chinese currency, which would mitigate inflationary pressures that would otherwise emerge from the increase in consumption demand. This will happen through two channels. First, appreciation would tend to reduce the pace of growth of exports and increase the pace of growth of imports, thus expanding domestic supply. Second, a more flexible exchange rate would allow the government greater flexibility in the use of interest rate policy (Goodfriend and Prasad, 2006). As will be argued below, higher real interest rates are almost certainly necessary to reduce China's excessive rate of investment, which in turn is a prerequisite to a successful transition to a more consumption-driven growth path.

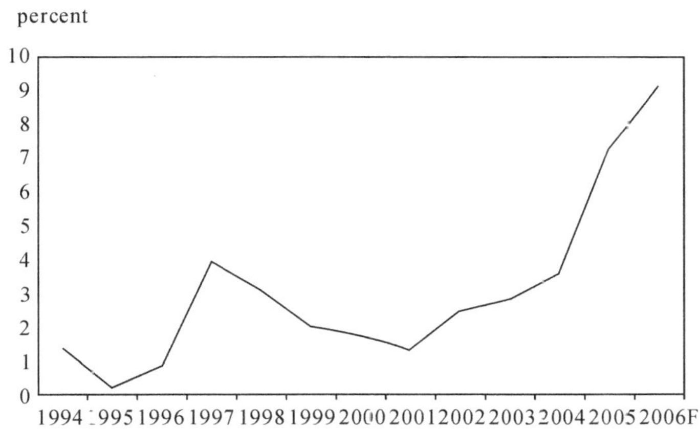

Figure 3 ***Current account balance as percent of GDP, 1994–2006F***

Source: National Bureau of Statistics of China, China Statistical Abstract 2006a; author's calculations.

■ Policies to Promote Consumption-Driven Growth

Promoting domestic demand as a source of economic expansion requires that the growth of household and/or government consumption increase relative to that of investment and net exports. Policies to promote consumption can be based on cutting personal income taxes or increasing government consumption expenditures (i.e. government noninvestment outlays). Shifting to a more consumption-driven growth path in China also will require significant changes in its exchange rate policy. Under current conditions a more flexible exchange rate regime would certainly lead to appreciation of the RMB, simultaneously tending to reduce net exports and, as will be explained below, increasing the flexibility of the government to raise interest rates. The latter is a prerequisite for slowing the rapid pace of investment spending of recent years. Changes in corporate tax policy, discussed below, also offer an opportunity to contribute to rebalancing the sources of economic growth in China.

In many economies, governments can increase personal consumption through fiscal stimulus in the form of tax cuts on household income. But, as will be discussed, this avenue is of limited relevance in China, where direct taxes on households are relatively small to start with and the government's cuts have been timid.

The alternative form of fiscal expansion is expenditure-based. If tax cuts cannot increase private consumption significantly, the government can increase its budgetary expenditures to add to domestic demand. Given already high levels of investment and the emergence of excess capacity in many industries, however, the government needs to increase its non-investment outlays, notably those on health, education, welfare, and pensions. There is enormous scope to do so, since governments at all levels combined in China spend only about 3.5 percent of GDP on these programs (National Bureau of Statistics of China, 2005, p.278).[1]

The government has considerable scope to increase its own consumption expenditures without raising taxes on households, which likely would depress household consumption, offsetting to some degree the increase in government consumption. The government could simply reduce its own

---

1 Excluding capital expenditures.

investment expenditures and reallocate the funds to consumption.[1] The government itself directly undertakes about 5 percent of all investment (National Bureau of Statistics of China, 2006a, p.52). In addition, the government budget allocates substantial additional funds, called "capital transfers," that are used to finance investment expenditures.[2] For 2003, the most recent year for which data have been released, these capital transfers were the equivalent of 10 percent of all fixed investment.[3] There is no evidence that capital transfers have been reduced in recent years, so the government's direct and indirect investment outlays combined probably amount to about 7 to 8 percent of GDP. A reduction in the government's direct investment and cutting capital transfers would free up resources to increase government consumption—i.e., outlays for health, education, welfare, and pensions. That would contribute significantly to a rebalancing of the structure of demand, away from investment and toward consumption.

An increase in household consumption as a share of GDP also could contribute significantly to the transition to a more domestic consumption-driven growth path. That, in turn, requires a reduction in the savings rate of households, which has increased significantly since the 1980s and has been running at about 25 percent of disposable income since 2000 (Kuijs, 2006). By contrast, in the United States in 2005 households spent more than their disposable income, i.e., the savings rate was slightly negative!

Any analysis of the likelihood of a reduction in the savings rate of households must begin by analyzing the motives for household savings. One motivation is clearly precautionary—to cope with life's uncertainties such as illness, unemployment, or injury. Increasingly, as the government and enterprises have reduced the support they provide, this expenditure has become an individual responsibility. In urban areas only about half the

---

1 This reallocation, of course, would reduce government savings since the latter are defined as current revenues less current (i.e. noninvestment) outlays.

2 Kuijs (2006, 7) believes these funds are transferred to enterprises in electric power, water, transport, and other infrastructure sectors.

3 See "Flow of Funds Table (Physical Transactions, 2003)", in National Bureau of Statistics of China (2006b, pp. 88-89).

population, for example, is covered by basic health insurance (OECD, 2005, p.185), and in rural areas less than a fifth of the population is covered by a cooperative health insurance program initiated on a trial basis in 2002. As the share of health expenditures paid directly by the government or borne by enterprises has waned, the share of total health outlays borne by individuals on an out-of-pocket basis increased from around 20 percent in 1978 to more than 55 percent by 2003 (IMF, 2006, p.49; National Bureau of Statistics of China, 2005, p.770). As a consequence, many households save to cover potential future medical expenses. Indeed, the reduction in the share of health expenditures provided through the government and by employers is likely a key reason that household savings as a share of disposable income increased significantly in the 1990s.

The share of China's workforce in 2005 covered by unemployment insurance is only 14 percent, and those covered by workers' compensation is even lower at only 11 percent (National Bureau of Statistics of China, 2006a, pp.43, 201). Thus the vast majority of workers have to save rather than rely on insurance to compensate for potential income interruption due to job loss or injury, adding further to the incentive for precautionary savings.

Another significant motivation for households to save is for retirement and for the education of their children. This is particularly true in China because the basic government pension scheme is extremely limited and government expenditures on education are modest. In 2005 the pension scheme covered 131.2 million workers, only 17 percent of those employed, plus 43.7 million retirees (National Bureau of Statistics of China, 2006a, pp.43, 201). Moreover, a worker must contribute for a minimum of 15 years before he or she is entitled to draw any benefits at retirement. And the basic pension scheme is designed to provide a pension equal to only 20 percent of average local wages, independent of a worker's lifetime earnings.[1]

Although the authorities in China over the past decade have repeatedly

[1] The basic pension scheme, the only one to which enterprises contribute, is the first of a three-pillar retirement program. There are, in addition, mandatory and optional individual contributory pillars. The basic scheme and the mandatory individual schemes combined are designed to replace about 50 percent of pre-retirement income.

asserted the goal of improving the social safety net, pension system coverage is expanding extremely slowly. Between 2000 and 2005 the share of those employed participating in the program rose by only 2.8 percentage points (National Bureau of Statistics of China, 2006a, pp.43, 201; 2005, p.117). At that pace universal pension coverage will not be achieved until 2155–2150 years from now!

Finally, households also save to finance education expenditures. Families are responsible for a significant share of national expenditures on education, since government expenditures on education amount to only 2 percent of GDP. In 2004 per capita expenditures on education of urban households amounted to RMB560 or 8 percent of total consumption expenditures (National Bureau of Statistics of China, 2005, p.352). Primary school fees are a large financial burden, particularly for poorer rural households.

In the long run, of course, increased provision of health care, unemployment compensation, and workers' compensation through the government budget can be expected to reduce precautionary savings on the part of households. As families gain confidence that the government will provide more of these services, they will reduce their own savings voluntarily, i.e., increase consumption as a share of their own disposable income. Similarly greater government provision of educational services and old age support could lead to a reduction in savings associated with lifecycle events, such as children's education and retirement.

In other countries, increased government provision of health services has led directly to an increase in household consumption (China Economic Research and Advisory Programme, 2005). For example, the introduction of National Health Insurance in Taiwan, China, which raised the fraction of the insured population from 57 percent in 1994 to 97 percent in 1998, substantially reduced household uncertainty about future health expenditures and thus stimulated increased consumption outlays. Households that previously enjoyed no health insurance coverage increased their consumption expenditures by an average of over 4 percent (Chou, Liu and Hammitt, 2002, p.1889).[1] Thus,

1 Consumption increased by 2.6 percent in households where one spouse was not in the labor force or unemployed and by 5.7 percent in households where both spouses worked.

China's transition to a more consumption-driven growth path will probably need to start with increased government consumption expenditures but with time is likely to be reinforced by changes in household consumption and savings decisions.

For China, exchange rate policy is an important third element potentially supporting the transition to a more consumption-driven growth path. The reason is that China's de facto fixed exchange rate system is a critical factor limiting the independence of monetary policy. Although China's central bank has had some success in sterilizing large foreign capital inflows, it has generally been reluctant to raise domestic interest rates for fear that these inflows could become unmanageably large. Fixed nominal domestic interest rates on loans in 2002–2003, when domestic price inflation was rising, led to a sharp decline in and ultimately to negative real interest rates on loans. Between the first half of 2002 through the third quarter of 2004, the real interest rate on loans fell by 13 percentage points, from almost 9 to 4 percent.[1] That fueled a very large increase in the demand for bank loans and thus a sharp increase in capital formation.

A more flexible exchange rate policy would allow the central bank greater flexibility in setting domestic interest rates and thus increase the potential to mitigate macroeconomic cycles by raising lending rates to moderate investment booms. That will lead, on average, to a lower rate of investment. A reduction in the rate of investment is a critical component of the policies to transition to a more consumption-driven growth path. In the absence of a reduction in investment, increased consumption demand would lead to inflation.

Finally, corporate tax policy should contribute importantly to the rebalancing of the sources of economic growth in China. As shown in Figure 4, from 1998 through the first half of 2006 profits of industrial enterprises in China soared from less than 2 percent to almost 9 percent of GDP (National Bureau of Statistics of China, 2005, p.494; People's Bank of China,

---

[1] The real interest rate is calculated as the one-year lending rate minus the inflation rate reflected in the corporate goods price index. The latter index is compiled and published by the People's Bank of China.

Monetary Policy Analysis Small Group, 2006, p.33). Although these profits are subject to a 33 percent corporate income tax, retained after-tax earnings of industrial firms in the first half of 2006 amounted to 5.8 percent of GDP compared with an estimated 1.6 percent in 1998.[1] In addition, industrial firms retain depreciation funds that amount to another 6 to 7 percent of GDP (Kuijs, Mako and Zhang, 2005).

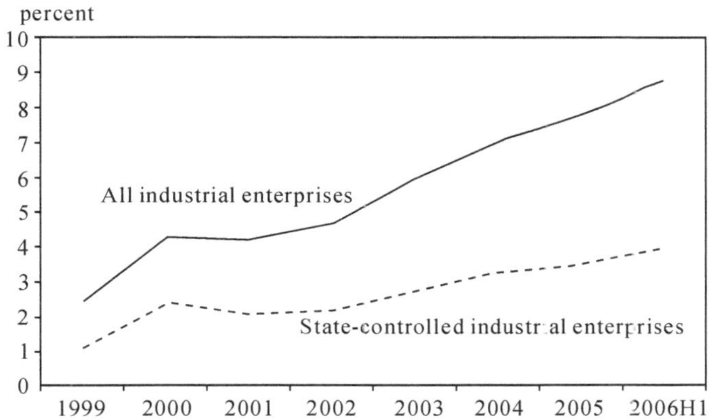

Figure 4 ***Industry profits as percent of GDP, 1999–2006H1***

Sources: National Bureau of Statistics of China, China Statistical Yearbook, 2005; People's Bank of China, Monetary Policy Analysis Small Group, 2006.

Unfortunately, in state-owned firms these funds are not subject to a significant rate of return test prior to being reinvested. The reason is that the only available alternative to reinvestment is low-yielding bank deposits. Taking into account the relevant measure of inflation, the real after-tax rate of return on corporate deposits is typically negative.[2] Given a negative real rate of return on deposits, from the point of view of a manager of a state

---

1 Industrial sector pretax profits were RMB810 billion in the first half of 2006 (People's Bank of China, Monetary Policy Analysis Small Group, 2006, p. 33). These profits are subject to the corporate income tax of 33 percent. In addition, China's three largest oil producers are also subject to a windfall profits tax, which amounted to RMB16.19 billion in the first half of 2006. Thus after-tax profits can be estimated at RMB530 billion or 5.8 percent of reported first half GDP of RMB9144 billion.

2 For example, starting August 15, 2006, the People's Bank of China raised the nominal interest rate on a one-year term corporate deposit to 2.52 percent. The corporate goods price index in August 2006 was up 2.9 percent compared with August 2005, making the real return—0.38 percent. Nominal returns on short-term deposits are less than 2.52 percent, as low as 0.72 percent for demand deposits, making the real return on deposits of less than one year as low as—2.18 percent.

enterprise, it is rational to reinvest retained profits and depreciation funds even when they have slightly negative anticipated rates of return.

Given the upward trend in profits as a share of GDP and apparent upward trend in depreciation funds as a share of GDP as well, retained earnings have become an increasingly important source of investment financing in China's corporate sector and have contributed to the rising investment share of GDP in recent years.

For a number of years, the authorities have been discussing requiring state-owned enterprises to pay dividends to their owner—the government (Kuijs, Mako and Zhang, 2005). This policy has the potential simultaneously to reduce the pace at which investment grows, or at least subject investment to a more demanding rate of return hurdle, and to provide the government with additional resources that could be used to enhance government-provided social services. In September 2006 Li Rongrong, chairman of China's State-Owned Asset Supervision and Administration Commission, announced that the government would begin collecting such dividends in 2007.[1] While the magnitude of required payments has not been announced, if state-owned companies were to pay half their after-tax income as dividends, this would have amounted to 1.3 percent of GDP in the first half of 2006.[2] The government could gain additional, larger amounts by reducing the depreciation rates used by firms in calculating their taxable income.

■ The Trajectory Thus Far

How aggressively is China adopting policies that could lead to a growth path that is more consumption-driven and less dependent on burgeoning investment and an expanding global trade surplus?

1 Rick Carew, "China Expects to Collect Dividends by Next Year", *Wall Street Journal*, September 18, 2006, http://online.wsj.com (accessed September 18, 2006).

2 Profits of the industrial sector in the first half were RMB810 billion. I assume the share accruing to state-owned and state-controlled firms was 45 percent of the total, the share they accounted for in 2004 (National Bureau of Statistics of China, 2005, 494 and 497). Deducting the windfall profits tax of state-owned oil companies and the corporate income tax results in an estimate of after-tax profits of RMB233.4 billion or 2.6 percent of GDP.

Even in advance of the 2004 Central Economic Work Conference, which formally endorsed the transition to a more domestic consumption-driven growth path, the government initiated a program to raise farm incomes by reducing the agricultural tax, long levied on farm income (Ministry of Finance, Ministry of Agriculture and State Tax Bureau). In 2004 the tax, which was set at 8.4 percent of average yields, was eliminated in two provinces and reduced by three percentage points in 11 provinces and by one percentage point in all other provinces.[1] By the end of 2005 the government had eliminated the tax in 28 provincial-level administrative units and had reduced it to less than 2 percent in the remaining three provinces, where the tax will be eliminated entirely in 2006 (State Tax Bureau, 2005b).

The early initiative to eliminate the agricultural tax was followed in 2006 with a doubling to RMB1600, of the monthly income exempt from the personal income tax levied on wage earners, who live almost exclusively in urban areas. The central government has encouraged local governments to raise the minimum wage in urban areas, potentially increasing the consumption of low-income workers.

All of these initiatives, however, are quite modest. Agricultural taxes collected fell from RMB33.7 billion in 2003 to RMB19.79 billion in 2004 and then to only RMB1.279 billion in 2005 (National Bureau of Statistics of China, 2005, p.281; 2006a, p.75). The tax burden on farmers was reduced by RMB23.4 billion in 2004 and an additional RMB22 billion in 2005 (Ministry of Finance, 2005; State Tax Bureau, 2005b). However, RMB23.4 billion is the equivalent of only 1 percent of rural consumption expenditure or 0.1 percent of GDP in 2004. More importantly, the cut in the agricultural tax was offset by record increases in other taxes levied on rural residents. In 2004 proceeds from the tax on occupied, cultivated land and the tax levied on contracts used to transfer land use rights or the sale, exchange, and inheritance of houses increased by one-half or RMB21 billion. The same

1 In 2004 the tax was eliminated in Jilin and Heilongjiang provinces, cut by 3 percentage points in 11 other grain-growing provinces (Hebei, Inner Mongolia, Liaoning, Jiangsu, Anhui, Jiangxi, Shandong, Henan, Hubei, Hunan and Sichuan), and reduced by 1 percentage point in all other provinces.

taxes rose by an additional one-third or RMB22 billion in 2005. These increases entirely offset the reductions in the agricultural tax (National Bureau of Statistics of China, 2005, p.281; 2006a, p.75).

Similarly, reductions in the personal income tax are not a very potent policy instrument. The proceeds of the personal income tax in 2005 amounted to RMB210 billion, only 1.1 percent of GDP (National Bureau of Statistics of China, 2006a, pp.20, 66). By comparison, the personal income tax in the United States prior to the major income tax cut under President George W. Bush in 2001 represented almost 10 percent of GDP. Tax cuts reduced this share to about 7 percent, translating into an increase in household disposable income of over 4 percent. China starts with an income tax one-tenth the relative size of that in the United States, and doubling the income tax exemption is a modest tax cut. The State Tax Bureau (2005a) reports that raising the exemption will reduce the total revenue of the individual income taxes by RMB28 billion in 2006. But this is an estimated 0.13 percent of GDP[1], a tiny amount compared with the Bush tax cuts, which reduced personal income taxes by 3 percentage points of GDP.

Finally, it is quite unlikely that the increase in minimum wages that went into effect on July 1, 2006, in most administrative jurisdictions will have a significant positive effect on household consumption expenditures. There are two reasons for this. First, the *Regulations on the Minimum Wage* of the Chinese Ministry of Labor and Social Security (2003) give local governments considerable leeway in setting the minimum wage. In practice, in most jurisdictions, the minimum wage is only about one-fifth to one-quarter the average wage prevailing locally.[2] Second, the share of the workforce earning the minimum wage appears to be quite small. In Beijing, for example, in 2002 minimum wage workers accounted for only 2.4 percent of

---

1 Assuming nominal GDP growth of 14 percent in 2006, based on GDP real growth of 10.9 percent and an implicit GDP deflator of 3.2 percent in the first half of 2006.

2 In Beijing, in 2002 and 2003, the minimum wage was 25.5 and 23.5 percent, respectively, of the average wage in those years. In 2004, in Shenzhen, the minimum wage was 18 percent of the average local wage (China's highest).

the workforce.[1] Given the low ratio of the minimum wage to the average wage and the small share of the workforce earning the minimum wage, the 6.5 percent rise in the capital's minimum wage in 2003 could not have had more than a minuscule effect on the total wage bill.[2]

More generally, the past decade's data suggest that China's minimum wage program has had a modest effect on household consumption. During this period the minimum wage in Beijing more than doubled, from RMB270 per month in 1996 to RMB640 in 2006. In Shenzhen's special economic zone the minimum wage doubled from RMB398 to RMB810 over the same period.[3] Presumably, minimum wages in other jurisdictions have had similar rates of increase. But over this period household consumption as a share of GDP has fallen significantly.[4]

It is unlikely that the further 10 percent increase in Beijing's minimum wage in July 2006, to RMB640 per month, and the similar increases in other cities will significantly increase wage income. Thus, even allowing for the likely higher marginal propensity to consume of minimum wage workers, the expected effect of China's minimum wage program on household consumption expenditures is likely to be small.

In summary, the cuts in taxes on rural and urban incomes instituted by the central government beginning in 2004 and the increases in minimum wage levels introduced by provincial and local governments have had and are likely to continue to have a modest effect on household income, and thus they are unlikely to lead to significantly higher levels of household consumption expenditures. The cuts in taxes on urban and rural incomes are too small, and in rural areas they have been offset by increases in other taxes.

---

1 China Statistical Information Net, "Wages of Beijing Workers and Staff Increase Steadily; Differentials Across Industrial Branches Expand", www.hebei.gov.cn (accessed July 10,2006).

2 In 2002 the share of Beijing's wage income earned by minimum wage workers can be estimated as 0.6 percent of total wage income (0.25×0.024). Assuming generously that the 6.5 percent increase in the minimum wage in 2003 had no effect on the number of minimum wage workers employed, the increase in the minimum wage would have raised total wage income by 0.04 percent.

3 See "Historical Minimum Wage Standards", available at www.labourlawyer.com (accessed July 3,2006).

4 China's minimum wage system was established in 1993.

On the expenditure side, at the annual meeting of China's legislative body in the spring of 2006 the government announced increased outlays on a number of social programs. The centerpiece of this effort is Premier Wen Jiabao's program to create a "new socialist countryside." The government has budgeted in 2006 for increased subsidies for grain producers, which will raise the incomes of some of China's poorest farmers; expanded coverage of the rural cooperative medical system, which was first rolled out in 2002; and announced that by 2007 it will eliminate educational fees for rural primary education. Other social initiatives were also unveiled.

But the budgeted increase in expenditures on these programs is far from impressive. The increase in grain subsidies is only RMB1 billion. The expansion of the rural cooperative medical system is modest, seeking to expand coverage to only 40 percent of the rural population by 2010 and increasing the annual per capita government subsidies for this expansion only by an equivalent of $2.50. Only the provision of free rural primary education, which is budgeted at RMB220 billion ($27.5 billion) over five years, is significant. But the overall increase in rural spending in 2006 is budgeted at only 14 percent, not a significant increase from the pace of recent years and only equal to the growth of nominal GDP in the first half of 2006. And unlike most years, the budget message of the minister of finance at the National People's Congress did not provide a figure for total budgeted outlays for social programs, so it is not clear whether the increase in social expenditures from the government budget in 2006 will be faster than the nominal growth of almost 18 percent in 2005 compared with 2004.

Finally, on the exchange rate, in July 2005 the Chinese authorities launched a reform program with several components: an initial revaluation by 2.1 percent vis-à-vis the US dollar; announcing that the currency could fluctuate by up to 0.3 percent per day and that its value increasingly would be determined by supply and demand in the market; and asserting that the RMB would be managed with reference to a basket of currencies rather than simply being pegged to the dollar. These reforms could have led to a more flexible exchange rate and thus given the People's Bank of China greater flexibility in adjusting interest rates.

But to date these reforms have not resulted in much flexibility. The potential for the currency's value to move by as much as 0.3 percent per day has been entirely theoretical, and massive government intervention in the foreign exchange market continues to prevent the currency from appreciating significantly. In the five months from July through December 2005, the authorities purchased an average of $19 billion per month, almost exactly the pace of intervention that occurred in the first six months of the year. In 2006 the average market intervention increased slightly to an average of $20.4 billion in the first half (State Administration of Foreign Exchange, 2006, p.6). This directly contradicts the People's Bank of China announcement of the new exchange rate system, which emphasized the increasing role of the market and supply and demand in determining the exchange rate. As a result, the cumulative appreciation of the RMB vis-à-vis the dollar in the first year of the "new" exchange rate system was less than 2 percent. Finally, there is little evidence of pegging to a basket of currencies. In short, China's exchange rate system remains a heavily managed peg to the dollar and does not provide the authorities with any significant increase in monetary policy independence.

One additional important development—a sharp decline in borrowing by consumers since 2003—suggests that the transition to a more consumption-driven growth path will be difficult, at least in the short run. The inability of consumers to borrow against future income historically has been an important factor contributing to a high rate of household savings in China. This began to change in the late 1990s, when banks started lending to consumers for the first time. Net annual lending to households grew rapidly from only RMB30 billion in 1998 to RMB510 billion in 2003. By the end of 2003, loans to households accounted for 10 percent of all bank loans outstanding. Subsequently, however, lending to households fell sharply to RMB435 billion in 2004 and then RMB200 billion in 2005, below the level of 2000.[1] Banks appear more than willing to lend to households, so the

[1] These data are for what Chinese sources call "household consumption loans", which include loans for mortgages, car purchases, tuition, and general consumer credit. They do not include what are called "household economic loans", which are working capital loans extended to Chinese peasants for the purchase of seeds, fuel, fertilizer, and other agricultural inputs.

slowdown in borrowing appears to reflect declining consumer confidence or perhaps a wait and see attitude on mortgage borrowing in many cities where sharp housing price increases of recent years have begun to moderate and in some cases reverse. In either case the implications for consumption growth are adverse since home purchases typically lead to increased expenditures on furnishings, appliances, and so forth, all of which are included in consumption expenditure.

■ Conclusion

The evidence to date suggests that the transition to more consumption-driven growth is off to a slow start. In the first half of 2006, it appears that investment grew more rapidly than GDP;[1] China's trade surplus expanded by more than half, meaning that net exports as a share of GDP are still rising rapidly. Thus China's external surplus continues to balloon and, short of a U.S. recession, seems likely to expand further in 2007. Government consumption expenditures appear to be growing roughly in line with nominal GDP growth. Since GDP is the sum of capital investment, consumption (household and government), and net exports, it can only mean that household consumption is growing more slowly than GDP. Thus household consumption as a share of GDP almost certainly continued to decline in the first half of 2006. Similarly, the government has acknowledged that the elasticity of energy consumption with respect to GDP continued to rise in the first half of 2006, extending the trend of the previous five years.[2]

The reasons government policy has thus far failed to put China onto a new growth path are clear. First, the tax burden on rural residents has not

---

1 China's high-frequency data on investment are for "fixed asset investment". Most observers believe that this measure includes the value of land sales, as well as the value of mergers and acquisitions transactions. Since these transactions reflect changes of ownership rather than additions to productive capacity, they should not be included in fixed investment. In 2005 capital formation, as reflected in the GDP expenditure accounts, grew by roughly three-quarters of the pace of growth of fixed asset investment. Assuming the same proportional relationship applies in 2006, the reported 30 percent growth of fixed asset investment in the first half would translate into an expansion of fixed capital formation by about 23 percent in nominal terms, well in excess of the reported pace of expansion of nominal GDP of 14.3 percent. That comparison strongly suggests that properly measured, the investment share of GDP continued to rise in the first half of 2006.

2 "A Failed Mid-Term Exam", editorial, *China Daily*, August 3, 2006, 4.

declined significantly. Second, income taxes paid by urban residents are too modest for cuts to have a perceptible effect on consumption. And despite much lip service to increasing the provision of social services financed through the budget, there is little evidence that a fundamental shift in government spending priorities is under way. Thus the precautionary demand for savings on the part of China's households persists.

Similarly, there is little evidence of a more flexible exchange rate and increased independence of monetary policy that would allow higher domestic interest rates. Government agencies issue repeated directives calling for reduced investment in sectors with excess capacity. But even after two modest increases in interest rates on loans in 2006, the rates paid by corporate borrowers remain very low in real terms.[1] In the first half of 2006 the increase in bank credit outstanding, almost entirely to corporate customers, was 50 percent greater than in the first half of 2005 (People's Bank of China, 2006b). Equally important, the real interest rate on corporate bank deposits remains negative, almost insuring that state-owned companies reinvest all of their retained earnings, even when expected returns are low or even moderately negative. Finally, consumer confidence seems to be waning, with a marked slowdown in borrowing starting in 2004. All of these factors suggest that China's transition toward more consumption-driven growth is likely to be substantially delayed.

References

China Economic Research and Advisory Programme (2005), China and the global economy: Medium-term issues and options (December)", On file with author.

Chou Shinyi, Liu Jintan and James K. Hammitt (2002), National health insurance and precautionary saving: Evidence from Taiwan", *Journal of Public Economics*, 87, 1873–1894.

Goodfriend, Marvin and Eswar Prasad (2006), "A framework for independent monetary policy in China", IMF Working Paper WP/06/11 (May), available at www.imf.org (accessed October 6, 2006).

IMF (International Monetary Fund) (2006), "Regional economic outlook: Asia and

[1] Effective August 15, 2006, the benchmark rate on a one-year loan was raised 27 basis points to 6.12 percent. The corporate goods price index in August 2006 rose 2.9 percent over a year ago, making the real lending rate faced by corporate borrowers only 3.22 percent, an extremely low rate in an economy growing at over 10 percent.

Pacific (May)", Washington, available at www. imf. org (accessed August 16, 2006).

Louis Kuijs (2006), "How will China's savings-investment balance evolve?", World Bank Research Paper 5 (May), Beijing: World Bank China Office.

Louis Kuijs, William Mako and Zhang Chunlin (2005), "SOE dividends: How much and to whom?", World Bank Policy Note (October 17), Washington: World Bank, available at www.worldbank.org (accessed August 9, 2006).

Louis Kuijs and Wang Tao (2005), "China's pattern of growth: Moving to sustainability and reducing inequality", World Bank Policy Research Working Paper 3767 (November), Washington: World Bank.

Ma Guonan (2006), "Who foots China's bank restructuring bill? In the turning point in China's economic development", in Ross Garnaut and Song Ligang (eds.), Canberra: Asia Pacific Press at the Australian National University.

Ministry of Finance, Ministry of Agriculture and State Tax Bureau (2004), "Notice concerning issues in lowering the agricultural tax rate and carrying out the reform of eliminating the agricultural tax in trial points", June 30, Beijing, available at www.mof.gov.cn (accessed July 21, 2006).

Ministry of Finance (2005), "Progress in the work of reforming rural taxes and fees in 2004 and the direction for work in 2005 (March 2)", Beijing, available at www.mof.gov.cn (accessed July 21, 2006).

Ministry of Labor and Social Security (2003), "Regulations on the minimum wage (December 30)", Beijing, available at www.trs.molss.gov.cn (accessed June 29, 2006).

National Bureau of Statistics of China (2005), *China Statistical Yearbook 2005*, Beijing: China Statistics Press.

National Bureau of Statistics of China (2006a), *China Statistical Abstract 2006*, Beijing: China Statistics Press.

National Bureau of Statistics of China (2006b), *China Statistical Yearbook 2006*, Beijing: China Statistics Press.

National Development and Reform Commission (2006), "Report on the implementation of the 2005 plan for national economic and social development and on the 2006 draft plan for national economic and social development (March 5)", Beijing, available at www.npc.gov.cn.

OECD (Organization for Economic Cooperation and Development) (2005), "China", OECD Economic Surveys, Volume 2005/13 (September), Paris.

People's Bank of China (2006a), Quarterly Statistical Bulletin, No.41, Beijing.

People's Bank of China (2006b), "Overall balance in financial circulation in the first half of 2006 (July 14)", Beijing, available at www.pbc. gov.cn (accessed July 14, 2006).

People's Bank of China, Monetary Policy Analysis Small Group (2005), "Report on the implementation of monetary policy 2005Q2 (August 4)", Beijing, available at www.pbc.gov.cn.

People's Bank of China, Monetary Policy Analysis Small Group (2006), "Report on the implementation of monetary policy 2006Q2", Beijing, available at www.pbc.gov.cn (accessed August 9, 2006).

State Administration of Foreign Exchange, International Income and Expenditure Analysis Small Group (2006), "Report on China's international balance of payments in the first half of 2006 (October 6)", available at www.safe.gov.cn (accessed October 6, 2006).

State Tax Bureau (2005a), "The adjustment of the individual income tax will bring RMB28 billion in benefit to tax payers (November 17)", Beijing, available at www.mof.gov.cn (accessed July 21, 2006).

State Tax Bureau (2005b), "The reduction in and exemption from the agricultural tax is estimated to reduce the farmers' burden by RMB22 billion (December 23)", Beijing, available at www.mof.gov.cn (accessed July 20, 2006).

Martin Wolf (2005), "Why is China growing so slowly?", Foreign Policy (January February), available at www.foreignpolicy.com (accessed August 4, 2005).

Three Poverties in Urban China

John Knight and Li Shi[1]

Introduction

During the period of central planning, and even during the early stages of economic reform, poverty in China was essentially a rural phenomenon. For instance, calculations based on a national survey in 1988 showed 12.7% of the rural population to be in poverty, but only 2.7% of the urban population. For 1995, calculations using a comparable survey and definition gave the proportions as 12.4% and 4.1%, respectively (Riskin and Li, 2001, pp.331, 336; Khan et al., 2001, p.129). Even these differences understate the rural-urban contrast: in real terms the urban poverty line was drawn at a level well above the rural one. Urban-dwellers were greatly protected from poverty by their "iron rice bowls"—guaranteed employment in state-owned enterprises operating mini welfare states—and they were defended against the potential competition of rural-dwellers by an "invisible Great Wall"—restrictions on

1 John Knight is the professor of Economics at the University of Oxford. Li Shi, Beijing Normal University. The paper was written when Li Shi was visiting the Department of Economics, University of Oxford. The financial support of the Ford Foundation and the UK Department of International Development is gratefully acknowledged, as are the helpful comments of a referee.

rural-urban migration and settlement (Knight and Song, 1999).

Since 1995, urban poverty has become an important issue. The reform of the loss-making, state-owned enterprises has produced vast redundancies, and a private and self-employment sector has been allowed to develop. Cracks have appeared in the iron rice bowl and in the invisible Great Wall. We use a household survey for 1999 to examine this new urban poverty. The proportion of households in poverty rose by 9%, and the "weighted poverty gap" (a measure of extreme poverty) by 89%, over the period 1995–1999, even though urban real income per capita increased by 25%. We distinguish three types of poverty and try to explain them in the light of the circumstances that now face urban-dwellers.

The poverty line identifies the group in poverty. When an absolute poverty line is drawn, the food poverty line and the non-food poverty line are normally defined separately. The conventional approach to the food poverty line is to select a basket of foods required to meet the minimum standard of nutrition of a normal adult, and then to evaluate it in terms of money. Given the food poverty line and assuming a ratio of the non-food to the food poverty line, the overall poverty line can then be derived straightforwardly. When an absolute poverty line is applied to income, the implicit assumption is that an individual with income equal to the poverty line would spend no less than the amount required to buy the selected basket of food and non-food. In reality, it is often found that some individuals with income above the poverty line have consumption below it (Deaton, 1991). They are usually defined as non-poor according to the income-based measure, but as poor according to the consumption-based measure. In this paper, we attempt to combine the two approaches in defining poverty.

The literature on poverty tends to use either income-based and consumption-based poverty concepts and measures. We develop three concepts: "consumption not income" poverty, "income not consumption" poverty, and "income and consumption" poverty. We also introduce "overall" poverty, encompassing all three measures. We explore why it is that some households fall into one of these three types of poverty, but not into the other two. In this way we attempt to explain not only the reasons for poverty in urban China, but also which sorts of poverty have the most adverse effects on economic welfare and which therefore deserve most attention in policy-making.

China's process of economic transition from a centrally planned to a market economy is generating new and greater uncertainties relating to various factors that govern economic welfare. For instance, employment has become less secure, social security protection has been weakened, and user charges for public services have become important. These insecurities are likely to impact on the consumption behavior of low-income households. One hypothesis of the paper is that this leads to a new, or an increasingly important, type of poverty in urban China—"consumption not income" poverty.

■ Concepts, Definitions, and Hypotheses

Poverty analysis is in principle concerned with economic welfare, or utility, but in practice poverty is normally measured in terms of income or consumption. Households can be assumed to maximize an intertemporal utility function, defined over current and future consumption (Deaton, 1997, pp.357-365). Intertemporal optimization requires that the marginal rate of substitution between consumption in any two periods should reflect the relative opportunity cost of funds in the two periods. On various simplifying assumptions, current consumption is equal to expected permanent income, and consumption remains constant except on account of stochastic shocks, the expectation of which is zero. However, this result is too simple in many respects, including the following. First, the real rate of interest r may differ from the rate of time discount δ. If $r>\delta$, consumption rises over time; and if $r<\delta$, it falls. Second, there may be changes in taste or need, for instance on account of changes in household composition or in health status. Third, there may be a binding borrowing or liquidity constraint, which can prevent consumption from being maintained in the face of a fall in current income. Fourth, uncertainty about future income can give rise to precautionary savings. If there is convexity in the marginal utility of consumption function (e.g. the marginal utility of consumption at the subsistence level is very high), an increase in uncertainty increases both precautionary savings and reluctance to borrow.

The income-based and consumption-based approaches to poverty have different advantages and disadvantages. If consumption is less than income, this savings reflect a preference for past or future consumption rather than current consumption. If consumption exceeds current income, this dissavings reflects a chosen transfer of past or future consumption to the present. Thus current income indicates the ability to command resources and allocate them across time. Consumption indicates current wellbeing, whereas income, being normally more volatile over time, may be a poor guide to current wellbeing.

The standard approach in the poverty literature is to distinguish "chronic" and "transient" poverty using the notion of permanent income, measured as intertemporal average welfare (income or consumption). A household is in chronic poverty if its intertemporal average welfare falls short of the poverty line; it is in transient, but not chronic, poverty if its current welfare falls short of the poverty line, but its intertemporal average welfare does not. Longitudinal data using a panel survey or a cross-section survey with recall information are necessary for the estimation of chronic poverty defined in this way.

There is, however, a possible alternative approach to these sorts of issues that is worth exploring as it requires only cross-section data on income and consumption. Avoiding the terms chronic and transient poverty because of their precise meaning in the literature, we use the terms persistent and temporary. We consider three cases: Figure 1 illustrates how they can be distinguished. *Y* is income, *C* consumption, and *PL* the poverty line. Three areas (*A*, *B*, and *C*) are shown in the figure. An individual (or household) falling in area *A*—that is, with both income and consumption below the poverty line—is in "income and consumption" poverty. An individual is defined as "consumption not income" poor if in area *B*, and as "income not consumption" poor if in area *C*. These three distinctions are different from the chronic/transient distinction: none of the three concepts corresponds either to chronic or transient poverty, nor even to our looser terms, persistent or temporary poverty.

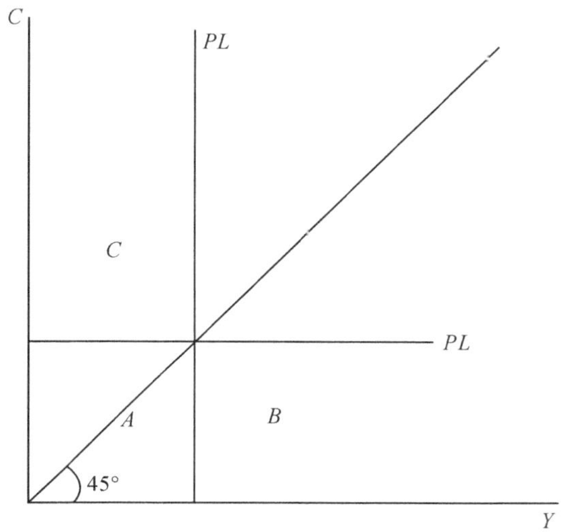

Figure 1 ***The three poverties***

The interpretation of the three poverties that we have distinguished depends on the extent of consumption smoothing or, in the face of changing needs, the extent of welfare smoothing that is practised. On the assumption that smoothing is complete, consumption represents permanent income. Those who make this assumption argue that, to be of interest, poverty should be persistent and therefore temporarily low income should not be the criterion for such poverty, that permanent income should be the sole criterion, and that the appropriate test of such poverty is whether consumption falls short of the poverty line. In Figure 1, households in areas *A* and *B* are therefore defined as persistently poor and those in area *C* are not. However, this approach can be misleading if consumption smoothing is incomplete. A household might have temporarily low income and yet fail to maintain consumption at the desired level (Morduch, 1994). It is likely that many people in urban China are unable fully to dissave or borrow if their income falls temporarily. On the consumption-based approach, they might be misleadingly classified as persistently poor.

Each of the three poverties is open to more than one interpretation. First, consider area *A*. If both consumption and income are below the poverty line, this suggests that the low current income reflects low permanent income, to which consumption is adjusted. That implies that poverty is persistent. However, with no consumption smoothing, or only weak smoothing, a negative temporary shock can reduce both income and consumption below the poverty line. Such poverty is temporary. The test of these alternative hypotheses requires a measure of permanent income other than current consumption. Household income predicted on the basis of household characteristics can provide such a measure, albeit imperfect. The difference between current and predicted income can have three components: measurement error, temporary deviations from normal income, and unobserved household characteristics that are rewarded or penalized. Use of predicted income as a proxy for permanent income appropriately corrects for the first two of these, but inappropriately eliminates the last component. Predicted income also fails to measure permanent income insofar as currently observable characteristics cannot show different expected future income based on current characteristics or on expected future characteristics. We therefore prefer to use the term predicted income rather than permanent income. At the least, it is likely to be more normal or persistent than current reported income, and thus potentially a better guide to consumption behavior. The liquid assets available to a household can also provide a means of choosing between the rival hypotheses concerning the nature of "income and consumption" poverty.

The interpretation of area *B* again depends on the scope for smoothing. Given the ability to even out welfare over time, this can be temporary income non-poverty concealing persistent poverty. For instance, people may be pessimistic about their expected future income. Looking forward, they save now so as to offset future low income. The expected fall in income thus induces current consumption-based poverty. Alternatively, consumption smoothing can be backward-looking. A previous temporary fall in income, resulting in accumulated debt, requires savings out of current income in order to pay back the debt. If credit and liquidity constraints prevent welfare from being protected against future negative shocks, the low consumption may reflect precautionary savings in the face of uncertainty about future income. If liquid assets were already at an equilibrium level, the low consumption may reflect an increase in uncertainty about the future. Some expenditures—such as house-building and children's education—are both predictable and in the nature of investment rather than consumption. In order to maintain welfare in a steady state they should be financed from savings or credit. Given capital market imperfections, these expenditures may be preceded by a period of designated savings, so giving rise to this type of poverty. Four types of variables suggest themselves for testing these alternative hypotheses about the nature of "consumption not income" poverty: predicted income; liquid assets and debt; proxies for uncertainty about the future, such as the probability of becoming unemployed; and indicators of the probability of future investment expenditures, such as the presence of a child.

Area *C* also has alternative interpretations. Insofar as there is complete or even partial consumption smoothing, consumption may be maintained above the poverty line when income falls temporarily below it: such income poverty will not persist. However, area *C* can represent persistent poverty if income is persistently below the poverty line, but consumption is temporarily raised above it. The purpose may be to meet a specific need, particularly if the need was not anticipated. For instance, expenditure on health care should constitute an addition to total expenditure if welfare is to be maintained from one period to another. These rival hypotheses relating to "income not consumption" poverty might be distinguished by examining the following variables: predicted rather than actual income; expenditures that could represent specific needs, such as spending on health care or education; and household demographics that might reflect life-cycle needs.

■ Data, Poverty Measures, and Setting

The data from a household survey in urban China enable us to investigate the scale of the three poverties and their causes. The survey was conducted in the spring of 2000 with the assistance of China National Bureau of Statistics (NBS), and related mainly to 1999. It covered five provinces, Liaoning, Jiangsu, Henan, Sichuan, and Gansu, and a province-level metropolis, Beijing. In addition to Beijing, 12 cities in the five provinces were selected according to a formula: three in larger provinces, such as Sichuan or Henan, and two in smaller provinces, such as Liaoning. Five provincial capital cities were included, so the sample may be biased towards large cities. The survey covers 4000 households with urban residence registration (*hukou*).

The questionnaires were designed by the research team with a research agenda in mind. Questions in the household questionnaires were divided into two parts, one part directed to individuals and the other to households. Thus, the survey data contain individual information, some of which are related to personal characteristics such as gender, age, educational attainment, party membership, employment status, and health status, and some of which are associated with job characteristics, such as ownership of work unit, occupation, job tenure, profitability of work unit, and sector of employment. An important part of the individual information is personal income and detailed income components. The household information is more concerned with consumption, wealth endowment, and housing conditions.

To measure poverty incidence and poverty intensity, a threshold or poverty line is required to identify poor households or individuals. As an absolute poverty line, it can be based either on income or on consumption. We draw on the work of the NBS. Researchers in the NBS estimated food poverty lines in the year of 1998 for different provinces in urban China by using the data from the national household survey in that year to obtain the cost of a minimum level of food consumption. The data cover 17,000 urban households, but exclude rural-urban migrants.

In approaching the poverty line, it is necessary to estimate the share of non-food spending in total consumption expenditure[1] for poor households:

---

1 We include expenditure on consumer durables because it is not possible to identify all expenditure on durables. Use of non-durable consumption alone would reduce consumption, so somewhat increasing the incidence of poverty involving consumption.

$$PL=PL_f+PL_{nf}=PL_f(1+R_{nf}) \quad (1)$$

where PL is the total poverty line, PL_f the food poverty line, PL_{nf} the non-food poverty line and R_{nf} the ratio of non-food expenditure to food expenditure. The NBS takes two-thirds as the ratio of non-food to food expenditure for the urban poor, based on the average value of Engel coefficients in developing countries. This approach is, however, not justified in the Chinese circumstances. Examining the consumption expenditure of the lowest 10% households in urban areas, the ratio of non-food to food expenditure was almost 90% in 1999. Applying this ratio, we get a rather higher poverty line than did the NBS. It is appropriate to adjust the poverty line for the existence of economies of scale within the household. The NBS provides "expenditure coefficients" for households of different size,[1] and these are adopted in this paper. Our poverty lines vary considerably by province, largely reflecting the provincial differences in the NBS's food poverty line.[2]

Economic reforms have resulted in dramatic changes for urban households in the 1990s. State-owned enterprise reform produced more than 24 million laid-off workers, referred to as *xia gang* employees,[3] over the period 1995–1999.[4] In addition, the number of officially registered unemployed increased from 3.8 million in 1990 to 5.8 million in 1999 (CLSY, 2000, p.86). The number of urban employees in state-owned and collective enterprises decreased by 28%, from 140 million to 100 million, in the same period (CLSY, 2000, p.14). The increased unemployment and redundancy inevitably reduced the income of some households, and generated insecurity and uncertainty for all of them.

---

1 One-person households have an expenditure coefficient of 1.5, two-person households 1.23, three-person households 1.00, four-person households 0.84, and five and more person households 0.75 (Wang, 2000).

2 The province poverty lines (in yuan per annum) that we use are: Beijing 3830, Liaoning 2296, Jiangsu 2709, Henan 1913, Sichuan 2328, and Gansu 2006.

3 *Xia gang* workers continue to be nominally employed by the enterprise, but do not attend work and, in principle, receive a low wage from the enterprise.

4 This may be a considerable underestimate. The annual China Labour Statistical Yearbooks (CLSY) for the years 1995 to 2000 show gross layoffs of 15.2 million in the period of 1998–1999 and net layoffs (gross layoffs minus re-employment or withdrawal from labour force) of 9.2 million in the period 1995–1997.

Accompanying enterprise reform, the traditional system of social security for urban workers has almost broken down and the new system is still in the making. The medical care of urban workers used to be the responsibility of their employers, but that is no longer generally the case, especially for enterprises in financial difficulty. The expectation is that households will increasingly have to pay for their medical services. Most unemployed people did not receive income support while unemployed because their enterprises could not afford to pay unemployment insurance.[1] Our data show that 49% of the laid-off workers received income below the (per capita) poverty line in 1999. Official statistics record that in 1999 nearly 40% of *xia gang* workers received either no benefits or less than the amount designated by the central government (CLSY, 2000, pp.410-411). A survey conducted in two cities, Wuhan and Shenyang, in 2000 shows that 46% of *xia gang* workers had not received any payments at all since becoming redundant (Institute of Labour Science, 2000). A study using the data that we analyse in this paper finds evidence that the unemployed and *xia gang* workers had experienced a significant fall in their income even after being reemployed (Appleton et al., 2004). One of the aims of the educational reforms has been to reduce the public subsidy for education in urban China. Urban households now have to pay school fees, and these have recently been rising.[2]

Increased uncertainty about job security and income prospects were likely to have a significant impact on the consumption behavior of urban households. The effect can be different for the different groups. People experiencing a fall in income which they expect to be temporary may not reduce their consumption. However, people with low expectations about their income prospects and job security in the long run are likely to consume prudently. According to Meng (2001), both income uncertainty, measured by the variation in household income over the last four years, and job

---

[1] Even in 1999, only 47% of the registered unemployed received unemployment benefits, recipients receiving on average 1174 yuan (CLSY, 2000, p. 480), equivalent to 12% of the average wage in urban areas.

[2] Household expenditure on education as a percentage of total expenditure in urban China rose from 4.5% in 1994 to 9.5% in 1999, according to official surveys (CLSY, 1995, p.63; CLSY, 2000, p.314). Moreover, the data from our 1999 survey show that household spending on the education of children accounts for 12% of total consumption.

uncertainty, measured by the predicted probability of becoming unemployed, have a significant negative effect on household consumption.

■ The Scale of the Three Poverties

In our 1999 sample, those defined as poor by either the income or the consumption approach account for 9.4% of the urban population (Table 1). Among this group, 29% are in "income and consumption" poverty, 20% in "income not consumption" poverty and 51% in "consumption not income" poverty. Our estimate of the poor population is higher than that obtained by either of the two approaches alone. If the income-defined approach is used, the incidence of poverty is 4.6%; on the consumption-defined approach, the incidence is 7.5%. Table 1 also shows the incidence of overall poverty and of the three poverties across the cities in the sample. There exists a considerable variation in poverty incidence—whichever concept is used—among the 13 cities.

Table 1 Poverty incidence in urban China, 1999

	Percentage of all individuals				Percentage of all poverty			
	Overall poverty	"Income and consumption" poverty	"Income not consumption" poverty	"Consumption not income" poverty	Overall poverty	"Income and consumption" poverty	"Income not consumption" poverty	"Consumption not income" poverty
Total sample	9.40	2.70	1.89	4.81	100	28 7	20.1	51.2
Beijing	3.95	1.76	0.33	1.87	100	44 6	8.4	47.3
Liaoning								
Shenyang	13.79	3.94	1.75	8.10	100	28 6	12.7	58.7
Jinzhou	12.97	6.81	2.11	4.05	100	52.5	16.3	31.2
Jiangsu								
Nanjing	1.91	0.24	0.64	1.03	100	12 6	33.5	53.9
Xuzhou	9.11	1.20	0.34	7.56	100	13 2	3.7	83.0
Henan								
Zhengzhou	8.06	1.40	4.73	1.93	100	17.4	58.7	23.9
Kaifeng	19.34	5.41	4.92	9.02	100	28.0	25.4	46.6
Pingding-shan	4.58	0.98	0.33	3.27	100	21.4	7.2	71.4

(To be continued)

(Table 1)

Sichuan								
Chengdu	11.09	2.73	1.71	6.66	100	24.6	15.4	60.1
Zigong	16.23	8.93	4.06	3.25	100	55.0	25.0	20.0
Nanchong	10.47	3.49	2.97	4.01	100	33.3	28.4	38.3
Gansu								
Lanzhou	8.45	1.20	2.47	4.78	100	14.2	29.2	56.6
Pingliang	15.67	2.10	0.97	12.60	100	13.4	6.2	80.4

Source: 1999 household survey.

To find out what sorts of people are likely to fall into poverty, we estimate the predicted probabilities of being in each of the three poverties for individuals with different characteristics, using a multinomial logistic model. The model includes the following explanatory variables: gender, age, educational level, employment status, and occupation of household head; health status, medical insurance, schooling and past experience of household members; and house ownership, location, and size of household. The predicted probabilities are presented in Table 2.

Table 2 Personal characteristics of the poor in urban China, 1999: Predicted probability of falling into each poverty group (%)

	Overall poverty	"Income and consumption" poverty	"Income not consumption" poverty	"Consumption not income" poverty
Characteristics of household head				
1. Gender				
Male	9.91	2.61	1.96	5.34
Female	8.33	2.89	1.70	3.74
2. Age distribution				
≤35	12.50	3.43	2.03	7.04
36–40	12.02	2.86	2.86	6.30
41–45	11.44	4.07	3.01	4.36
46–50	6.73	2.57	1.24	2.92

(To be continued)

(Table 2)

51–55	5.84	1.89	0.24	3.71
56–60	8.85	1.65	2.24	4.96
61–65	4.22	0.57	0.46	3.19
≥66	9.83	2.72	1.60	5.51
3. Educational attainment				
College and above	1.42	0.38	0.28	0.76
Professional school	3.58	0.14	0.72	2.72
Middle-level professional school	5.84	1.37	0.14	4.33
Upper middle school	7.56	2.44	0.24	4.88
Lower middle school	13.64	4.72	2.82	6.10
Elementary school	15.62	4.05	3.24	8.33
4. Status of employment				
Working or employed	7.8	1.94	1.51	4.35
Retired	7.71	1.68	1.29	4.74
Laid-off and unemployed	35.81	15.81	8.95	11.05
Other	24.62	12.31	5.97	6.34
5. Occupation				
Private owner/self-employed	10.81	2.03	0.00	8.78
Professional	3.99	0.85	0.47	2.67
Manager	2.30	0.00	0.88	1.42
Department manager	3.84	0.87	1.16	1.81
Clerical/office staff	5.32	0.99	1.41	2.92
Skilled (4 grade and above)	13.32	3.42	2.90	7.00
Skilled (3 grade and below)	15.57	6.25	1.64	7.68
Unskilled worker	18.51	4.66	4.52	9.33
Commercial/service worker	16.85	7.74	1.14	7.97
Characteristics of household				
6. Having member in poor health				
Yes	13.4	4.40	2.67	6.33
No	8.29	2.25	1.66	4.38

(To be continued)

(Table 2)

7. Having a school pupil				
Yes	10.57	2.87	2.43	5.27
No	7.95	2.51	1.21	4.23
8. Having a member not covered by public health care				
Yes	11.55	3.51	2.36	5.68
No	3.40	0.50	0.53	2.37
9. Having a member who has experienced unemployment or has been laid-off				
Yes	19.71	7.09	4.78	7.84
No	6.41	1.45	1.04	3.92
10. House ownership				
Rented public housing	12.16	3.87	2.23	6.06
Purchased public housing	5.76	1.46	0.84	3.46
Purchased private housing	10.34	3.98	3.04	3.32
Own-built private housing	22.17	5.96	6.12	10.09
Rented private housing	14.50	0.00	5.34	9.16
Other	13.70	1.52	4.06	8.12
11. City				
Large city	7.58	1.91	1.67	4.00
Small-medium city	12.03	3.81	2.28	5.94
12. Household size				
1 person	8.85	3.78	2.93	2.14
2 persons	6.68	2.11	1.74	2.83
3 persons	9.41	2.81	2.11	4.49
4 persons	10.36	2.85	1.66	5.85
5 persons	10.76	2.26	0.91	7.59
6 persons	14.58	4.52	0.44	9.62

Note: Computation of the predicted probability is based on the multinomial logistic model estimates and the assumption that a continuous variable takes its mean value and dummy variables take their omitted values.

The multinomial logistic analysis generates some interesting results. The educational level of the household head is highly correlated with the incidence of overall poverty and of all three types of poverty as well: the higher is education, the lower is the predicted probability of poverty. In the case of overall poverty, for instance, an individual living in a household whose head has college education has a predicted probability of being poor of 1.4%, whereas she has a probability of 21% if her household head is illiterate. Households with uneducated heads have lower income and consumption and are thus more likely to fall into "income and consumption" poverty; they are also more likely to fall into "consumption not income" poverty, suggesting that they face greater uncertainty in their income and employment. The unemployment or the *xia gang* status of the household head significantly increases the incidence of poverty. The predicted probability of an individual falling into overall poverty is 4.4 times higher if her household head is unemployed or *xia gang*. Moreover, she is more likely to be "income and consumption" poor and "consumption not income" poor. She is more likely to be poor if her household head is an unskilled worker, in terms of both these poverties. As expected, owners of private firms and self-employed persons have a strong motivation to save for investment and thus have a higher predicted probability of being in "consumption not income" poverty. Households facing greater liability in respect of health or education are more likely to fall into poverty. For example, a household with a member in ill-health has a predicted incidence of overall poverty that is 60% higher than for other households; if a household has a member not covered by public health care, the probability is more than trebled; a household with a child in primary or middle school has a motive to save for further education and therefore has a higher predicted probability of being poor than a household without a child. A household living in inherited (and therefore old) or rented private housing has an incentive to save for house improvement or purchase and so is more likely to be "consumption not income" poor than one living in public housing.

■ The Low-Income Consumption Function

Our hypotheses imply that the reasons why households enter "income not consumption" poverty and "consumption not income" poverty are related to their consumption (and savings) behavior. Banerjee (2000) has argued that the poor may behave differently from the non-poor. There are numerous possible reasons, including greater risk-aversion, poorer access to credit, and a "culture of poverty". This can justify estimating separate behavioral equations for relatively poor people. Our estimates below relate to "low-income households", i.e., the sub-sample with both income and consumption per capita below the sample mean values.

To explain the consumption behavior of the low-income households, we specify the following household consumption function:

$$C=c(S, P, I, N, Z) \quad (2)$$

where C is household consumption; S is a set of variables measuring the smoothing effect that predicted income and financial assets can have relative to actual income;[1] P is a set of variables measuring the precautionary effect, which includes the predicted probability of working members falling into unemployment and the number of household members in poor health; I stands for proxy variables capturing the investment effect, such as expenditure on education and the purchase of housing; N is a set of variables measuring household spending on special needs such as health care and savings for a wedding; permanent income plus transitory income were substituted for actual income in the equation; and Z is a set of control variables, including city dummies and household size. Each of the explanatory variables represents an effect that we wish to capture.

The coefficients of the consumption function for the low-income households

---

1 When predicted income is regarded as equivalent to permanent income, the coefficient of actual income is equal to that of transitory income, defined as the deviation of actual from permanent income. The proof is as follows. $C=\alpha+\beta Y_p+\gamma Y_t$, where Y_p, Y_t are permanent and transitory income, respectively. Actual income $Y=Y_p+Y_t$, so $C=\alpha+\beta Y_p+\gamma(Y-Y_p)=\alpha+(\beta-\gamma)Y_p+\gamma Y$.

are presented in Table 3.[1] Actual income has a significant coefficient, but it implies a low marginal propensity to consume (0.35). Predicted income as a proxy for permanent income (Y_p) has a significantly positive coefficient. If permanent income plus transitory income were substituted for actual income in the equation ($Y_p+Y_t=Y$), the marginal propensity to consume out of predicted income would be 0.38 (see endnote 6). The financial asset variable, measured by the difference between actual and predicted household financial assets,[2] also has a significantly positive coefficient, suggesting that assets above the predicted level discourage and assets below encourage savings, and that assets tend to smooth household consumption.

We obtain the expected results for the variables associated with precautionary savings. The predicted probability of working members becoming unemployed has the right sign and is also significant:[3] the unit probability of having an unemployed member causes a reduction of household consumption by 1042 yuan, equivalent to 11% of the average consumption of low-income households, even ignoring the effect of unemployment in reducing household income. Another variable leading to precautionary savings is poor health status of household members. This has a negative and significant sign.

---

1 We estimated the equation with the consumption and income variables expressed both in levels and logarithmic form. There were no sign changes in the coefficients, but fewer were significant in the latter, and the Box-Cox test favored the former. As the levels equation also simplifies the subsequent decomposition exercise, it is the one reported.

2 The predicted household assets are estimated in the equation, $A=0+1Y+2Y^2+3age_i+4owner_i+5hea_i+6stu_i+7size+8city_i$, where A=household assets; Y=household income; age_i=age group dummies for household heads; $owner_i$=private owner dummies (1, if a household has a private owner; 0 if it has not); hea_i=health status dummies (1 if a household has a member in poor health; 0 if it has not); stu_i=student dummies (1 if a household has a child in school; 0 if it has not); size=household size; $city_i$=city dummies.

3 The predicted probability refers to the sum of probabilities of household working members, which is based on predicted value of each working member falling into unemployment using a probit model. The model is specified as U (U=1 if unemployed; U=0 if employed or working)$=\beta_0+\beta_1 sex_i+\beta_2 age_i+\beta_3 par_i+\beta_4 edu_i+\beta_5 hea_i+\beta_6 own_i+\beta_7 job_i+\beta_8 occ_i+\beta_9 sec_i+\beta_{10} ent_i+\beta_{11} city_i$, where sex_i=gender dummies; age_i=age group dummies; par_i=party membership dummies; edu_i=education dummies; hea_i=health status dummies; own_i=ownership dummies; job_i=job status dummies; occ_i=occupation dummies; sec_i=employment sector dummies; ent_i=enterprise type dummies; $city_i$=city dummies.

Table 3 Estimates of the consumption function for low-income households

	Mean	Coefficient	*t*-value
Intercept	1.00	2,009.13***	5.46
Actual income	11,031.0	0.349***	19.24
Predicted income	11,011.0	0.026**	2.14
Difference between AFA and PFA	0.000	0.023***	8.04
Predicted probability of unemployment	0.255	−1,042.35***	−4.07
Member in poor health	0.238	−247.01**	−1.74
Expenditure on education	926.2	0.92***	17.89
Private owner	0.018	−875.25**	−2.11
Housing expenditure	1,047.7	−0.02***	−3.78
Medical expenditure	670.4	0.95***	15.23
Unmarried member aged 25–35	0.045	−382.70	−1.37
Household head aged 36–40	0.187	−261.58	−1.37
41–45	0.1977	3.01	0.39
46–50	0.162	−206.18	−1.04
51–55	0.077	120.86	0.49
56–60	0.072	−320.40	−1.23
61–65	0.047	13.70	0.05
66–	0.098	−563.96**	−2.32
Number of household members	3.273	497.85***	5.45
adj-R^2		0.623	
F-value		79.4	
Mean of dependent variable		9,438.5	
Number of observations		1,442	

*Notes: (a) The dependent variable is household consumption. (b)***, **, and * denote statistical significance at 1%, 5% and 10% level respectively. (c) The omitted dummy variable categories are household head aged up to 35, household without private owner or self-employed worker, household without a member in poor health, and Pingdingshan city. (d) AFA=actual financial assets, and PFA=predicted financial assets. (e) City dummies are included, but not presented.*

We have three variables to capture the effect of household investment on consumption. Expenditure on education, included in consumption, has a highly significant positive coefficient which approaches unity (0.92). If a household contains an owner of a private enterprise or someone involved in self-employment, consumption is substantially and significantly reduced on account of the household's motivation to save for business investment. Housing investment expenditure, including purchasing and improving housing, has a significantly negative effect on household consumption.

To measure the effects of special needs on household consumption, we include in the function two variables, expenditure on health care and having an unmarried member aged 25–35. The first variable, like expenditure on education, has a highly significant and remarkably large coefficient (0.95). The coefficients of expenditure on education and on health care—both almost unity—indicate that households which spend heavily on these items do so at the expense not of other consumption, but of savings.[1] The second special needs variable, not significant, has the expected negative sign, hinting that households have a motive to save for a wedding and new household formation. We include age of household head in the consumption function to capture life-cycle effects, and city dummies and household size as control variables. The marginal expenditure per household member (498 yuan) is small in relation to the corresponding average (2884 yuan).

■ Explaining the Three Poverties

Using the consumption function for the low-income households, we predict the consumption of the three poverty groups. Our stage-by-stage approach can be illustrated in Figure 2. $C=F(Y, E_i)$ is the household consumption function, with income Y and other household characteristics E_i as the independent variables. Applying the estimated coefficients to the mean characteristics of the low-income group, we obtain predicted consumption given a level of income.

Take the households in "income not consumption" poverty as an example. Suppose that the actual consumption of these households is C_a, and that the predicted consumption is C_Y given their mean actual income $\bar{Y}$

---

1 Although these components of expenditure are potentially endogenous, the size of their coefficients suggests that causation runs from them to total expenditure.

(when predicted income is set equal to actual income) and the mean values of other household characteristics set equal to those of the low-income group as a whole, $\bar{E}_i$. The difference between C_a and $\hat{C}_Y$ needs to be explained. According to the permanent income hypothesis, it is permanent rather than current income that determines consumption. We use instead income predicted on the basis of human capital and other income-generating characteristics. The predictive equation is obtained from an income function estimated for individual workers and aggregated to households. The predicted income of poor households may be higher or lower than their actual income. In the case of the "income not consumption" poor, mean predicted income exceeds mean actual income by 56% (Table 4). When the predicted income is Y, a household is predicted to have consumption $C_{\hat{Y}}$ The difference between $C_{\hat{Y}}$ and C_Y is explained by the difference between the means of predicted and actual income, applying the coefficient on Y to the divergence of Y from $\hat{Y}$. We also need to know how large a part of the residual C_a–$C_{\hat{Y}}$ can be explained by the additional variables E_i. Suppose that $\hat{C}_{\hat{Y}x}$. is the consumption of the households in "income not consumption" poverty derived from their predicted income and their mean values of other determinants of consumption. For illustration, refer to these other determinants as financial assets. The difference between $\hat{C}_{\hat{Y}x}$ and $\hat{C}_{\hat{Y}}$ is, thus, that part of consumption explained by the fact that the "income not consumption" poor possess more financial assets than do the low-income group as a whole.

We are thus able to decompose the consumption of this poverty group into four parts, as illustrated in Figure 2: (i) that predicted by their actual income (when actual and predicted income are held at the mean value of actual income for this group, but they have the mean financial assets of the low-income gap as a whole): $\hat{C}_Y$; (ii) that explained by the difference between the mean values of the predicted and the actual income of this group: C_a–$\hat{C}_{\hat{Y}}$; (iii) that explained by the difference between the mean values of the financial assets for this group and for the sub-sample as a whole $C_{\hat{Y}x}$–$C_{\hat{Y}}$; and (iv) the unexplained residual: C_a–$C_{\hat{Y}x}$. This decomposition enables us to identify which variables are important determinants of each type of poverty, and in this way to test the alternative hypotheses about the nature of each poverty.

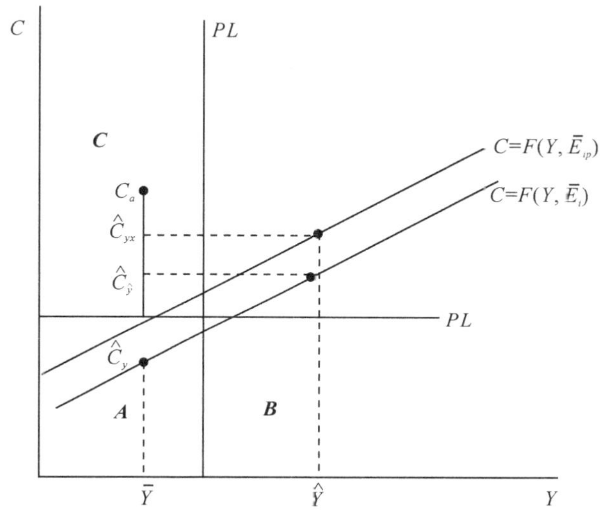

Figure 2 Prediction and decomposition of the consumption of a poverty group

The group in "income and consumption" poverty consume almost all their income: their savings rate is only 1% (Table 4). Table 5 reports the results of a decomposition analysis applied to this group. On the assumption that both actual and predicted income are equal to the mean value of actual income, but that the mean value of other variables in the consumption function are the same as for the low-income group as a whole, the difference between actual and predicted consumption ($C_a - \hat{C}_{\hat{Y}}$) is −1449 yuan. Why is the consumption of the "income and consumption" poor almost 20% lower than we might expect at the first sight? When all the variables are held at the mean values of this group, the explained difference ($\hat{C}_{\hat{Y}x} - C_{\hat{Y}}$) is −419, accounting for 29% of the total difference.

Table 4 Mean values of key variables for the three poverty groups and the low-income group

	"Income and consumption" poverty	"Income not consumption" poverty	"Consumption not income" poverty	Low income
Actual income	6,288	5,183	11,575	11,031
Predicted income	9,190	8,089	11,456	11,011
(When actual income=100)	(146)	(156)	(99)	(100)
Actual financial assets	6,225	9,802	7,205	9,579
Predicted financial assets	7,603	6,069	10,583	9,579
Predicted probability of unemployment	0.393	0.261	0.278	0.255
Member in poor health	0.379	0.294	0.237	0.238
Expenditure on education	495	1,087	462	926
Private owner	0.024	0.012	0.029	0.018
Housing investment	3,066	356	1,243	1,048
Medical expenditure	630	883	470	670
Unmarried member aged 25–35	0.065	0.047	0.072	0.045
Household head aged 36–40	0.161	0.247	0 203	0.187
41–45	0.242	0.235	0.126	0.197
46–50	0.161	0.118	0.135	0.162
51–55	0.073	0.035	0.077	0.077
56–60	0.089	0.106	0.092	0.072
61–65	0.000	0.024	0.048	0.047
66–	0.105	0.082	0.135	0.098
Number of household members	3.484	2.929	3.541	3.273
Household consumption	6,212	9,050	6,747	9,439
Savings rate (%)	1.21	74.61	41.71	14.43

The explained difference (set as −100%) can be decomposed further, as shown in Table 5. The net smoothing effect goes the wrong way (+11%), as the income and financial asset effects account for +18% and −7%, respectively: predicted income exceeds actual income, but predicted financial assets are lower than actual. The precautionary effect accounts for −42% of the explained difference. In particular, the relatively high predicted probability of unemployment pulls down consumption. The largest explanatory factor (−107%) is the investment effect, mainly because this group spend relatively little on education, but also because their relatively high investment in housing depresses consumption. The larger size of these households actually raises consumption rather than helping to explain why it is low.

The group in "income not consumption" poverty have an actual mean consumption well in excess of mean income: the dissavings rate is 74% (Table 4). In this case, mean consumption far exceeds—by over 20%—the initial predicted consumption. Only 28% of the total difference (C_a−$\hat{C}_y$) can be explained ($\hat{C}_{\hat{Y}x}$−$\hat{C}_{\hat{Y}}$) (Table 5). The smoothing effect is important here: predicted income exceeds actual income by 56% and predicted financial assets are lower than actual financial assets by nearly 40% (Table 4), and these together contribute 33% of the explained difference. The other two important reasons for the high consumption of this group are their relatively high expenditure on education and on health care, contributing 30% and 41% of the explanation respectively (Table 5).

The households in "consumption not income" poverty display a savings rate of no less than 42% (Table 4). However, assuming that their actual and predicted income equal the mean value of their actual income and that the mean values of the other explanatory variables are the same as for the low-income group as a whole, we predict their mean consumption ($\hat{C}_y$) to be over 40% higher than it actually is. Table 5 also reports the decomposition results for the "income not consumption" poor. Only 23% of the total difference (C_a−$\hat{C}_{\hat{Y}}$) can be explained ($\hat{C}_{\hat{Y}x}$−$\hat{C}_{\hat{Y}}$). The smoothing effect is −12%: predicted mean income is only 1% below actual mean income, but the relatively low financial assets pull down consumption. Nor is the precautionary effect important. The crucial reasons for the low consumption of this group are their low expenditure on education and on health care, accounting for 64% and 28% of the explained difference, respectively.

Table 5 Explaining the consumption of the poor

	"Income and consumption" poverty		"Income not consumption" poverty		"Consumption not income" poverty	
	Yuan	%	Yuan	%	Yuan	%
1. Total difference $(C_a - \hat{C}_y)$	−1,449	−100.0	1,803	100.0	−2,881	−100.0
2. Explained difference	−419	−28.9	496	27.5	−658	−23.2
$(\hat{C}_{yx} - \hat{C}_y)$		(−100.0)		(100.0)		(−100.0)
due to:						
Smoothing effect	44	(10.5)	161	(32.5)	−81	(−12.0)
(1) Income	76	(18.1)	76	(15.3)	−3	(−0.5)
(2) Financial assets	−32	(−7.6)	85	(17.2)	−78	(−11.5)
Precautionary effect	−178	(−42.4)	−20	(−4.0)	−24	(−3.5)
(3) Predicted prob. of unemployment	−143	(−34.1)	−6	(−1.2)	−24	(−3.5)
(4) Health status	−35	(−8.3)	−14	(−2.8)	0	(0.0)
Investment effect	−449	(−107.2)	170	(34.2)	−441	(−65.6)
(5) Expenditure on education	−397	(−94.8)	148	(29.8)	−427	(−63.5)
(6) Private enterprise	−5	(−1.2)	6	(1.2)	−9	(−1.4)
(7) Housing	−47	(−11.2)	16	(3.2)	−5	(−0.7)
Special needs effect	−46	(−11.0)	201	(40.6)	−201	(−29.8)
(8) Expenditure on health care	−38	(−9.2)	202	(40.8)	−190	(−28.2)
(9) Savings for wedding	−8	(−1.8)	−1	(−0.2)	−11	(−1.6)
Life-cycle effect	0	(0.0)	−11	(−2.1)	−31	(−4.5)
(10) Age of household head	0	(0.0)	−19	(−2.1)	−31	(−4.5)
Control variables	210	(50.0)	−6	(−1.2)	104	(15.3)
(11) Household size	105	(25.0)	−171	(−34.5)	134	(19.8)
(12)City	105	(25.0)	165	(33.3)	−30	(−4.5)

■ Expenditure on Education and Health Care

We saw that additional expenditure on education and on health care raises total consumption expenditure by almost the same absolute amount, i.e., such expenditures are not made at the expense of other consumption. This helps to explain a remarkable pattern to emerge from the analysis: the importance of differential expenditures on education and health care in distinguishing the three poverty groups. It has the interesting implication that poverty may have to be judged not by some uniform standard, but according to the particular needs of each household. In order to explore the reasons for these differences we estimated educational and health care expenditure functions for low-income households (Table 6). An important underlying question is: to what extent are these expenditures discretionary and to what extent are they governed by need, e.g., having children of school-going age or sick members of the household?

Our best indicator of educational need is the presence of children of school-going age in the household. We see that the coefficients in the educational expenditure function are significant and rise monotonically with the relevant age group for successive educational levels Eq.(2). That there is a discretionary element is indicated by the corresponding coefficients on the number of children enrolled at each educational level Eq.(1). These are our best estimates of the marginal private cost of education. Beyond the compulsory (13–15) level, the coefficients reflecting potential education are substantially lower than the coefficients reflecting actual education. There are other signs that educational expenditure is discretionary. Predicted income significantly raises educational expenditure, implying a marginal propensity to spend on education of 0.04, ceteris paribus. The predicted probability of becoming unemployed has a negative effect, as expected, but it is not significant. The educational attainment of the household head has a monotonically increasing effect. This may reflect the stronger preference for education of better-educated parents or their expectation of higher returns to educational investment. The importance of some city dummy variables could reflect different rates of return (discretion) or different degrees of subsidy (need).

Table 6 Explaining household expenditure on education

Variable	Eq.(1)		Eq.(2)	
	Estimate	t-value	Estimate	t-value
Intercept	−270.82	−1.55	−333.10	−1.83*
Predicted income	0.0364.95***	0.038	5.03***	
Financial assets in 1998	0.001	0.82	0.002	1.26
Predicted probability of unemployment	−68.44	−0.56	−166.90	−1.31
Student aged 6–12	—	—		
Student aged 13–15	539.15	7.48***		
Student aged 16–18	918.97	11.41***		
Student aged 19–23	1,231.75	9.49***		
Child aged 6–12		—	—	
Child aged 13–15		515.41	6.75***	
Child aged 16–18		775.21	9.62***	
Child aged 19–23		186.24	2.28**	
Education of household head:				
College	485.53	4.39***	540.20	4.72***
Upper middle school	287.83	3.06***	311.89	3.20***
Lower middle school	63.07	0.68	94.07	0.98
Primary school	—	—	—	—
adj-R^2	0.189		0.131	
F-value	16.73		11.13	
Mean of dependent variable	925		925	
Number of observations	1,416		1,416	

*Notes: (a) The dependent variable is household expenditure on education. (b)***, **, and * denote statistical significance at 1%, 5% and 10% level respectively. (c) City dummies are included but not presented.*

Several variables indicate need for health care expenditure (Table 7). The number of household members in poor health has a large, positive and significant coefficient. There is also a tendency for health care expenditure to rise with the age of the household head, being lowest for the youngest and highest for the oldest age group. Some urban households, by virtue of employment, are entitled to free or subsidized medical services, some have compulsory medical insurance, some choose to buy insurance, and others simply pay user-fees. It is apparent from this set of coefficients that the nature of access to health care affects household expenditure, it being lowest for those with free or subsidized access. Neither predicted income nor the predicted probability of unemployment has a significant effect. We conclude that there is a strong non-discretionary element in medical expenditure.

Table 7 Explaining household expenditure on health care

Variable	Coefficient	T-value
Intercept	200.32	1.26
Predicted income	0.010	1.17
Financial assets in 1998	0.001	1.05
Predicted probability of unemployment	14.13	0.13
Number of members in poor health	399.93	9.97***
Number of children aged 1–3	522.69	5.18***
Number of members in health care I	54.85	0.90
Number of members in health care II	166.19	2.30**
Number of members in health care III	309.00	3.09***
Number of members in health care IV	114.14	2.01**
Household head aged ≤35	—	—
36–40	146.90	1.78*
41–45	81.46	0.99
46–50	200.67	2.33**
51–55	284.38	2.70***
56–60	326.06	3.01***
61–65	253.56	2.04**
66–	595.39	5.90***

(To be continued)

(Table 7)

Number of household members	2.34	0.04
adj-R^2	0.191	
F-value	2.54	
Mean of dependent variable	670	
Number of observations	1,422	

*Notes: (a) The dependent variable is household expenditure on health care. (b) ***, **, and * denote statistical significance at 1%, 5% and 10% level respectively. (c) Health care I=public medical services; Health care II=compulsory medical insurance for serious diseases; Health care III=privately paid medical insurance; Health care IV=privately paid medical services. (d) City dummies are included, but not presented.*

From Table 4 we can find that the "income not consumption" poor households spend on average 120% more on education than the "income and consumption" poor households and 135% more than the "consumption not income" poor households. Moreover, the "income not consumption" poor spend 40% and 88% more on medical services and medicines than do the other two groups, respectively. These differential expenditures suggest the need for disaggregation of consumption in the analysis and assessment of poverty.

■ Conclusions

The ideal instrument for exploring consumption and poverty dynamics is a good panel data set. China—in common with many developing countries—does not possess such a panel.[1] We have, however, shown that cross-section data—much more commonly available in developing countries—are capable of yielding helpful insights into consumption and poverty issues. It was particularly apposite to examine these issues at a crucial time of radical reform, rapid marketization, and social and economic flux in urban China.

It is helpful to use both income and consumption measures of poverty.

---

[1] The national household survey of the NBS has a rolling sample: no household is retained for more that four years. In the past household identification numbers were changed every year. It would thus be a major project to make even a four-year panel available.

Different groups of the poor can be distinguished on that basis, and our understanding of the nature of poverty in urban China can be advanced. By combining income and consumption criteria, we have distinguished three types of poverty in urban China: "income and consumption", "income not consumption" and "consumption not income". The most surprising feature of this classification was the large proportion of the poor who had income above the poverty line, but consumption below it. We attempted to explain the differential consumption behavior of these groups. The benchmark was the estimated consumption function of the "low-income" group (with both income and consumption below their means). Our methodological contribution was to introduce a method of decomposing the divergence in the consumption of each poverty group from their benchmark consumption.

Our consumption function for the low-income group shows solid evidence of a degree of consumption smoothing. Consumption is influenced positively by predicted income (a weak proxy for permanent income) and by the difference between predicted and actual assets. In the increasingly insecure urban environment—with the iron rice bowl disintegrating—consumption is held back by precautionary considerations, such as health status and the likelihood of unemployment. Reflecting the imperfect credit market, investment opportunities also curb consumption—whether that of the self-employed and business-owners or that of households intending to purchase or improve their housing. In this period of economic transition, uncertainty and expected needs thus encourage savings.

The presence of children and of sickness in the household involves additional expenditure on education and health care. Both these expenditures are made almost entirely at the expense of savings, representing future consumption, and not at the expense of other current consumption. This is an unexpected finding, and apparently not one reported in the literature on consumption behavior. Theoretical explanations for this behavior are possible: school costs can be viewed as an investment in human capital and health care costs as necessary to smooth consumption standardized for healthiness. Surprisingly much of the consumption difference among the three poverty groups can be traced to their differences in educational and medical expenditures. The underlying determinants of these expenditures are partly inescapable and partly discretionary in the case of education, and largely inescapable in the case of health care.

We could explain the relatively high consumption and the dissavings of the "income not consumption" poor reasonably well. Much of it was due to the fact that their predicted income greatly exceeded their actual income, i.e., they were able to smooth their consumption. Additional contributing factors were their relatively high financial assets and expenditures on education and medical care. The "income and consumption" poor, who consumed almost precisely what they earned, consumed less than our benchmark prediction for them. The main part of the explained difference was an investment effect: their low spending on education (included in consumption) and their high investment in housing (excluded from consumption) both depressed consumption. A precautionary effect—the relatively high predicted probability of unemployment—also cut their consumption. The remarkable high savings rate of the "consumption not income" poor is explained partly by their unexpectedly low financial assets, but mainly by their low expenditure on education and on health care. These households had few children of school-going age and few members in ill-health, and therefore less need to spend. Contrary to our expectations, the precautionary motive for savings was not important for them.

For each poverty group, a considerable part of their differential behavior remained unexplained. Consumption and income are generally measured with error. This is especially true of rural households and self-employed urban households—given the problems of imputing values for own production and of estimating costs and revenues when accounts are not kept. Nevertheless, there are difficulties of measurement and incentives for misreporting in any survey, even an urban one conducted as well as this one was. The large residuals in our decomposition analyses could reflect unobserved heterogeneity, but they could also reflect measurement error.

Finally, consider the policy implications of our analysis. We saw that high consumption relative to income is due partly to consumption smoothing (income being temporarily low) and partly to special needs (particular consumption expenditures being high). If the latter were not briefly high, there would be a strong case for poverty targeting. We saw that both low income and low consumption are associated in particular with low expenditure on education and a strong precautionary effect. The high risk of unemployment drives households to cut their consumption in anticipation, so indicating a need for greater public support of the unemployed. Those with low consumption relative to income are partly smoothing their consumption, but mainly they have relatively low expenditures on education and health care. Such households choose to save even though their consumption is thereby depressed below the poverty line. The case for poverty targeting appears weak in these circumstances. More generally, the different types of poverty suggest different types or strengths of policy intervention, which single income—or consumption-poverty measures based on cross-section surveys would miss.

References

Appleton, Simon, John Knight, Lina Song and Qingjie Xia (2004), "Contrasting paradigms: Segmentation and competitiveness in the formation of the Chinese labour market", *Journal of Chinese Economic and Business Studies*, 2, 185-205.

Banerjee, Abhijit (2000), "The two poverties", Working Paper Series, Department of Economics, Massachusetts Institute of Technology.

Deaton, Angus S.(1991), "Saving and liquidity constraints", *Econometrica*, 59, 1221-1248.

Institute of Labour Science (2000), "Analytical report of situation of xiagang workers in Shenyang and Wuhan using sample data", Research Forum, No. 19, August (in Chinese).

Jalan, Jyotsna and Martin Ravallion (1998), "Transient poverty in post-reform rural China", Journal of Comparative Economics, 26, 338-357.

Khan, Aziz, Keith Griffin and Carl Riskin (2001), "Income distribution in urban China during the period of economic reform and globalisation", in C. Riskin, R. Zhao and S. Li (eds.), China's retreat from equality: Income distribution & economic transition, New York: M.E. Sharpe.

Knight, John and Lina Song (1999), "The rural-urban divide", *Economic Disparities and Interations in China*, Oxford: Oxford University Press.

Meng, Xin (2001), "Unemployment, consumption smoothing, and precautionary saving in urban China", Australian National University, manuscript.

Morduch, Jonathan(1994), "Poverty and vulnerability", *American Economic Review*, 84, 221-225.

National Bureau of Statistics, China Labour Statistical Yearbook (CLSY), Beijing: China Statistics Press (annual).

Riskin, Carl and Li Shi (2001), "Chinese rural poverty inside and outside the poor regions", in C. Riskin, R. Zhao and S. Li (eds.), *China's retreat from equality: Income distribution and economic transition*, New York: M.E. Sharpe.

Wang Youjuan (2000), "Measuring poverty in urban China", National Bureau of Statistics, PRC, manuscript.

Environmental Stressors and Food Security in China

Jerry McBeath and Jenifer Huang McBeath[1]

■ The Problem of Food Security and Environmental Change

Food is the material basis to human survival, and in each nation-state, providing a system for the development, production, and distribution of food and its security is a primary national objective. Many forces have influenced the food security of people since ancient times, with particular challenges from natural disasters (floods, famines, drought, and pestilence) and growing populations globally. From the late twentieth century to the early twenty-first, however, analysts have riveted their attention on environmental change and crises, for example pollution of arable land and water, insufficiency of water, deforestation, desertification, and over-fishing among others. Our focus is on the food security of the world's most populous nation, China, and the impact on food security of vast environmental change in the

1 Jerry McBeath and Jenifer Huang McBeath are the professors in economics at the University of Alaska.

last 50 years. First, however, we explain why China must be considered in any global discussion of food security.

China has 22% of the global population but just 7% of the world's arable land. Food security has been a chief mission of the Chinese state since early in the dynastic era. It remains a primary state objective in the early twenty-first century. China in 2008 is largely self-reliant in food supplies, and its farmers produce about 95% of the staples consumed. Yet, any large disturbance in supply would have global ramifications, for example, by increasing world food prices.

China's environmental conditions directly impinge on its food security. Many observers believe China's environment is in crisis.[1] Population increases reduce arable land and water sufficiency; indirectly, population stress increases deforestation and desertification as well as over-fishing. New environmental stress such as climate warming has an impact on plant diseases, pests, and invasive species too.

China is a developing country, and its food security and environmental protection regimes are relatively new and untested. It was this combination of factors—a huge population with limited agricultural land, severe environmental challenges, and political, social, and economic systems in the process of modernizing—which prompted Lester Brown's 1995 book *Who Will Feed China*? [3].

■ Loss of Arable Land

Brown's alarmist prediction that China would have to import 200 million tons of grain by 2030[2] initiated a debate among scholars as well as government officials on grain sufficiency. This debate focused on the amount of arable land in China, and whether it was sufficient to sustain agricultural production of staples. In the late 1990s, the official government estimate (now revised upward) was approximately 95 million ha; on a per

---

1 For early studies, see [1] and [2].

2 Brown focused on what he believed was stagnating grain production in China of the early 1990s because of reduced arable land, lack of significant productivity gains, and environmental problems such as water insufficiency and large-scale soil erosion. He contended that China would need to import massive quantities of grain in future years to feed its population.

capita basis, this would equal 0.08 ha per person, making China's land availability about one-fourth of the global average [4].

The major critic of the Brown hypothesis has been Vaclav Smil, a geographer at the University of Manitoba. Smil makes a convincing argument that grain sufficiency pessimists underestimate the amount of China's arable land by at least 50% [5]. He points out the several reasons why official statistics are wrong: (1) a non-standard accounting unit is used for the areal measurement of land—the *mu* (there are about 15 *mu* to the hectare[1]); (2) there were large incentives to underreport land in the Maoist era, for underreporting reduced land taxes and also allowed peasants (and collective leaders) to claim higher harvests per *mu*; and (3) under the somewhat more privatized system of land use in China today, underreporting land allowed fairer apportionment of marginal, less productive land; it reduced the quotas required for delivery to the state at fixed prices; and it reduced taxes as well.[2]

In the last two decades, analysts have made two improvements in land measurement: remote sensing and detailed land surveys. These have produced a consensus among researchers that the range of arable land is between 131 and 137 million ha.[3] (As we note below, government officials in 2008 used the figure of 121.8 million ha.) Smil finds confirmation for the recent estimates of Chinese researchers and officials in results of the MEDEA study, a multi-disciplinary scientific program using U.S. intelligence satellites and a methodology employing stratified, multi-stage area estimation.[4]

Even this approach is too conservative, in the view of Smil, because it omits measurement of non-traditional land uses, which nevertheless produce goods serving nutritional needs of modern Chinese. Specifically, traditional land measurement does not include fish ponds and orchards, and both

---

1 The hectare is approximately 2.47 English acres. The *mu* (also spelled mou) is approximately one-fifteenth of a hectare. However, historically the *mu* has not been standardized. See [6].

2 Smil [5], p. 417. See also [7].

3 Smil [5], p. 419. See also [8] and [9].

4 Smil [5], pp. 419-20.

farmed fish and fruits play an increasingly important role in Chinese nutrition. By adding these surfaces, Smil estimated that land devoted to intensive food production was in the range 146 to 160 million ha in 1997—an average of 153 million ha or 63% higher than official estimates (and on a per capita basis higher than figures for Japan, South Korea, or Taiwan region).[1]

In 2007, China listed the area of cultivated land as 130,039,200 ha. This is based on the situation surveyed as of late 1996. Estimates of the National Bureau of Statistics for 2001 show 127,082,000 ha. Of this amount, "regularly cultivated land" comprised 105,826,020 ha and "temporarily cultivated land" was 21,256,000 [10]. As mentioned throughout this article, attention focuses both on loss of arable land to other purposes and attempts to increase arable land. For example, in 2006 China lost 307,000 ha, mostly for new construction [11]. In the National Agricultural and Rural Economic Development Program for the Eleventh Five-Year Plan (2006–2010), the Ministry of Land and Resources predicted that grain-producing land would decline by 0.18% annually (based on loss of 8 million ha of arable land from 1999 to 2005). It estimated the need for at least 103.33 million ha in 2010 to reach a target production of 500 million tons of grain [12]. Simultaneously, the Ministry of Land and Resources announced that between 1999 and 2006, China gained 2.4 million ha of arable land (and during this period, grain production increased by 10% to 20% in pilot areas) [13].

As we note below, this information does not close the debate, which has refocused on the ways to increase production of both plant and animal foods. Moreover, it is abundantly clear that whatever the areal measurement of China's land in 1949, since the late 1970s, China has lost lands formerly used for production of food crops. We now seek an explanation for this loss.

■ Causes of Arable Land Loss

Three interrelated factors are the source of pressure on arable land in China: population, urbanization, and economic development. As Ho and Lin note,

---

1 Smil [5], pp. 423-424.

they explain about three-fourths of the variation in the share of land employed for nonagricultural uses [14]. We treat each in turn.

Population Growth and Pressure

China is the world's most populated nation-state and has been so since the dynastic era. Table 1 reports the growth of population, in selected years:

China's population more than doubled in the 50-year period from 1949 to 1999. Only since 1979 has a clear population limitation strategy been in effect. It was obvious from the results of the first national census in 1953, when population increases clearly exceeded rises in agricultural productivity, that some form of national birth control planning effort would be needed. However, Mao Zedong was at best ambiguous on the subject of birth control [15]. He made several statements to the effect that he favored birth control, but he also said (in 1958) that a population of more than one billion would be "no cause for alarm." [15]

Table 1 China's population, selected years

Year	Population (in millions)
1949	541.67
1954	602.66
1959	672.07
1964	704.99
1969	806.71
1974	908.59
1979	975.42
1984	1,043.57
1989	1,127.04
1994	1,198.50
1999	1,257.86
2004	1,299.88
2006	1,314.48

Source: China Statistical Yearbook, 2007, 105.

Mao's actions on population questions, however, sent a clear message. In 1957, demographer and Peking University president Ma Yinchu warned, based on the 1953 census, that China's rapid population growth would jeopardize development if not checked. For his forthright views, which contradicted state policy and Mao's many statements that China's strength lay in its huge and growing population, Ma was silenced, forced to resign from the university, and stripped of his academic and government posts.[1]

The size of China's population, which is now expected to peak at 1.6 billion in 2030,[2] puts immense pressure on the land, but this pressure is uneven. In the deserts of western China, population pressures are slight; Tibet, too, is lightly populated. The eastern coastal provinces, however, while occupying only 15% of China's expanse have 41% of China's total population. These differences are summarized in population density statistics. China's population density in 2000 was 351.3 persons per square mile, by no means the highest in the world (in Bangladesh, density was then 1,520 persons per square mile). Yet, in Jiangsu province, the most densely populated region, the statistic was 1,567 persons per square mile, as compared to Tibet and Xinjiang, with fewer than four persons per square mile [17].

Growth of China's population brings a corresponding increase in use of land for housing and human settlements. Although population growth has slowed, it is still increasing. Moreover, the improvement in economic conditions has released a pent-up demand for more, better, and larger housing. The housing construction boom, noticeable in cities as well as in the countryside, has used a large amount of land, including cultivated land.[3]

Urbanization

The fast pace of urbanization in China has swallowed up huge areas of arable land. In the first 20 years of economic reforms, the number of cities in

---

[1] See [16].

[2] This is an estimate only. Several sources predict that population will not peak at the 1.6 billion level until 2050.

[3] Ho and Lin [14], p. 762.

China increased from 193 to 666 [18]. In 1995, the rural population of China peaked at about 750 million, while the urban population continued to grow. By the early twenty-first century, China's urban population was greater than 500 million. As cities became more populous, they expanded into the countryside, consuming land once used for agricultural purposes. One estimate is that urban sprawl and transportation networks took up 1.4 million ha annually, just in the period of the Eighth Five-Year Plan (1991–1995) [19].

Li Diping reports results of landsat mapping for Chengdu, the capital of Sichuan Province. From 1988 to 1996, the city doubled in size [19]. Ho and Lin discuss changes in Guangzhou, which illustrates the combined impact of rural—urban migration, rapid industrialization, and urbanization. From 1988 to 2000, the amount of land used for non-agricultural purposes doubled, from 35,000 to nearly 70,000 ha. They remark: "With a negligible amount of unused land in the region, the increase in non-agricultural land was largely at the expense of agricultural land."[1] The same pattern can be observed not only in other cities, but also in rural towns.

Urban residents have more disposable income than most rural residents in China (a global pattern). Members of China's growing middle class expect to be able to use their leisure time in recreational activities. Much farmland near cities and towns has been converted into golf courses, parks, and other recreational uses. Yet, critics of conventional wisdom regarding urbanization's adverse impact on cultivated areas suggest that under certain conditions urbanization may save arable land, and produce more efficient land uses than if rural residents were left in rural areas (or if the central government promoted development of small cities and towns, with less concentrated populations).[2]

Economic development

There were large pressures of people on the land during the Great Leap Forward and Cultural Revolution. These events had disastrous consequences

1 Ho and Lin [14], p. 766. For a case study using different methods, see [20].

2 See [21].

for China's environment, but they were of limited duration. The economic reforms unfolding since 1978 have spurred economic development in all parts of China, at the cost of China's arable land.

Factories, office buildings, hotels and resorts, and shopping centers consume space in China's cities and suburbs. They are as important as human settlements in accounting for loss of arable land. One estimate is that loss of agricultural land to industrial development has been underreported by as much as 61% [22]. Perhaps the clearest example of land loss is to what is called "development zone fever (kaifa qu re)."

At the outset of reform, central planning authorities established experimental special economic zones (SEZ) on the south coast of China. Planners established four SEZs in Guangdong and Fujian provinces and in 1988 declared Hainan Island a SEZ. In 1989 the state created two additional special zones in the Xiamen SEZ (Haicang and Xinglin) for investors from Taiwan region. In 1990 SEZ status was extended to the Pudong New District in Shanghai. Then in 1994, the China—Singapore Suzhou special zone for industrial development was established. By 1995, some 422 zones had been approved by the central government [23].

The state gave SEZs several privileges and advantages in order to spur rapid development, and high officials visited them, such as in Deng Xiaoping's highly publicized "Southern Tour" of 1992. One measure of the impact of industrial development zones is seen in the 1997 provincial survey of Fujian Province. It revealed that in the previous 7 years, more than half of the 700,000 ha being used for industrial development had been arable land.[1] Cartier reports the egregious example of a large seaport industrial zone associated with Liem Sioe Liong, the head of the Salim Group and Indonesia's leading industrialist. Local authorities allege that the provincial government sold him 800 ha of farm land for "virtually nothing."[2]

An unintended consequence of the SEZ model was widespread copying of the concept in rural counties and towns [24]. The chief force has been the

---

1 Cartier [23], p. 452.

2 Ibid.

Township and Village Enterprise (TVE, siangjen qiye). In the initial stages of economic reform, TVEs were owned collectively by all rural residents of the township or village in which the enterprise was located. Many are now owned by local governments (or their subsidiaries), and a large number have been privatized and are under the control of owner—managers. By the early 1990s, there were 1.3 million TVEs, and they then produced about 30% of national industrial output (rising to 40% by the late 1990s) [25]. Most of the TVEs are small factories, and they have taken up land once used for farming in rural areas. A large number of TVE factories sit in industrial parks covering more than a hectare of land. We discuss the effects of these and other types of economic development in the next section.

Illegal land acquisition, which implicates local governments throughout China, is perhaps the gravest threat to China's diminishing arable land. Gan Zangchun, the deputy state land inspector-general of the Ministry of Land and Resources stated "Violations of land laws and regulations have cropped up recently in some areas." He directly accused local governments, remarking that "Some local governments have arbitrarily expanded development zones in violation of the master plan for land use, and encroached on land using various pretexts." [26] The root of the problem is the lack of a property right to land of farmers. Local governments illegally lease land, the prices of which have become inflated due to a booming land and property market, which makes land sales and leases a lucrative business for local governments. Corruption has become rampant through officials' siphoning off land sale proceeds and abusing land use powers to improperly allot land. Xu Shaoshi, Minister of Land and Resources, said "The illegal acquisition of arable land (for purposes other than agriculture) has endangered both food safety and social stability." He emphasized in a pessimistic voice: "Given the growing population and fast industrialization and urbanization, illegal land acquisition will probably continue." [27]

Senior researcher Li Guoxiang of the CASS Rural Development Institute said "Local governments don't get any incentive for protecting arable land, even though the central government wants them to do so." Establishing industrial units produces higher revenues than what could be derived from agriculture. Local officials see urbanization and industrial production as a solution to poverty, low rates of literacy, economic backwardness, and the other ills of rural life. "Agriculture isn't considered important in their policymaking because it can't bring quick returns that can improve their careers." [28]

■ Effects of Socioeconomic Change

Increased population, urbanization, and economic development have had some benign effects on food production in China. Certainly, rapid economic development has pushed China to the rank of the world's third largest economic power, and earned it the foreign exchange to purchase whatever food it cannot produce to sustain the population. But our focus is on domestic food security in China, and economic development and industrialization in particular have had mostly adverse impacts on food production. Our two large topics here are degradation of land and of water.

Land degradation

By degradation of the land, we mean reducing or eliminating its ability to generate plant life and sustain humans and animals. The immediate causes of such despoilation are erosion, changes to the nutrient balance of soils, and pollution of the land with toxic substances. Erosion occurs naturally in most ecosystems, but our concern is with erosion caused by human actions, such as through deforestation. Changes in nutrient balance of soils occur through weather and climate changes but also through excessive use of chemical fertilizers and other poor farming practices. Pollution of soils occurs primarily through human action.

Several reports in 2006 pointed out the serious extent of land degradation. The Ministry of Water Resources stated that 37% of China's total territory suffered from land degradation. This despoliation included soil erosion, deforestation, salinity, reduced fertility and sand storms, affecting 3.56 million km^2 [29]. The study China Ecological Protection issued by SEPA in this year reported continued deterioration of China's ecology.

Major problems included excessive logging, degradation of natural pasture land, shrinking wetlands, overuse of pesticides and fertilizers in farmland and contaminated coastal areas. The study reported these specific findings:

The ecology of 60% of China's territory was considered fragile;

About 90% of natural pasture land (accounting for more than 40% of China's territory) faced degradation and desertification; desertified pastures had become major sources of sand and dust storms;

Only about 40% of China's wetlands were under effective protection [30]. We treat erosion, deforestation, desertification, and land pollution, giving examples of each form. (Air pollution and particularly acid rain are somewhat less important factors in agricultural production, and for this reason we make only passing reference to them.)[1]

Erosion

Erosion of soils is a general problem of ecological degradation in China. We provide examples from three regions: the Northeast, the Northwest, and the South. Northeast China—including the provinces of Heilongjiang, Liaoning, Jilin and part of the Inner Mongolia Autonomous Region—is China's breadbasket. It is an area of black soil, covering more than 35 million ha, and one of the world's three largest black soil regions (the others being the Ukraine and the U.S.). The black soil belt accounts for 30% of China's total grain output, and its yields feed 10% of the population. Research institutes of the Chinese Academy of Sciences in Harbin and Shenyang recently demonstrated that the thickness of the soil had dropped radically from more than 80 cm to less than 30 cm in the past six decades. The density of organic substances in the soil declined from 12% in the 1940s to less than 2%; about 85% of the soils lacked sufficient nutrients. Causes of soil erosion and degradation included excessive farming, overuse of fertilizers and excessive logging. Soil erosion, in turn, has brought about more frequent drought, floods and sandstorms. Zhang Xudong, an expert with the Shenyang-based Institute of Applied Ecology, commented that "Soil erosion and degeneration

---

1 One example of a recent study is: [31].

will jeopardize the nation's grain security." [32]

Soil erosion has become a large problem in northwestern China's Xinjiang Uygur Autonomous Region as excessive herding and farming have outpaced state conservation efforts. Remote sensing surveys show 1.03 million km^2 of land degraded by soil erosion. Xinjiang itself accounts for about 30% of China's total acreage of soil erosion. A local soil conservation official remarked: "The region has a vulnerable ecology. Besides natural factors, human activities (excessive herding on pastureland and farming along the Tarim River) are largely to blame for the deteriorating soil erosion." [33] As noted below, this is a primary cause of desertification, which affects most of Xinjiang's counties and cities and nearly two-thirds of its territory.

Soil erosion is even a problem in prosperous Guangdong province, ranking second on the mainland for this form of land degradation. The provincial water conservancy bureau reported that more than 2,200 km^2 of soil had eroded during the Tenth Five-Year Plan period (2001–2005) alone, with expected worsening during the next plan period. Experts feared that soil erosion would spread to 5,748 km^2 of land (or about 3.2% of the province's farmland) by 2010. In the case of this province, industrial developments have been the primary factor damaging soils [34].

Deforestation

Population growth and the timber industry are the major factors causing a substantial reduction in forests. About half of China's forests have been destroyed since 1949. Today, forests cover 134 million ha, 14% of the land area, but few virgin forests remain. In recent years, they have decreased at an annual rate of 5,000 km^2. Mining and logging have deforested mountains, which causes erosion, reduced water storage capabilities, and severe sandstorms in northern China.

Agricultural development and housing settlements have also reduced forest and vegetative cover. As will be noted below, government policies of afforestation, reforestation, and converting cropland to grassland and forests have ameliorated some of the deleterious effects of deforestation, but because they replace natural forests, they have "altered the variety, quality, and the pattern of delivery of plant and wildlife habitats that had been provided previously." [35] The massive reforestation and afforestation programs have not yet curbed soil erosion, which as discussed threatens more than one-third of China's territory [36].

Starting in the late 1980s, the central government developed a natural forest protection program (also known as the National Greening Campaign). After massive flooding of the Yangtze River in 1998, this program was strengthened. It included a complete logging ban in the upper reaches of the Yangtze River and the upper and middle reaches of the Yellow River. Also, the program called for a reduction or adjustment of timber output in state-owned forest farms of the Northeast and Inner Mongolia, as well as rehabilitation and development of natural forests in other regions.

However, illegal logging continues, notwithstanding the ban. One of our respondents, a forest ecologist, estimated that one-third of industrial wood in China is harvested illegally. Most of this timber was harvested above the official quota level. He remarked:

On the recommendation of the State Forestry Administration (SFA), the State Council fixes and approves a five-year quota, which is adjusted annually. There is an extensive network of checking stations. At these stations, permits to log are checked. But the system is corrupted. Loggers give money to local officials to register a lower amount than that actually logged. Thus, they avoid the quota limit and also avoid paying heavy taxes. The end result is that five years later, at the end of that quota period, a national inventory will be taken. SFA will do surveys; they'll use remote sensing. Then they discover that the inventory doesn't match the quota.[1]

In a highly publicized case of 2004–2005, the environmental NGO Greenpeace attacked Asia Pulp & Paper (APP), a multinational pulp and paper production giant, for illegal logging in Yunnan Province. Greenpeace charged the firm with logging a large section of natural forests, violating the state's Forest Law as well as the national natural forest protection program [37]. The firm then replanted 183,000 ha with eucalyptus plantations. Local

1 Personal interview, Beijing, May 18, 2004.

farmers claimed their land had been requisitioned at yearly rents of only $1.45 per ha. In this case, Greenpeace enlisted the collaboration of the Zhejiang Hotels Association in a boycott of APP products, which led the corporation to modify its actions [38].[1]

Desertification

Sand and desert cover about 27% of China's land area. The expanse of deserts has increased dramatically in the contemporary period. Desertification annually claims an additional 3,400 km^2 [40]. Desertification has dried up rivers and lakes (leading to salinization of the soil, which then cannot be used for growing crops), shriveled plants and vegetative cover, and led to dropping levels of ground water, posing a direct threat to more than 100 million people. Specifically, it degrades farmland and pastures, and leads to the reduction of crop production.[2] Desertification also has threatened national treasures such as the Great Wall [42] and the Mogao grottoes [43].[3]

Desertification in parts of China is attributable to deforestation as well as to poor protection and overutilization of water resources in arid and semi-arid regions of the North and West. Increased desertification in some parts of China also is attributable to agriculture, commercial, industrial, and residential development.

Grasslands degradation is a principal form of desertification. It refers not just to degradation of the grass but also the soils, with a despoilation of the entire ecosystem. China's many steppes have undergone extensive degradation as a result of land reclamation, grazing, and wood cutting. In the estimate of experts, the productivity of plant communities on steppes has declined 60% since the 1950s, with particularly obvious degradation in the last decade.[4]

---

1 Also, see [39].

2 See [41].

3 The Mogao caves are located in Dunhuang, Gansu province and are famous for their 1,000 year old Buddhist statutes and wall paintings. They are threatened by the encroaching Kumutage desert, China's sixth largest.

4 See [44]. See also [45].

A special case of desertification is erosion around the world's highest and largest wetlands, the Sanjiangyuan Nature Reserve in Qinghai province. Sanjiangyuan means "source of the three rivers" (the Yangtze, Yellow River, and Lancang River), but in recent years the region has become increasingly sandy because of overgrazing, increased human activity, and climate change. Although ecological restoration work began in 2005, a conservative estimate is that efforts will need to continue for 10 years to bear fruit [45].

Desertification is correlated with the increase of sandstorm activity in North China [47].[1] Most of the sandstorms blowing into Tianjin and Beijing originate in Inner Mongolia [51]. Inner Mongolia has China's four largest deserts—Otindag, Horqin, Moo-Os and Hulun Boir—with a combined area of 15 million ha. The Otindag desert in Xilingol League once was mostly grassland and produced few sand storms (only one recorded from 1930 to 1960). However, population increases and over-grazing (an increase in livestock from one million in 1947 to 24 million in 2000) severely increased pressure on the land; by 2000, the region produced 14 sand storms alone [52].

While it is clear that sandstorm activity has increased consequent to China's rapid industrial development, scientists suggest that spring sandstorms are a "fact of nature" in North China. Qin Dahe, director of the China Meteorological Administration, introduced a note of caution in the discussion of sandstorm activity: "The public should have a full understanding of sand and dust, which have complex effects on nature and society....Without sandstorms, Chinese society would not have arisen." Qin maintained that sandstorms contributed to creation of nearly 1 million km^2 of loess plateau. It was the Yellow River, he remarked, whose course over the plateau washed away huge amounts of dust, forming the North China Plain [53].

There is consensus that some of the causes of erosion should be addressed, and several mitigation strategies have been employed to reduce desertification. The regime's re- and afforestation policy was the original strategy to reduce soil erosion and desertification, but lack of water in desert

---

[1] See also [48-50].

regions frustrated this policy. A major recent method has been fencing in grasslands to protect vegetative cover against advancing deserts. While this has been superior to planting trees, which require more water resources than available in most desert areas, it has a large impact on the ecosystem. Migratory species are then restricted in their movement.[1] Another mitigation strategy used in Inner Mongolia has been erecting sand barriers and planting soil-stabilizing shrubs.

Land pollution

Three types of pollution afflict agricultural lands in China: industrial plant waste, mining operations, and use of chemical fertilizers and pesticides. Chemical and other industrial facilities pollute land with toxic contaminants, diminishing or exterminating plant growth. Pollution caused by rural industries is far more severe than that caused by urban industries. Second, China has a large number of small-scale mining operations, particularly coal mines, for China is reliant on coal for nearly 70% of its energy needs. Mine waste dumps including sulfides as well as other toxic chemicals have had adverse impacts on the soil microbial communities in adjacent areas [54]. A third cause of land pollution is from excessive use of chemical fertilizers and pesticides by farmers, which degrades soils.

Reports from the Ministry of Land and Resources in 2007 indicated that about 12.3 million ha—more than 10% of China's arable land by current government estimates—is contaminated by pollution, and the situation is worsening [55].[2] The ministry acknowledged that heavy metals alone had contaminated 12 million tons of grain and caused losses of $2.6 billion each year, and that the contaminated grain would ultimately be a health hazard.

Land pollution concerns prompted the State Environmental Protection Administration (SEPA) to conduct the first soil survey of China's farmlands to insure food safety, beginning in mid-2006. The survey has focused on

---

1 Personal interview with government-organized NGO representative involved in desert control activities, Beijing, May 18, 2007.

2 Also see [56].

main grain-producing and industrial areas: Jiangsu and Zhejiang provinces in the Yangtze River Delta and Guangdong Province in the Pearl River Delta and also Liaoning Province in the Northeast and Hunan in central China. In addition to pollution of grain production regions by wastewater, solid waste and other pollutants, vegetables and fruits have also been polluted by excessive nitrates in the soils [57].

Air pollution

Some 2,000 tons of mercury, from more than 2 billion tons of coal burned every year, enter the soil and pose threats to agricultural production and human health [58], and this is one indication of the serious impact air pollution has on agricultural land. In 2005, one third of China's land mass was affected by acid rain; in some regions of the nation, all rainfall was acidic. With 26 million tons of sulfur dioxide discharged in 2005—27% greater than in 2000—China became the world's largest sulfur dioxide polluter [59].[1] Coking plants and coal-burning power stations were primarily responsible for these emissions.

Air-borne pollution particles have cut rainfall in many regions of China, particularly in the Northeast and Northwest. Scientists studying mountain regions have noted a particular kind of precipitation called orographic, which occurs when moist air is deflected upwards by a topographic feature such as a mountain, which cools the air and causes cloud droplets and then raindrops to fall. Polluted air carries more particles that divide cloud droplets into smaller ones. The smaller cloud droplets are slower to combine into rain drops, reducing precipitation [62].

Air pollution is a major cause of lung cancer, as harmful particulates enter the lungs and cannot be discharged. As noted below, water pollution also is a cause of cancer, which in recent years has been the most lethal disease for China's residents. In China, a 2007 survey administered by the Ministry of Health (of 30 cities and 78 counties) indicated that death rates

---

[1] In Guangzhou, eight out of every ten rainfalls was acidic in 2007; see [60]. China is a major source of transboundary air pollution reaching its neighbors. Even in Los Angeles, city officials estimate that on some days, one-quarter of the city's smog comes from China. See [61].

from cancer had risen to 19% in cities and 23% in rural areas [63]. In recent years, reports on "cancer villages," where residents describe high rates of deaths from cancer, have increased. The World Bank reports that deaths resulting from water-related pollutants and bad air reach 750,000 a year [64].

However, optimistic reports from government agencies in 2007-2008 said the high rate of air (as well as water) pollution might be lowering somewhat. SEPA noted that there were fewer sandstorms in 2007 than in the previous year, that key cities in North China were less seriously polluted, and that "good air" days were more frequent than in the previous year [65]. Further, SEPA noted that although the total amount of pollutant discharges rose in 2006, the rate of increase was slower than in the previous year. Sulfur dioxide emissions fell 0.3% in the first quarter of 2007 [66].[1]

Degradation of China's waters

While degradation to China's land is serious and worsening, water degradation, in the view of many observers, has reached crisis proportions. We consider first the issue of water sufficiency in China, and then treat respectively pollution to fresh waters and to the oceans off China's coasts.

Water sufficiency

Lester Brown directly connected the nature of China's water system with global food security when, in 1998, he commented: "As rivers run dry and aquifers are depleted, the emerging water shortages could sharply raise the country's demand for grain imports, pushing the world's total import needs beyond exportable supplies." [68][2] As in his previous critique of China's loss of arable land, he maintained that if China were not to address this problem, world grain prices would rise, creating instability in Third World

---

1 NGO activity targeting air pollution became more public in 2007. Ma Jun, author of China's Water Crisis and head of the Institute of Public and Environmental Affairs, set up a China Air Pollution Map to mirror the China Water Pollution Map. Its blacklist in late 2007 included 40 multinational corporations among 4,000 firms on the roll. See [67].

2 See also [69]. For a generic response to Brown's argument, see [70, 71].

cities.

China ranks fifth in the total water resources of nations in the world, but on a per capita basis, China's water supply is 25% below the global average. Future projections are more troubling. By 2030, per capita supply is expected to drop from 2,200 to below 1,700 m^3, and at this level would meet the World Bank's definition of a water-scarce country [72]. Agriculture consumes from 70% to 80% of China's water resources, but as supplies tighten, agricultural use of water is threatened by rising industrial and household consumption. However, most observers of China's water sufficiency believe that shortage of water has not yet led to a substantial loss of irrigated area or industrial production [73].

Thus, on a national basis, China's water resources currently seem to be sufficient; however, water is not evenly distributed throughout China. It is relatively scarce in the North and West, and is abundant in the humid South. Although the dry North produces more than 40% of China's grain supplies, it has less than a quarter of China's water resources and parts have been subject to drought conditions, for example Shaanxi in 2007 [74]. The North China Plain (Huabei pingyuan) is the heartland of Chinese civilization, and is traversed by three major rivers: the Yellow, the Hai, and the Huai. The Yellow River (affectionately dubbed the "mother river") is the most obvious example of water scarcity in the North. In 1972, for the first time in Chinese history, the Yellow River dried up before water could reach the sea. In 1997, for 330 days of the year, water from the Yellow River did not reach the ocean [75]. Causes of water loss included extensive upriver exploitation of water as China rapidly industrialized; future threats include melting of glaciers and depletion of underground water systems feeding the river [76]. Both the Hai and Huai rivers suffer from depleted flow, leaving entire valleys short of water, notwithstanding construction of thousands of large- and small-scale reservoirs.[1]

With less available water (and because most water from rivers is polluted), the people of the North and West have turned to use of ground water. In

1 As a number of studies have indicated, the crop structure of regions in the North China Plain, affecting the amount of water consumed through irrigation systems, strongly influences water sufficiency prospects. See, for example, [77].

recent years, however, the ground water tables through most of North China and parts of the South have dropped, making it necessary to drill deeper wells. A recent survey indicated that the water tables beneath much of the North China Plain have fallen an average of 1.5 m per year in the last 5 years.[1] The dropping water tables have caused large areas of subsidence.

Not only is water in limited supply in China, but it also is used inefficiently. One estimate suggests that only 43% of the water used in agriculture is used efficiently, as compared to 70%–80% of irrigated water in developed countries. Moreover, about 25% of the water transmitted through pipes is lost through leakage, much higher than the 9% lost in this way in Japan, and 10% in the United States[2]. In China's irrigation systems overall, much water is lost through evaporation.

A final factor affecting water supply is the pricing system for water use. Until recently, prices for commercial, industrial, and household use were not well-differentiated. Moreover, prices for water in most of China's regions and cities did not vary in proportion to the amount of water used.[3] Lohmar et al. comment: "Despite increasing water prices, current pricing policies do not effectively encourage water savings and in fact contribute to China's water problems in other ways."[4] Also, researchers have identified challenges as well as opportunities in the transition from collective management of water to water user associations and contracting systems.[5] In a country that remains communist, with clear policy goals of egalitarianism, the transition to a market-based system for water use is especially difficult. Only in 2007, did the regime gingerly begin planning to deregulate prices of water, to reflect its scarcity [79]. For these reasons, the water use system encourages over-use of water instead of careful conservation.

---

1 Brown [68], p. 2.

2 Turner & Otsuka [72], p. 3.

3 Personal interview with water engineer, Beijing, May 15, 2007.

4 Lohmar et al. [73], p. 17.

5 Most of the analyses suggest that incentive systems and not the development of new water management institutions are most likely to produce water savings. See [78].

Water pollution

The consensus of water specialists is that water sufficiency currently is less of a problem in China than water pollution.[1] One obvious indicator is that 16 of the world's 20 most polluted rivers are in China. Moreover, air and water pollution combined with widespread use of food additives and pesticides have made cancer the leading cause of death in China. Chen Zhizhou, a health expert with the cancer research institute of the Ministry of Health noted: "The main reason behind the rising number of cancer cases is that pollution of the environment, water and air, is getting worse day by day." He continued: "Many chemical and industrial enterprises are built along rivers so that they can dump the waste into water easily. Excessive use of fertilizers and pesticides also pollute underground water. The contaminated water has directly affected soil, crops and food." [80][2]

There are three major sources of water pollution: industrial contaminants spewed into rivers and lakes, chemical pesticide and insecticide run-off from crop fields, and human waste and garbage disposed into waterways. A 2006 study examined 30 of China's major rivers carrying processed water to the sea, accounting for 82% of the total run-off volume. Results showed a large increase over the previous year in levels of pollutants discharged via the Yangtze, Pearl, Yellow, Minjiang and several other rivers. Of the total volume of major pollutants, chemical oxygen demand accounted for 86.3%, nutritive salts some 12.5%, with the remainder distributed among oil, heavy metals, and arsenic [84].

Industrial pollution events hit the news repeatedly in 2006 and 2007. In late 2006, a chemical spill caused by an explosion at the Jilin Petrochemical Corporation (in the Northeast, China's rustbelt), created a toxic slick on the

---

1 Based on personal interviews with officials of the Ministry of Water Resources, professors of hydrology, and NGO representatives, Beijing, March 15, 22, May 18, 22, 30, 2007.

2 Environmental degradation also has been linked to birth defects, which increased by nearly 40% between 2001 and 2007. See [81]. The health effects of contaminated water are both direct and indirect. Farmed fish raised in contaminated waters may lead to higher rates of cancer as well as liver disease and other afflictions. See [82]. Eel farmers called the times accusation that fish farmers had mixed illegal veterinary drugs and pesticides into fish feed "totally groundless." Local environmental protection bureau officials said strict regulations since 2003 had made drug use illegal, and that "The major pollutants in eel breeding are nitrogen, phosphorous and excrement which are found naturally" and that 97% of aquatic products met standards during random tests. See [83].

Songhua River, forcing downstream cities in Heilongjiang to suspend their normal water supplies [85]. In fact, the Ministry of Water Resources (MWR) labeled water quality at level 5, the poorest, equivalent to raw sewage. The basin of the 1,900 km Songhua River spreads to Jilin and Heilongjiang provinces, Inner Mongolia, and it flows into Russia (and its level of pollution nearly created an international incident). This event prompted the resignation of the minister. Government officials planned to let the river "rest in peace and rehabilitate itself" for 10 years [86], but experts were not sanguine about the prospects of full recovery in this period, given lack of clean-up success in other rivers, such as the Huai. Pollution on this river, which authorities have been attempting to clean up for 10 years, has become significantly worse [87].[1] The pollution situation in the Liaohe River of the Northeast is equally bleak. In Shenyang, capital city of Liaoning Province, some 400,000 tons of sewage were released into a major tributary of the Liaho River daily, and emissions of chemical oxygen demand have steadily increased since 2001 [89].

Pollution levels in the Yellow River have increased rapidly during the reform era. Between the 1980s and 2005, the volume of wastewater flowing into the river increased from about 2 billion tons to 4.3 billion tons [90]. Much of this pollution has been caused by industrial enterprises, which produce large amounts of sewage, but untreated household waste also has been released in the river. For example, the city of Lanzhou, capital of Gansu Province, had released millions of tons of household sewage into the Yellow River because the city's sewage treatment facilities were out-of-date and inefficient [90]. Tributaries of the Yellow River are similarly affected. For example, the Weihe River, the largest tributary, is seriously polluted. Cities along the Weihe such as Baoji, Xianyang and Weinan dump sewage into it daily; Xian, capital of Shaanxi Province, dumps nearly one million tons of sewage into the Zaohe River, a tributary of the Weihe. The Weihe

---

[1] The Huaihe River is China's third longest and stretches through Henan, Anhui, Jiangsu, and Shandong provinces. In early 2008 wastewater treatment plants treated just 60% of daily wastewater from industrial plants and households. Its chemical oxygen demand level was still 80% higher than the accepted standard, and a MEP report faulted provincial governments for inadequate pollution monitoring and enforcement [88].

River basin covers one-third of the province's total area. Home to 63% of the Shaanxi population, it contains 56% of the farmlands and generates about 89% of the province's GDP [91].

Pollution levels also have increased enormously in the Yangtze River, which (including its tributaries) accounts for about one-third of China's total fresh water resources. In a 2007 report, the Yangtze River Water Resource Commission stated that one-tenth of the 6,211 km main course of the river was in critical condition. In addition, about 30% of the major tributaries of the Yangtze—including the Minjiang, Tuojiang, Xiangjiang, and Huangpu rivers—were heavily polluted by excessive ammonia, nitrogen, phosphorous and other pollutants [92]. High levels of pollution led to a shrinking of fish catch, and threatened endangered species.[1] Other industrial pollution reports included a cadmium spill along the Beijiang River in Guangdong Province, spills from factories in Gansu Province, and factories in Hunan Province flushing waste water with high concentrations of arsenide into the Xinqiang River [94].

Both the Yangtze and Pearl River estuaries were listed as "dead zones" in a study released in late 2006 by the United Nations Environment Programme (UNEP) [95]. Dead zones are water areas where nutrients from fertilizer runoff, sewage, human and animal waste and the burning of fossil fuels trigger algae blooms. The blooms require oxygen and remove it from the water, a condition called eutrophication, which endangers all water life. The number of deoxygenated areas has increased each decade since the late 1970s; they are a major threat to fish stocks and people depending on the fisheries.

In the summer of 2007, many lakes in China experienced major algae outbreaks. High concentrations of nitrogen and phosphorus in the waters caused spurts of blue-green algae that threatened the safety of the water supply of Wuxi in Jiangsu Province, a city with a population of nearly six million [96].[2] Resembling a sheen of green oil paint, the canopy of algae

---

1 The white-fin dolphin, with a history of 20 million years along the Yangtze, has practically died out because of pollution and over-fishing. See [93].

2 Also see [97, 98], for a report of an outbreak of blue algae in the water supply of Changchun in northeast China.

covered 70% of the lake's surface. To dilute the polluted lake water, local officials diverted water from the Yangtze River and also seeded clouds to bring rain [99].[1] China's natural lakes are estimated to be disappearing at the rate of 20 a year because of eutrophication.

Pollution has increasingly affected groundwater supplies throughout China. A recent report found that 90% of the groundwater of China's cities is polluted to some extent, which poses huge problems because nearly three-quarters of the population of China relies on ground water for drinking.[2] SEPA Vice-Minister Pan Yue reported in 2007 that the quality of potable water in key cities had dropped by five percentage points as compared to the previous year; only 66 cities had source water meeting national environmental standards [103]. Groundwater contamination is a more serious problem in North than in South China, because abundant rainfall flushes out contaminants in the South. Yet even in the South, pollution remains a serious problem. A study of drinking water in Guangdong province by the Guangzhou Institute of Geography indicated that 17,000 m^3 of sewage were being discharged into rivers every year. At least 16 million residents of the province faced water shortages because of pollution [104].[3]

Most of these reports come from urban areas in China, but the situation in rural areas doubtless is worse. Primary pollutants in rural areas are poisonous fertilizers and discharge of untreated sewage water. China uses more than 360kg of fertilizer per ha, much higher than developed nations' usage rates, and fertilizer is used inefficiently. Fertilizer runoff after rains causes contamination of water and water life. Most of the 280 million tons of sewage generated each year is untreated and directly discharged into rivers. Some 9 billion tons of sewage water is discharged every year. Overall,

---

1 An environmental activist who protested about the impact of the chemical industry in pollution of Lake Tai sought retribution from the government. See [100]. Yet five of the nine "Green Chinese," winners of environmental awards sponsored by seven ministries in 2007 won the prizes because of their service in reducing water pollution, including Zhang Xiaojian, who treated polluted water of Lake Tai in Wuxi. See [101].

2 Turner and Otsuka [72], p. 4; also see [102].

3 This region too was afflicted by algae blooms. See [105].

about one-third billion rural Chinese use unsafe drinking water [106].

Government officials, particularly in the national SEPA and MWR, as well as provincial and local environmental protection bureaus, have addressed these problems by tightening regulations and increasing inspections.[1] Yet the problems persist and are increasing in frequency and severity.[2] A senior engineer working in an institute affiliated with the Ministry of Water Resources commented "The water environment is not good, and this influences the quality and quantity of cereals production in China."[3] The security of China's drinking water and purification of major rivers and lakes—together with major pollution and emissions control and urban waste treatment measures—were highlighted in the Eleventh Five-Year (2006–2010) Plan. Total investment in environmental protection will increase to 1.35% of GDP, and the new investment will focus on treating pollution sources [111].[4]

Ocean pollution

China's coastline extends 18,400 km and abuts four seas: the Bo Hai (considered an "inland" sea), the Yellow Sea, the East China Sea, and the South China Sea. In 2006, China's seas generated $270 billion or just over 10% of GDP [114], yet development of a booming regional economy along

---

1 For example, in 2007 SEPA announced that it was launching an automated system to closely monitor key polluters, who account for 65% of the country's industrial waste (to respond to environmental activists who complain that many industrial plants shut off expensive sewage disposal facilities after SEPA inspections and resume dumping wastes into rivers). The agency claimed it had reached a "turning point" in this year because the rate of increase in pollutant discharges increased at a slower rate than in the previous year. See [107, 108].

2 In 2007, SEPA reported that despite an increase in funding on pollution control, amounting to 1.23% of China's GDP, "China is under increasing pressure to cope with environmental pollution." Of 842 pollution accidents reported for 2006, more than half were water related. Moreover, half the country's population lived in an environment where sewage was not treated. Orders from SEPA to reduce pollution routinely were disregarded by some cities. See [109, 110].

3 Personal interview with Senior Engineer, Institute of Water Resources, Beijing, May 30, 2007.

4 SEPA official Zhou Shengxian gave an optimistic projection, claiming that "the quality of China's key drinking water resources should meet national standards by next year." He also believed that pollution of waterways would decline: "The ecological system should maintain a virtuous circle and all rivers should flow calmly along their natural course." See [112]. It seems unlikely that either goal will be realized without greater government coordination and enforcement actions. The immediate plan was to inaugurate the first national pollution census to examine sources of industrial, agricultural and residential pollution without, however, linking results to either punishment or evaluation of derelict officials. See [113].

this coastline is jeopardized by increased degradation of the ocean. Threats to China's oceans include overfishing, destructive fishing methods, pollution, and the reclamation of coastal lands. Marine fisheries are nearly 75% of China's total fisheries, and overfishing has resulted in a serious decline of take in recent years. The mariculture industry has caused degradation of water quality as well as put pressure on fish fry, small crustacea, and shellfish [115]. Moreover, the use of dynamite and poison fishing has damaged coral reefs and mangrove forests. At least 50% of the coral reefs off China's coasts have disappeared in the past 20 years. Loss of coral reefs in turn increases the risk of typhoon damage to China's coasts.

Pollution from industries, agriculture, domestic sewage, oil and gas exploration, and fish farming has degraded China's ocean environment, as has extensive runoff of silt from rivers and seabed dredging. As one NGO representative remarked: "All the coastal cities of China dump their wastes in the sea."[1] A State Oceans Administration official stated: "The coastal marine ecosystem is worsening, the quality of ocean water is deteriorating, and large amounts of pollutants are infiltrating from land to sea."[2] The loss of coastal wetlands to agriculture, aquaculture, and reclamation projects has devastated both wildlife and marine resources. Several species already have become extinct: sea cows, species of kelp, and the habitat of sea turtles has been threatened. Enforcement of existing regulations and laws on pollution remains problematical.

Red tides have increased in frequency and range, with 80 or more occurrences in recent years. The tides are caused by buildup of marine plankton that consume oxygen while releasing toxic substances into the water, killing fish and plant life in the coastal regions. The third appearance of a red tide in Shenzhen bay caused serious pollution in mid-2007, which marine experts said was the largest ever appearing off the city's coast [117].

---

1 Personal interview with NGO representative, Beijing, January 11, 2005.

2 Personal interview with official, State Oceanic Administration (SOA), Beijing, January 1, 2006. A SOA report issued in August 2007 and based on more than 500 pollution outlets monitored by the agency found that 77% of the outlets were discharging more pollutants than permitted, some 18% more than in the previous year. See [116].

Problems of ocean pollution have attracted less attention even than those of land and freshwater systems in China. Director of the Guangdong Oceanic and Fishery Administration, Li Zhujiang, said problems of the Pearl River estuary were the product of years of ineffective protection measures: "The government has spent so much on cleaning the river, but it never set up a special financial foundation to deal with pollution near the sea." [118]

In 2008, Director of the State Oceanic Administration, Sun Jhihui, pledged to address these concerns. He said the agency would tighten monitoring of the ecology of waters offshore China, conduct experiments to restore the marine ecosystem, and establish seven special protection zones [119]. However, the agency is small and not well regarded for its enforcement capability.

■ State Responses to Environmental Stressors

The environmental challenges to China's food producing lands and waters have been huge, and the state has responded in kind with standard bureaucratic routines as well as large-scale projects. Space limitations prohibit our consideration of pests and plant diseases, the food safety system, and implementation issues—all of relevance to China's food security. Here, we examine six different examples of state responses: policy restricting arable land conversion, China's one child policy, investment in irrigation systems, the South—North Water Diversion Project, large-scale afforestation and reforestation campaigns, and the program to convert marginal agricultural lands to forests and grasslands.

Restriction on arable land conversion

In the 1980s and early 1990s, the central government employed an hierarchical system to regulate conversion of agricultural lands to other purposes—primary industrial, commercial, and residential. The regulatory system had several loopholes, however. Moreover, local level officials had large incentives to bend the rules because of the benefit to provinces, counties, and municipalities of the conversion of collective land to commercial and industrial purposes. The most recent change to policy was through adoption of a revised Land Management Law, promulgated in 1998.[1]

Under the revised law, the central government resumed decision-making control on land conversions from agricultural to other uses. The land utilization plan for the period 1996 to 2010 called for a reduction in land allocated to human settlements and industrial sites, and specified that very little agricultural land would be converted for any purpose in the coastal provinces. Also, the central government imported sophisticated remote sensing technology from France, which made it less dependent on provincial and local governments for information on land use.

Ho and Lin believe these goals are overly ambitious, given the expected pressure of population increases and increased industrial and commercial activity in the coastal areas.[2] Cartier has a more sanguine view of the revised law, believing that it may resolve some of the internal contradictions (between different interests in land conservation and development of different levels of government in China),[3] and that it may promote fiscal stability by cooling speculative fever in land transactions.

These measures did not reduce pressures on arable land, which reached a high point by the end of the Tenth Five-Year Plan in 2005. To curtail conversion and safeguard future food security the regime responded in three ways: (1) it set a limit on the minimum amount of cultivatable land, (2) it tightened regulations on land conversion, and (3) it sought ways to increase the amount of arable land. We discuss each in turn.

At the 17th Congress of the CCP, Premier Wen Jiabao announced that China could not have less than 120 million ha (about 1.8 billion *mu*) of arable land. Reiterating this point, Minister of Land and Resources Xu Shaoshi stated: "The red line of 120 million ha of arable land cannot be crossed." [120] (At the end of 2006, official accounts reported that the arable land total was 121.8 million ha, compared to 122 million ha in 2005.)

In 2006, the Ministry of Land and Resources established a new classification system for lands. It strictly barred any construction of villas,

---

1 This discussion follows Ho and Lin [14], pp. 776-778.

2 Ibid., p. 778.

3 Cartier [23], pp. 466-469.

golf courses, or race tracks taking up large amounts of arable land [121]. Then, it initiated a process to define lands into four different regions: those where urbanization was "prioritized," "encouraged," "limited," and "forbidden." At the completion of this national blueprint, provincial governments would be given greater freedom to plan their own development projects in accord with the national plan [122].

The land approval process was tightened in 2007 to force local governments to make better use of their available land and spur disposal of land already approved for use. In mid-2007, the Ministry of Land and Resources began a 3-year national land-use survey, to ascertain changes in land utilization and management. A previous survey had been done from 1984 to 1996, but a number of local officials camouflaged land status or fabricated data during the inspection, leading to many cases of illegal land acquisition, as mentioned above. The ministry planned random checks and strict penalties for manipulation of land data [123].[1]

The ministry also increased fees and penalties for illegal conversions. It doubled the land-use fee for arable land for new construction projects, which reduced the incentive for local governments to sell land (as they would receive less income for doing so). The ministry also set a minimum pricing standard for land sales for industrial use, as a means to stop local governments from attempting to attract investors with heavily discounted land prices [125]. Finally, the ministry announced a campaign to check land law enforcement, and to hold provincial governments responsible for diverting farmland to other uses in excess of quotas [126].[2]

China's land authorities also have made efforts to increase the amount of

---

[1] A State Council regulation of 2008 required greater cooperation among land survey participants and further tightened penalties for falsifying or distorting information. See [124].

[2] Nearly half of the rural protests in China were triggered by illegal land seizures or expropriations. The State Council ordered local governments to raise compensation for farmers losing land to development projects, as one means to address protests; increasing enforcement of land law violators including local government officials is another. See [127]. Some 22,000 cases of illegal land use covering more than 328,720 ha were reported between January 2005 and September 2006. Late in the next year, land inspectors in the Ministry of Land and Resources ran a 100-day campaign to detect major rule violators, catching a few local government officials. See [128]. The ministry promised to station inspectors in every province as part of a pilot project to curb illegal land acquisitions involving local authorities. See [129]. During 2007, about 2,700 local officials were arrested; they either failed to seek permission before developing land or ignored rules on expansion of development zones.

arable land. From 1999 to 2006, China added 2.4 million ha of arable land, which was a greater amount than land made available for construction projects. In the expanded, pilot areas, grain production increased by 10% to 20%.[1] A second plan, announced in mid-2007, was to convert at least 5.5 million ha into cultivable land through two forms of consolidation: (1) re-planning of random, scattered and small plots, and (2) merging villages and returning land used to build houses and other structures to farming [131].

Altogether, these measures were designed to insure sufficient arable lands for production of staples in the near-term. They seemed to be having some effect, as the rate of arable land loss in 2007, a reduction of 40,700 ha to a total of 121.73 million ha, was the smallest annual decrease since 2001 [132].

China's one-child policy

Population pressures figure in each of the environmental stressors discussed above, and this is a problem to which the regime responded radically. In 1979, China introduced the one-child family policy, which is the single most important reduction of environmental stress to have occurred globally in the past generation. The policy was designed primarily for urban areas, where there were incentives for residents to have small families. In rural areas, the policy effectively was an "one child with exceptions" policy. The army of enforcement officials (at least one million) usually tolerated families with two, and sometimes three children. The policy also was not applied to minority households at all. Recently, an additional exception to the policy has allowed married couples, both of whom are single children, to have two children. The onus of policy implementation fell on women and led to horrible abuses such as forced abortions and sterilizations [133].[2] Preference for male offspring resulted in cases of female infanticide and under-reporting of births, as well as skewed sex ratios and large future

---

1 For example, authorities in Jilin Province expected to increase rice output through converting large areas of salina lands to paddy fields. The plan was to make the salt-encrusted land arable by flooding it with nearby river water. See [130].

2 For a critical perspective see [134], and Greenhalgh and Winkler [15]. Also, party officials, celebrities, and the rich have ignored the policy, and enforcement has had little effect in deterring this in recent years. See [135].

problems as millions of men lack marriage partners.

Notwithstanding these serious defects, the policy has sharply reduced the rate of growth in China's population as compared to relatively unconstrained population growth in other large developing countries such as India and Indonesia. Demographic experts estimate that the population would have reached 1.7 billion instead of the current 1.3 billion had the policy not been implemented [136].

Repeated calls for a loosening of the one-child policy have had no effect. In March 2008, Zhang Weiqing, Minister of the State Population and Family Planning Commission, ruled out any policy change for the next decade. He noted that China faced a new birth peak in the coming 10 years, when nearly 200 million would enter childbearing ages:

Given such a large population base, there would be major fluctuations in population growth if we abandoned the one-child rule now. It would cause serious problems and add extra pressure on social and economic development [137].

State investments in irrigation systems

One of the factors typically used to explain China's ability to achieve food self-sufficiency is the huge investments the state has made in irrigation infrastructure. In the 1960s and 1970s particularly, spending on water control played a very important role in rural development. Fan et al. note that government spending on irrigation was 30% of total expenditures in rural China in 2000 [138]. Whether in poor or rich areas, spending on irrigation systems has been the most important form of agricultural investment. They mention that the state invests more than ten times as much in irrigation as it does in agricultural research.

Approximately 51% of the cultivated area in China is irrigated; nearly two-thirds of the irrigated areas used surface water, while the rest is irrigated with groundwater [139]. Several studies of the impact of irrigation on crop yields as well as household incomes report positive findings. For example, Huang et al. point out the "strong and robust" effect of irrigation on agricultural performance [140].

The South-North Water Diversion Project

Another very large-scale project, which if continued would be one of the world's largest, is the plan of the central government to address water scarcity in northern and western regions by transferring water there from the South. Mao Zedong proposed the grand plan in 1952, and it has been in the discussion stage for decades.

The South-North Water Diversion Project (SNWDP) includes three water transfer routes—east, central, and west—which will link the Yangtze River of central China to the Huai, Yellow, and Hai Rivers of North China. The project plan includes "four latitude and three longitudinal water courses regulating and distributing water not only from south to north but also from east to west." [141] Construction began on the first (eastern) phase in late 2002 and is scheduled for completion in 2008. This section is the easiest to construct, as it can take advantage of existing rivers and lakes, including the Grand Canal and its parallel rivers. However, it has required construction of nearly two dozen new, upgraded and expanded pumping stations, many reservoirs, and extensive water treatment facilities for polluted water.[1] The cost for just the first, eastern section is estimated to be $6 billion (with the cost of the total project running to $72 billion in 2007 dollars).

The second phase is not expected to be completed so quickly, as the route is longer and more new construction will be required. The western route project is still in the design stage, and many observers believe it will not be built. The plan to divert Qinghai-Tibet plateau water resources away from the Mekong and other international rivers is extremely controversial.[2] The size of the projects is gargantuan. Objections come from provinces losing water to the North and the West, particularly Hunan and Hubei; from scientists who question whether at the time of greatest need for water (in winter months of the North), there will be sufficient water to transfer; from those fearing the disruptive displacement effects on people along the

---

1 Ibid., 21. For example, pollution in the Huai River poses a threat to diversion of water from the south to the north. See [142].

2 Personal communication to the authors from T.J. Cheng, October 8, 2007.

proposed routing; from environmentalists; and from China's neighbors to the southwest who object to loss of water resources from their rivers.[1]

Large-scale afforestation and reforestation projects

We discussed one of the largest afforestation programs above, in the context of the Yangtze flooding of 1998. This was one of seven different afforestation programs since the 1970s. The others include:

1. The "Three Norths" Shelterbelt program involves establishing plantations in north, northeast, and northwest China (from 1978 to 2050) with the objective of afforestation of 35 million ha;
2. Protective afforestation in the upper and middle reaches of the Yangtze (1989–2000) involved planting and restoration of 6.8 million ha;
3. Coastal shelterbelt (1991–2000) led to planting trees in 3.6 million ha;
4. Cropland protection and agro-forestry in the plains (1988–2000) covered nearly 1,000 counties in four provinces;
5. Afforestation of the Taihang Mountain (1990–2010) involved planting trees on 4 million ha; and
6. Combating desertification (1991–2000) had as its objective control of desertification in over 7.2 million ha [144].

In 1998, China Daily proudly announced "China now ranks first in the world in both the speed and scale of afforestation." [145] A 2007 report proclaimed that 20% of China would be forested by 2020.[2] Nevertheless, Harkness commented that "Increases in forest cover have coincided with decreases in the actual amount of wood available for harvesting", which has pushed Chinese logging firms abroad [148].

Several problems have been identified in the afforestation programs, particularly the development of monocultural plantations, which limit species diversification. A forestry management official said that this needed to be kept in perspective:

---

1 See Economy [143], p. 126.

2 China has planted 53.3 million ha of forests since 1949, more than any other country in the world, with forest coverage rising from 8.6% to 18.2%. See [146, 147].

We are now looking at species diversity. We are emphasizing hardwood species, and this is a positive sign. Yes, there are problems, but the scale is unparalleled. We are converting sloping farmlands into forests, and enlarging wetlands. There is massive afforestation, which is good for carbon sequestration.[1]

Yin et al. point out additional difficulties. They object to the top-down nature of campaigns, and insufficient attention paid to local interests and conditions. Often those who have lost access to forests and logging have been inadequately compensated. Finally, the lack of long-range planning and development of good practices may increase other problems, such as erosion and introduction of invasive species.[2] Notwithstanding the criticism, the afforestation and reforestation programs have brought about a significant reduction in erosion, which benefits agricultural productivity.

Forests occupy 280 million ha and about half of China's rural population depends on them to some extent for a living. In August 2007, the State Forestry Administration (SFA) announced plans to reform the management structure of forests—now owned exclusively and managed either by the state or village collectives (jiti). Similar to reforms in management of agricultural lands, the SFA proposal would extend management rights to individual farmers, contractors and in some cases overseas investors, for periods as long as 60–70 years [149].

Restoration of forests and grasslands

The final state program is also the most recent, launched just in 1999–2000. With an overall budget of more than $40 billion, the sloping lands conversion program is perhaps China's most ambitious environmental initiative; without a doubt it is one of the world's largest land conservation programs [150]. It was designed after the Yangtze flooding to deal directly with erosion, which is particularly serious on sloped lands. Many of these lands in the Yangtze and Yellow River basins were originally forested, but in

---

1 Personal interview with forestry manager, State Forestry Administration, Beijing, May 18, 2004.

2 See [144], pp. 28-30.

previous campaigns of the Maoist era were converted to farmlands. With slopes of 25° or greater, they were especially subject to erosion, and for this reason the original plan was to convert 5.3 million ha of croplands on steep slopes to forest and grass coverage.

The program began with trials in Sichuan, Gansu, and Shaanxi provinces in 1999, and was then formally inaugurated in 2000 as the Slope Land Conversion Program (SLCP, also known as "Grain to Green"; in Chinese Tuigeng huanlin. The goal of SLCP expanded to convert about 14.7 million ha of fragile cropland to forests (or grasslands) by the completion date of 2010. Under the SLCP plan, the state provided extensive benefits to participating farmers. They received 1.5 to 2.55 tons of grain per year (depending on location) for retiring 1 ha of cropland. Also, they received a one-time cash subsidy of RMB750 yuan per ha to purchase seedlings or seeds, and RMB300 yuan per year for miscellaneous expenses for the duration of the program [151].[1] By 2004, some 7.2 million ha of land had been converted, the result of a very rapid expansion of the program from 2001 to 2003.[2]

These incentives made the project quite popular with participating farmers, some of whom received more in food subsidies than they would have through their own productive work. The costs to the state, however, have been in the neighborhood of $1.4 billion per year, making this one of the most expensive major environmental programs in China. The program has been effective in increasing the value of marginal lands, but its sustainability is in question because of the high cost and continuing questions about its effects on rural household income.[3]

The most penetrating (and obvious) criticism of the Slope Land Conversion Program has been that it has reduced arable land and led to lowered grain productivity and increased grain prices. In late 2003 and 2004, grain prices rose sharply in response to falling grain production, and the

---

1 Also see [144], pp. 22-23. The importance of economic compensation for farmers' support of the SLCP is presented in [152].

2 Xu et al. [153], p. 117.

3 See [153].

Ministry of Land and Resources and several researchers hypothesized that the SLCP program was responsible for this price rise [154]. The ministry successfully argued for a slowing of the conversion program.

Researchers have found a co-variance between the SLCP reductions and a reduction in land area sown with grain. However, most findings indicate that SLCP has had a relatively small effect, particularly given that most of the converted land was sloped and of poor quality. Xu et al. attribute just about 1% of the price increase in cereals to SLCP, also noting the large impact it has had in reduction of the build-up of silt in irrigation networks and reservoirs and reduction in downstream flooding [155].[1] In other words, there does not appear to have been a trade-off between land conversion and agricultural productivity. Nevertheless, the policy is an expensive one and has created new dependencies. Said a policy analyst with the Chinese Academy of Sciences:

Investment in Tuigeng huanlin means a reduction of investment elsewhere. As to people's income, what happens after the policy ends? Now, about 50% of the people in affected areas are reliant on government subsidies.[2]

By 2007, the SLCP had returned 24 million ha to forest and grass cover, accounting for about 60% of China's new forest area and benefiting 124 million farmers. However, as arable land neared the 120 million ha threshold, official attention focused again on SLCP, and the government suspended a plan to convert 1.07 million ha into forest [158]. Agriculture ministry officials said the program curtailment was solely for the purpose of making adjustments in it, and the project seems likely to continue, but at a reduced level.[3] The State Council did fine-tune the program, by limiting the period during which subsidies would be provided, based on category of land, and by making special provisions for "ecological immigrants," especially in minority areas [161].

---

[1] See also [156]. For a study of the impact of converting cropland to grassland, see [157]. Also, personal interview with former staff member, Chinese Academy of Forestry, Beijing, May 21, 2007.

[2] Personal interview with policy analyst, CAS, Beijing, May 25, 2007.

[3] See [159, 160].

■ Conclusions: Overall Impacts on Current Food Security

During China's reform era (from 1978 to the present), arable land has declined, due to pressures of population growth, urbanization, and exceedingly rapid economic development. These pressures have increased erosion, deforestation, desertification, pollution to land, air, fresh water, and China's marine coastal environment. Nevertheless, through improvements in agricultural technology and practices, China has been able to feed its 1.3 billion inhabitants. (In 2007, China produced 500 million tons of staples [162],[1] more than sufficient to provide food nationwide.) Yet the regime pays close attention to the amount of arable land and particularly to grain sufficiency. At the 2007 meetings of the National People's Congress, Premier Wen Jiabao announced that China must maintain 120 million ha of arable land.[2]

Some Chinese scientists and policy elites are worried about the reduction of arable land; a number of foreign observers, such as Lester Brown, have made alarmist predictions, suggesting China will not be able to feed itself in the future. Our sense from a reading of the large literature on this topic and interviewing agricultural scientists, land resources experts, and policy-makers is that the amount of arable land is sufficient for the present, and with appropriate changes in policy,[3] grain security can be assured in the near-term. However, without significant changes, land resources will not sustain food production when population increases to 1.6 billion in 2030 and when demand for food increases among China's increasingly well-off population. Space does not permit consideration of climate change as well as plant and animal diseases here, but they may adversely affect food

---

1 This was the fourth consecutive year of increase in grain output, and it allowed China to meet 95% of domestic demand. A shortage in production was not expected until 2010. See [163]. However, rising global grain prices and shortages of corn and soybeans spurred grain officials to eliminate the export tax rebates on major grains. Also, the State Council enacted an export tax on grains both to insure adequacy of domestic supply and curb food price inflation. See [164-166].

2 An official of the Ministry of Land and Resources indicated that Wen's statement did not reflect policy of the State Council, which did not believe that the cited amount of land needed to be retained in the arable land category (personal interview, Beijing, May 27, 2007). A land resources researcher at a university land management institute opined that Wen's statement was "a slogan," designed to outline a conservative approach (personal interview, Beijing, May 23, 2007).

3 See [167]. See also [168, 169].

production too.

We have discussed several strategies adopted by the regime to counter environmental stressors and their impact on food security. The recent focus of attention in China has been on increasing the efficiency in use and productivity of available arable land. This entails the improvement of cultural practices of farmers, use of improved seeds, more efficient utilization of crop enhancements such as fertilizers, and the like.[1] Indeed, in mid-2007, a coordination group of four ministries—Science and Technology, Agriculture, Finance, and the State Administration of Grain—signed responsibility contracts with 12 major grain producing provinces pledging to make greater efforts to increase crop yields through science and technology [172]. Another area of importance, which space limitations do not permit us to cover, is biotechnological responses of the regime, primarily through the development of genetically-modified foods, which are targeted directly at increasing agricultural productivity.

Based on our research, to the present and into the near-term, China has been successful in feeding its large and growing population, notwithstanding huge environmental stressors.

References

[1] Ross, Lester (1998), *Environmental policy in China*, Bloomington, IN: Indiana University Press.

[2] Smil, Vaclav (1993), *China's environmental crisis: An inquiry into the limits of national development*, Armonk, NY: Sharpe.

[3] Brown, Lester (1995), *Who will feed China? Wake-up call from a small planet, Washington*, DC: Worldwatch Institute.

[4] World Resources Institute (1999), *World Resources 1998–1999*, New York: Oxford University Press.

[5] Smil, Vaclav (1999), "Research note: China's arable land", *China Quarterly*, 158, June, 414-429.

[6] Pannell, Clifton W. and Runsheng Yin (2004), "Diminishing cropland and agricultural outlook", in Hsieh Chiao-min and Max Lu (eds.), *Changing China: A Geographic Appraisal*, Boulder, CO: Westview.

[7] China Development Brief, Statistics: Seeking truth from (tonnes of) facts. Retrieved February 15, 2006, from: http://www.chinadevelopmentbrief.com.

[8] Wu Chuanchun (1984), "Land utilization", in Geping Qu and Woyen Lee Dublin

[1] See, for example, [170, 171].

(eds.), *Managing the environment in China*, Tycooly International, 68, See [167]. See also [168, 169], 69, See, for example, [170, 171], Environmental Stressors and Food Security in China, 75.

[9] Heilig, Gerhard K. (1997), "Anthropogenic factors in land-use change in China", *Population and Development Review*, 231, 142.

[10] National Bureau of Statistics (2007), *China statistical yearbook 2007*, Beijing: China Statistics, 464.

[11] Li Fangchao (2007), "Arable Land Bank continues decline", *China Daily*, 3, April 13.

[12] Zhao Huanxin (2006), "Bottom line set for grain production", *China Daily*, 1, August 4.

[13] Xie Chuanjiao (2007), "1.7 m Hectares of arable land 'by 2020'", *China Daily*, 2, June 22.

[14] Ho Samual P.S. and George C.S. Lin (2004), "Non-agricultural land use in post-reform China", *China Quarterly*, 179, September, 776.

[15] Greenhalgh, Suzan and Edwin A. Winckler (2005), *Governing China's population: From Leninist to neoliberal biopolitics*, Stanford, CA: Stanford University Press, 74.

[16] Shapiro, Judith (2001), *Mao's war against nature: Politics and the environment in revolutionary China*, Cambridge, UK: Cambridge University Press, 37.

[17] Hsieh, Chiao-min (2004), "Changes in the Chinese population: Demography, distribution, and policy", in Chiao-min Hsieh and Max Lu (eds.), *Changing China: A geographic appraisal*, Boulder, CO: Westview, 204.

[18] Wang L. (1995), "The degree, characteristics, and trends of China's urbanization", *People's Daily*, October 31, 4.

[19] Di Liping (2004), "Land-use patterns and land-use change", in Chiao-min Hsieh and Max Lu (eds.), *Changing China: A geographic appraisal*, Boulder, CO: Westview, 19.

[20] Liu Guifen and Diao Chengtai (2006), "Current situation of cultivated land resources and food security in Jiangjin City", in Liu Yancui (ed.), *Study of the strategy of land resources and regional coordinated development in China*, in Chinese, Beijing: Meteorology.

[21] Huang Jikun, Zhu Lifen, Deng Xiangzheng and Scott Rozelle (2005), "Cultivated land changes in China: The impacts of urbanization and industrialization", *Society of Photo-Optical Instrumentation Engineers* 5884, 58840I, 1-15.

[22] Gar-On Yeh Anthony and Li Xia (1997), "An integrated remote sensing and GIS approach in the monitoring and evaluation of rapid urban growth for sustainable development in the Pearl River Delta, China", *International Planning Studies*, 22, 193-210.

[23] Cartier, Carolyn (2001), "'Zone Fever', the arable land debate, and real estate speculation: China's evolving land use regime and its geographical contradictions", *Journal of Contemporary China*, 1028, August, 454-456.

[24] Yang, Dali L. (1997), *Beyond Beijing: Liberalization and the regions in China*, London: Routledge, 54-55.

[25] Oi, Jean (1999), *Rural China takes off: Institutional foundations of economic reform*, Berkeley: University of California Press, 37.

[26] Li Fangchao (2007), "Illegal land use poses major threat", *China Daily*, September 18, 1.

[27] Wu Jiao (2007), "Land loss threatens food safety", *China Daily*, December 26, 1.

[28] Xin, Zhiming, Fu Jing, Zhu Ping (2008), "Security of food calls for serious thought", *China Daily*, January 16, 7.

[29] Guan, Xiaofeng (2006), "Experts discuss answers to land degradation", China Daily, August 28, 2.

[30] Li Fangchao (2006), "Ecological degradation continuing", *China Daily*, June 5, 1.
[31] Huang Yizong, Li Zhixian, Li Xiangdong, Yang Wenmiao, Liang Zhaoyong, Li Huafeng, Liu Dinglan and Lu Bisheng (2007), "Effects of acid deposition and atmospheric pollution on forest ecosystem biomass in Southern China", *Ecology and Environment*, in Chinese, 161, 60-65.
[32] Xinhua (2007), "Erosion threatening grain security", *China Daily*, August 28, 2.
[33] Xinhua (2007), "Xinjiang losing land to soil erosion", *China Daily*, July 3, 4.
[34] Zheng Caixiong (2007), "Soil erosion targeted in Guangdong", *China Daily*, November 20, 4.
[35] Rozelle, Scott, Huang Jikun and Vince Benziger (2003), *Forest exploitation and protection in reform China*, in Hyde, Belcher, and Xu, 20.
[36] Liang Chao (2005), "Probe launched into erosion threat", *China Daily*, July 5, 2.
[37] Greenpeace China (2004), *Investigative report on APP's forest destruction in Yunnan*, Hong Kong: November.
[38] China Development Brief (2006), Greenpeace, Zhejiang Hotels, S*tand Firm against Paper Giant*, March 31, 2005, Retrieved February 14, from: http://www.China developmentbrief.com/node/77/print.
[39] Liang Chao and Cui Ning (2005), "Authorities crack down on illegal logging", *China Daily*, March 31, 2.
[40] Cao Desheng (2004), "Nation fighting ever-engulfing deserts", *China Daily*, June 18, 2.
[41] Li Xiang-yun, Yang Jun and Wang Li-xin (2004), "Quantitative analysis on the driving role of human activity on land desertification in an arid area: The case of the Tarim River Basin", in Chinese, *Resources Science*, 265, September, 30-37.
[42] Ma Lie (2007), "Water rule will protect great wall, Gansu Oasis", *China Daily*, August 7, 5.
[43] Wang Shanshan (2007), "Creeping desert threatens Mogao Grottoes", *China Daily*, November 6, 3.
[44] Han Nianyong, Jiang Gaoming and Li Wenjun (2002), *Management of the degraded ecosystems in Xilingol biosphere reserve, Chinese and English*, Beijing: Tsinghua University Press, 120-134.
[45] Biodiversity Working Group of China Council for International Cooperation on Environment and Development (2001), "Restoring China's degraded environment: The role of natural vegetation", Beijing, 2-7.
[46] Xinhua (2007), "10-Year plan needed to save wetlands from desert", *China Daily*, September 18, 4.
[47] Gluckman, R. (2004), "The desert storm", *Asiaweek*, October 13, 2000, 3-6.
[48] Ma Lie, (2003), "Desertification threatens northwest areas", *China Daily*, September 6, 2003.
[49] Jiang Weiyu and Fanglin Chan (2004), "Controlling desertification in North China", *Journal of Arid Land Resources and Environment*, in Chinese, 265, September, 30-37.
[50] Gao Qianzhao, Qu Jianjun, Wang Run, Li Yuan, Zu Ruiping and Zhang Kecun (2007), "Impact of ecological water transport to green corridor on desertification reversion at lower reaches of Tarim River", *Journal of Desert Research*, in Chinese, 271, January, 52-58.
[51] Zhao Huanxin (2007), "Inner Mongolia's green efforts aid Beijing", *China Daily*, July 26, 3.
[52] Wu Yong (2007), "Playing with nature or helping it is the question", *China Daily*, August 22, 12.

[53] Sun Xiaohua, "Sandstorms a fact of nature", *China Daily*, March 15, 2007, 6.
[54] Liao Guolan and Wu Chao (2005), *Heavy metal pollution and control in mining environment*, in Chinese, Changsha, Hunan: Central South University Press.
[55] Li Fangchan (2008), "Official: More than 10% of arable land polluted", *China Daily*, April 23, 2007, 1.
[56] Xinhua, "Bitter harvest", *China Daily*, May 19, 3.
[57] Sun Xiaohua (2008), "SEPA sets sights on polluted soil", *China Daily*, January 9, 3.
[58] Sun Xiaohua (2007), "Soil survey to monitor pollution", *China Daily*, May 9, 1.
[59] Liu Li (2006), "One third of nation hit by acid rain", *China Daily*, August 28, 2.
[60] Chen Hong (2008), "Guangzhou swamped by acid rain", *China Daily*, March 28, 4.
[61] Doug Struck (2008), *Washington post national weekly edition*, February 25-March 2, 10.
[62] Wu Chong (2007), "Researchers: Polluted air causes less rainfall", *China Daily*, March 9, 3.
[63] Xie Chuanjiao (2007), "Pollution makes cancer the top killer", *China Daily*, May 21, 1.
[64] Kahn, Joseph and Jim Yardley (2007), "As China roars, pollution reaches deadly extremes", *New York Times*, August 26, A13.
[65] Sun Xiaohua (2007), "SEPA publishes Q1 report", *China Daily*, May 22, 3.
[66] Wu Jiao (2007), "Pollution picture to brighten", *China Daily*, June 6, 1.
[67] Wang Zhuoqiong (2007), "Global giants on pollution blacklist", *China Daily*, December 14, 1.
[68] Brown, Lester R. (1998), "China's water shortage could shake world food security", *World Watch*, July 1.
[69] China Development Brief (2001), *Thirsty cities and factories push farmers off the parched earth*, June 1.
[70] Xu Jianxin, Zhang Zezhong and Liu Fa (2005), "The analysis of the water resource's assurance of grain production security", *Water Conservancy Science and Technology and Economy*, in Chinese, 1110, October, 611-614.
[71] Lohmar, Bryan and Wang Jinxia (2003), "Will water scarcity affect agricultural production in China", *In China's food and agriculture: Issues for the 21st century*, Washington, DC: Economic Research Service, USDA, 41-43.
[72] Turner, Jennifer and Otsuka Kenji (2006), *Reaching across the water*, Washington, DC: China Environment Forum, Woodrow Wilson International Center for Scholars.
[73] Lohmar, Bryan, Wang Jinxia, Scott Rozelle, Huang Jikun and David Dawe (2003), "China's agricultural water policy reforms", Economic Research Service, Agriculture Information Bulletin, No. 782, 1.
[74] Ma Lie (2007), "Shaanxi reels from drought", *China Daily*, May 11, 50.
[75] Ma Jun (2004), *China's water crisis*, Norwalk, CT: Eastbridge, vii.
[76] Yardley, Jim (2006), "China's path to modernity, mirrored in a troubled river", *New York Times*, November 19, A1, 14-15.
[77] Liao Yongsong and Huang Jikun (2004), "Impact of crop structure change on irrigation water demand in the basins of Yellow River, Huahe River and Haihe River", *Journal of China Institute of Water Resources and Hydropower Research*, in Chinese, 23, September, 184-188.
[78] Wang Jinxia, Xu Zhigang, Huang Jikun and Scott Rozelle (2005), "Incentives in water management reform: Assessing the effect on water use, production, and poverty in the Yellow River Basin", *Environment and Development Economics*, 10, 769-799.
[79] Fu Jing (2007), "High prices to 'persist' next year", *China Daily*, September 18, 2.
[80] Xie, Chuanjiao (2007), "Pollution makes cancer the top killer", *China Daily*, May

21, 1.
[81] Hu Yinan (2007), "Rural environmental protection plan released", *China Daily*, November 22, 5.
[82] Barboza, David (2007), "In China, farming fish in toxic waters", *New York Times*, December 15.
[83] Hu Yinan and WuJiao (2008),"Fishing in 'troubled waters' leads to big losses", *China Daily*, January 3, 1.
[84] Xinhua (2007), "Volume of pollutants exceeds 13 m tons", *China Daily*, May 11, 4.
[85] Li Fangchao (2007), "Provincial officials promise to close loopholes", *China Daily*, May 11, 4.
[86] Li Fangchao (2007), "Rehabilitation effort for country's dirtiest waterway to last a decade", *China Daily*, May 11, 4.
[87] Sun Xiaohua (2007), "SEPA publishes Q1 report", *China Daily*, May 22, 3.
[88] Sun Xiaohua (2008), "3 Provinces fail on river targets", *China Daily*, April 22, 4.
[89] Sun Xiaohua (2007), "Polluters face stiff penalties", *China Daily*, August 27, 1.
[90] Wang Zhuoqiong (2007), "River is 10% sewage: Official", *China Daily*, May 11, 4.
[91] Ma Lie (2007), "Shaanxi tackles river pollution", *China Daily*, May 15, 5.
[92] Sun Xiaohua (2007), "Pollution takes heavy toll on Yangtze", *China Daily*, April 16, 1.
[93] Liu Xiao (2007), "Swift action needed to save Yangtze, forum says", *China Daily*, September 18, 3.
[94] Xinhua News Service (2007), "Sepa to get tough on gov't violations", *China Daily*, March 2, 3.
[95] Sun Xiaohua (2006), "Yangtze and Pearl River Estuaries now 'dead zones'", *China Daily*, October 20, 2.
[96] Zhang Kun (2007), "Experts identify algae afflicting Taihu Lake", *China Daily*, June 13, 4.
[97] Li Fangchao (2007), "Official warns of major algae outbreak", *China Daily*, July 14-15, 3.
[98] He Na (2007), "Blue algae hits city's water supply", *China Daily*, July 18, 4.
[99] Zheng Lifei and Zhao Huanxin (2007), "Water better, but not drinkable", *China Daily*, June 2-3, l.
[100] Kahn, Joseph (2007), "In China, a lake's champion imperils himself", *New York Times*, October 14.
[101] Wang Zhuoqiong (2007), "Turning back the tide", *China Daily*, December 31, 8.
[102] Jiang Zhuqing, "Groundwater quality 'deteriorating'", *China Daily*, October 10, 2.
[103] Sun Xiaohua (2007), "SEPA publishes Q1 report", *China Daily*, May 22, 3.
[104] Chen Hong (2007), "Guangdong water woes 'to worsen'", *China Daily*, November 28, 5.
[105] Liang Qiwen (2007), "Algae blooms watched", *China Daily*, December 28, 4.
[106] Wu Joa and Li Fangchao (2007), "Rural water woes to be addressed", *China Daily*, August 23, 1.
[107] Xinhua (2007), "Big polluters face strict monitoring", *China Daily*, May 11, 4.
[108] Wu Jiao (2007), "Pollution picture to brighten", *China Daily*, June 6, 1.
[109] Xinhua (2007), "Spending failing to solve pollution problems", *China Daily*, September 25, 4.
[110] Xin Dingding (2007), "278 Cities suffer untreated sewage", *China Daily*, August 31, 3.
[111] Sun Xiaohua (2007), "Drinking water gets top priority in new plan", *China Daily*, November 27, 3.

[112] Zhu Wutai (2007), "SEPA chief outlines vision for clean drinking water", *China Daily*, November 22, 5.
[113] Sun Xiaohua (2008), "1st National pollution census starts", *China Daily*, January 5-6, 1.
[114] Sun Xiaohua (2007), "10% of GDP now comes from sea, says report", *China Daily*, April 10, 4.
[115] Mackinnon, John, Sha Mang, Catherine Cheung, Geoff Carey, Zhu Xiang and David Melville, A biodiversity review of China, Hong Kong: World Wide Fund for Nature (WWF) International, 495.
[116] Sun Xiaohua (2007), "Offshore water quality deteriorates", *China Daily*, August 4-5, 2.
[117] Yeung, Jonathan (2007), "Red tide returns to Shenzhen coastal area", *China Daily*, June 7, 4.
[118] Qiu Quanlin (2007), "Pearl River waste harming the sea", *China Daily*, July 25, 5.
[119] Xinhua (2008), "Official vows to cut offshore pollution", *China Daily*, February 26, 4.
[120] Zhao Huanxin (2007), "No yielding on arable land: Minister", *China Daily*, July 13, 1.
[121] Li Angchao (2007), "Arable Land Bank continues decline", *China Daily*, April 13, 3.
[122] Fu Jing (2007), "Land plan to preserve countryside", *China Daily*, September 25, 1, 2.
[123] Li Fangchao (2007), "Minimum land bank to stay in effect", *China Daily*, June 26, 3.
[124] Xin Dingding (2008), "Authentic land data promised", *China Daily*, February 28, 3.
[125] Li Fangchao (2007), "Protection of arable Land Banks a joint responsibility: Minister", *China Daily*, July 13, 4.
[126] Li Fangchao (2007), "Illegal land use poses major threat", *China Daily*, September 18, 1.
[127] Zhao Huanxin (2007), "Farmers' protests decline sharply", *China Daily*, January 31, 1.
[128] Wu Jiao (2007), "Crackdown on illegal land use", *China Daily*, December 11, 3.
[129] Wu Jiao (2008), "Illegal land use in cross hairs of new nationwide scheme", *China Daily*, February 2-3, 3.
[130] Xinhua (2007), "Salt lands may offer solution to land shortage problem", *China Daily*, December 27, 2007, 3.
[131] Xie Chuanjiao (2007), "1.7 m Hectares of additional arable land 'by 2020'", *China Daily*, June 22, 2007, 2.
[132] Wu Jiao (2008), "Arable land reserves continue to decline", *China Daily*, April 17, 2008, 3.
[133] Saich, Tony (2004), *Governance and politics in China*, New York: Palgrave, 246-268.
[134] Greenhalgh, Susan (2005), "Missile science, population science: The origins of China's one-child policy", *China Quarterly*, 182, June, 253-276.
[135] Xinhua (2008), "Hubei Luminaries fined for flouting family rules", *China Daily*, January 2, 5.
[136] Xie Chuanjiao (2007),"Baby boom set to start next year", *China Daily*, December 12, 3.
[137] Xing Zhigang (2008), "Population policy will stay for now", *China Daily*, March 10, 1.
[138] Fan, S., L. Zhang and X. Zhang (2004), "Reforms, investment, and poverty in rural China", *Economic Development and Cultural Change*, 522, 417.
[139] National Statistical Bureau of China (2007), *Statistics yearbook of China*, Beijing: China Statistics.

[140] Huang Qiuqiong, Scott. Rozelle, B. Lohman, J. Huang and J. Wang (2006), "Irrigation, agricultural performance and poverty reduction in China", *Food Policy* 31, 30-52.

[141] State Council (2004), "Construction Committee of the South-North Water Diversion Project", *China South-to-North Water Diversion Project*, Beijing, 15.

[142] Sun, Xiaohua (2007), "Polluters face stiff penalties", *China Daily*, August 27, 1.

[143] Economy, Elizabeth (2004), *The river runs black: The environmental challenge to China's future*, Ithaca, NY: Cornell University Press.

[144] Yin, Runsheng, Jintao Xu, Zhou Li and Can Liu (2005), China's ecological rehabilitation: The unprecedented efforts and dramatic impacts of reforestation and slope protection in western China, Woodrow Wilson Center, China Environment Series, Issue 7, 19.

[145] *China Daily* (1998), Afforestation tops priority list among former loggers, June 10, 3.

[146] Sun Xiaohua (2007), "More nature reserves to protect forests", *China Daily*, December 5, 4.

[147. Liang Chao (2005), "China 2020: A greener and leaner landscape", *China Daily*, August 1, 2.

[148] Harkness, James (1998), "Recent trends in forestry and conservation of biodiversity in China", *China Quarterly*, 15651, December, 924.

[149] Fu Jing (2007), "Forest reform on horizon", *China Daily*, August 16, 3.

[150] Xu Zhigang, M.T. Bennett, Ran Tao and Jintao Xu (2004), "China's sloping land conversion programme four years on: Current situation and pending issues", *Internatinonal Forestry Review*, 63-4, 317.

[151] Xu, J. T. and Y. Y. Cao (2001), "Converting steep cropland to forest and grassland: Efficiency and prospects of sustainability", *International Economic Review*, in Chinese, 2, 56-60.

[152] Zhi Ling, Li Nuyun, Wang Juan and Fanbin Kong (2004), "A discussion on the economic compensation system for conversion of cropland to forestland in western China", *Scientia Silvae Sinicae*, in Chinese, 402, March, 1-8.

[153] Xu Jintao, Ran Tao and Xu Zhigang (2004), "Sloping land conversion program: Cost-effectiveness, structural effect and economic sustainability", *China Economic Quarterly, in Chinese*, 41, October, 160.

[154] Ministry of Land and Resources (2004), "2003 China national report on land and resources", Beijing.

[155] Xu Zhigang, Xu Jintao, Deng Xiangzheng, Huang Jikun, Emi Uchida and Scott Roelle (2006), "Grain for green versus grain: Conflict between food security and conservation set-aside in China", *World Development*, 341, 130-148.

[156] Deng Xiangzheng, Huang Jikun, Scott Rozelle and Emi Uchida (2006), "Cultivated land conversion and potential agricultural productivity in China", *Land Use Policy*, 23, 372-384.

[157] Su Yongzhong and Su Peixi (2006), "Ecological effects of converting crops to grass in the marginal lands of Linze Oasis in the middle of Heihe River Basin", in Liu (ed.), 445-450.

[158] Wu Yong (2007), "Reforestation plan put on hold", *China Daily*, September 12, 2.

[159] Sun Xiaohua (2007), "Tree plan being retooled", *China Daily*, September 20, 3.

[160] Sun Xiaohua (2007), "Returning farmland to forests to protect income, farmers told", *China Daily*, October 11, 2.

[161] State Council (2007), Notification on the completion of the Tuigeng Huanlin policy, August 9.

[162] Xinhua (2007), "Grain yield exceeds 500 m ton", *China Daily*, December 24, 3.
[163] Wang Ying (2007), "Country is able to meet grain needs", *China Daily*, November 22, 3.
[164] Diao Ying (2007), "Grain export tax rebate dumped", *China Daily*, December 18, 13.
[165] Diao Ying (2008), "Gov't sets export tariff on grains", *China Daily*, January 2, 14.
[166] Wu Jiao (2008), "Tight supply may hit grain stability", *China Daily*, January 4, 4.
[167] Huang Jikun (2004), "Is China's grain security facing great challenge?", *Science & Technology Review*, in Chinese, 17.
[168] Wu Jiao (2007), "Ministry forecasts bumper harvest", *China Daily*, July 12, 3.
[169] Fu Jing (2007), "Agriculture Chief has thought for food and plenty on his plate", *China Daily*, October 15, supplement 1.
[170] Zheng Chao, Liao Zongwen, Liu Kexing and Mao Xiaoyun (2004), "Effects of fertilizer on agriculture and environment", *Ecology and Environment*, in Chinese, 131, 134-138.
[171] Tan Shukui and Peng Buzhuo (2003), "Examination of cultivated land utilization to guarantee our grain security", *Economic Geography*, in Chinese, 233, May, 371-374.
[172] Wang Ying (2007), "Hi-tech measures to increase grain yield", *China Daily*, July 17, 3.

China R&D: A High-Tech Field of Dreams[1]

Kathleen A. Walsh[2]

■ Introduction

The odds are that the next new commercial Research and Development (R&D) centre announced by Intel, Microsoft, Motorola, Ericsson, Nokia or other leading multinational corporations (MNCs) are located in Mainland China. In fact, establishing an R&D programme in the Middle Kingdom is considered an essential part of doing business in today's global economy and, in particular, for success in the strategically important China market. For this reason, China ranks first—among both developed and developing economies—in international surveys asking MNCs where their future R&D centres are likely to be located (EIU, 2004; UNCTAD, 2005b). Instead, the

---

1 The views expressed herein are the author's alone and should not be taken to represent official views of the US Government, Department of Defense, or Naval War College.

2 Kathleen A. Walsh, Department of National Security Decision Making, US Naval War College.

more difficult decision many chief executive officers (CEOs) face today is exactly where on the Mainland to locate their R&D centre(s) and what form of R&D to pursue, not whether or not to conduct R&D in China.[1]

Although the number of multinational R&D centres in China and several other developing economies has multiplied rapidly over the past decade, the trend toward outsourcing and offshoring R&D to these new destinations has only recently captured the attention of the mainstream media, industry analysts and policy makers. Weekly newspaper headlines and magazine reports now highlight this growing trend and often comment on whether it poses long-term economic, technology, or security concerns for the home countries of these companies.

As reflected in the growing number of press stories, there is little doubt that offshore commercial R&D is expanding into new frontiers; the key question that remains unanswered, however, is to what effect? In other words, are there winners and losers (that is, a zero-sum game), or can there be mutual advantage to offshore R&D, particularly in still-developing economies such as China? What impact does this new form of R&D investment have on domestic economic and technological development as opposed to merely enhancing a MNC's bottom line? And, over the long run, will the trend toward globalized R&D significantly change the way engineers innovate in Silicon Valley or in Beijing's Zhongguancun equivalent? As a growing recipient of foreign R&D investments and one of the few countries with the potential to become a future peer competitor to the United States, this debate is particularly important as it applies to China.

This study seeks to look beyond the numbers to analyse first, what is driving foreign R&D investment to China, how this rapid increase is influencing the Mainland's own long-term technology development strategy, and the impact this trend could have on future Asia-Pacific relations.

---

1 This is not to say that the question should not be asked (whether or not it is wise to invest in R&D in China), but that the answer is often taken as a given among industry leaders.

■ China's Field of Dreams

By 2005, there were reportedly as many as 750 foreign-invested R&D centres on the Chinese Mainland (*China Daily*, 2005; *Xinhua News Agency*, 2006a). This number is significant given the apparent fast rate of growth evidenced in this type of foreign investment. U.S. R&D investment, for instance, shot up from a mere $7 million in 1994 to over $500 million by 2000, placing China 11th among foreign destinations for U.S. R&D investments (NSB, 2004). In fact, the actual amount is likely to be far higher today (Walsh, 2005). The pace at which foreign R&D centres have spread across China is also startling, representing a six-fold increase, if official figures are accurate, in just the past three years (Walsh, 2003a).

The majority of these R&D programmes are today wholly foreign-owned enterprises and are frequently located in China's major cities along the eastern coast: Beijing, Shanghai, Guangzhou, Shenzhen and their environs (Walsh, 2003b). The reasons behind this geographical bias are obvious. China's vast central and western regions remain largely poor and underdeveloped, while its east coast provinces have enjoyed unprecedented levels of foreign investment, much of which has been funnelled into urban development. In conjunction with large amounts of state and municipal funding, foreign capital has underwritten—and in some cases foreign companies have actually conducted—the building of modern, high-tech infrastructure in the form of western-style office buildings and residential housing, expanded energy and power supplies, improved roads and transportation systems, as well as advanced fibre-optic communications in China's major metropolitan hubs. In short, China's strategy applies the "Field of Dreams" adage: "if you build it, they will come".

As the rising number of foreign R&D programmes in China attests, this strategy appears to be working reasonably well (Hu, 2005). This is true despite the fact that one could reasonably argue that the nature of China's labour force should deter foreign R&D investment due to persistent security concerns in the form of political-military relations and intellectual property rights challenges.

Yet, important "pull" factors continue to attract foreign R&D investment to China (for example, a substantially lower-cost, sizeable and increasingly skilled labour force). But it is China's investment in infrastructure at the national, provincial, municipal and local levels which sets the Mainland apart from other prospective R&D locales emerging across the developing world.

China is taking a similar approach in its efforts to fashion regional high-tech innovation centres to that found in the United States' Silicon Valley. Chinese municipalities, provinces and local officials today compete with one another to build the most modern, innovatively attractive, technology-themed development parks in order to attract high-profile, high-tech foreign investors. As a result, new technology parks in China come complete with not only modern office buildings, relatively reliable electricity, potable water, security, sewers and advanced communications, as well as with universities, research institutes, technology incubation centres (to assist local entrepreneurs), hospitals, customs offices, and whatever else is likely to spur increased investment, trade, technology transfer and innovation. China's premier high-tech park, Beijing's Zhongguancun Science Park, for instance, hosts 40 universities, 130 research institutes, over 40 foreign R&D centres, and many domestic R&D firms as well. New and more specialized parks are springing up elsewhere across China's mainly eastern regions (UNCTAD, 2005a). The extent of this competition among local Chinese officials, however, has proved counter-productive in some respects, causing Beijing to promote development of more specialized high-tech zones in different areas of the country based on regional resource and competitive advantages in order to ensure continued high levels of foreign investment across China's high-tech eastern corridor. Multinational corporations seeking access to overseas markets through offshore R&D programmes are drawn to these ready-made high-tech and specialized industry zones, as well as by China's loose regulatory environment, tax incentives and other investment-related enticements. It is not wholly surprising, therefore, that as globalization has promoted enhanced levels of international trade, investment, travel and communication that the Chinese market has attracted many MNC-sponsored R&D centres.

More important than the overall number of R&D centres, however, is the rate of growth in this form of investment and technology transfer. The expansive growth in foreign R&D investments over a relatively short period of time to a marketplace not obviously conducive to high-tech R&D (considering China's continuing IPR problems, among other liabilities) suggests there is something unique going on.

Why are so many MNCs investing in R&D in China so suddenly? The reasons for doing so have grown over time and as the number of R&D programmes has expanded (Walsh, 2003b; UNCTAD, 2005a). A first-order rationale and "push" factor is to establish an innovative "listening post" in what is clearly an important and potentially sizeable consumer market. Another key reason for establishing an R&D presence in China is to appease PRC officials who demand it; doing so is viewed by many foreign investors as essential to furthering other, long-term interests in the China market. Alas, where technology leaders go, others follow. Thus, as industry heavy weights Intel, Microsoft, Motorola, General Motors (GM) and others began to invest in R&D assets in China, competitors, partners and suppliers took note, with many establishing their own R&D programmes on the Mainland. These three basic rationales help explain the initial emergence of high-tech investment and R&D in the China market. But over time, the purpose has become more complex. A fourth and more recent justification for R&D investment in a developing economy such as China's is in order to locate R&D functions alongside already offshored manufacturing and production. Because so much lower-end manufacturing moved to China a decade or more ago, MNCs had found by the mid-to late-1990s that the ideas, designs and technologies they had established in China no longer met the needs of the local or regional markets. New ideas, re-designs, and innovations would be needed to maintain what market share they had gained and to keep Chinese competitors at bay. Globalization made this possible; Chinese policy makers made it easy, particularly once the PRC joined the World Trade Organization (WTO) in 2001 and removed additional market barriers. Another oft-cited rationale affecting a CEO's decision to invest in R&D in China (or anywhere else for that matter) is the ready supply of skilled engineers. In China, in contrast with many other countries, this supply is abundant and is likely only to grow and mature over time. Given these compelling and compounded rationales (one or more of which can influence MNC R&D investment decisions), it is no wonder the number of foreign R&D centres in China has exploded.

Unfortunately, this is often where the discussion ends, providing little insight into how these R&D inputs are in fact impacting China's own developmental efforts—if they are at all. Many pundits and commentators who note the rise in offshore investment and R&D in China tend to assume it is having a profound and positive impact on China's technology development capabilities. Many also suggest a corollary argument that it necessarily weakens or threatens America's own technological strength and leadership (Pillsbury, 2005; NAS, 2006). Industry representatives typically take the opposite view or else consider the offshoring of R&D a necessary evil in an age of globalization in which the Chinese market plays an increasingly vital role. It should be noted as well that some in industry find the trend troubling even though they feel compelled to participate (BCG &KW, 2004). A third group sees little cause for concern and tends to dismiss the potential this form of foreign technology transfer holds for China's indigenous technology development capacity based on China's long and largely unspectacular S&T development efforts over the past half-century, which include numerous failed attempts at foreign technology assimilation (China's missile, nuclear and space breakthroughs are considered, by these adherents, exceptions to the general rule). Finally, a large constituency remains confident in the USA's capacity to stay ahead of any potential technological up-and-comers regardless of whether China benefits from rising U.S. and other foreign R&D investments (Gilboy, 2004).

For their part, the Chinese populace is also divided, with many advocating the promise that foreign investment affords while others feel overly exploited by foreign interests (a theme persistent throughout Chinese history). PRC officials and analysts also appear to disagree on whether MNC investments in R&D can or will contribute value to China's own science and technology capabilities. However, an issue on which they do agree is that the PRC continues to need foreign technology and R&D investment but must make better use of these inputs or risk falling prey to foreign exploitation with little innovative indigenous capacity to show for it (another underlying theme running through China's past efforts at S&T modernization). In fact, this latter sentiment underlies China's latest long-term S&T development plans, which place great emphasis on the need to exploit foreign technology investments better.

This discord and mutual uncertainty with regard to the significance of R&D in China arises in large part due to a continuing lack of good, hard data. PRC officials have only in recent years published figures on the level of foreign R&D investment, and the methods used to collect and analyse the data remain unclear.[1] The data does, however, appear to support external estimates and analyses that find a substantial increase over the past decade in foreign R&D investment on the Mainland (Xue & Wang, 2001; Walsh, 2003b; Moris, 2004). U.S. government data, though slow to reflect the trend and still not well equipped to collect accurate, complete, or timely information on overseas R&D investments, also show a sharp increase in U.S. corporate investment in R&D in China over the past decade (Weber, 2005). This is significant given the fact that U.S. companies are the largest foreign investors in China's information technology (IT), computer and electronics sectors, which dominate (along with biotechnology) overseas R&D investment on the Mainland. Several international studies also depict the rising investment in China R&D by foreign multinationals, including studies by the Organization for Economic Cooperation and Development (OECD) and the United Nations Conference on Trade and Development (UNCTAD) (OECD, 2005; UNCTAD, 2005a).

Yet again, however, these studies provide few insights into how the growing amounts of foreign R&D investment are affecting China's

---

1 The methodology employed by China's Ministry of Commerce is uncertain. However, the latest World Investment Report 2005 states that China's statistics on foreign R&D investment are based on registered R&D programmes, mandated for all new R&D investments as of 2003. The survey, therefore, might exclude R&D programmes established prior to the rule and depend on whether or not companies have complied with the mandate as well as the degree to which it has been effectively enforced (see UNCTAD, 2005a, p. 141).

indigenous science, research and development efforts. This is true both at the macro (national) level as well as on a micro (firm) level. While numerous studies exist on the spillover effects that foreign direct investment (FDI) has on host nations, comparatively few studies examine these effects in developing or transitioning economies and even fewer focus on foreign-invested R&D in these countries, specifically China (Fan, 2003; Myer, 2004). Some notable exceptions exist (Sun, 2002; Li & Yue, 2005; von Zedtwitz, 2005; Assimakopoulos & Yan, 2006; Yuan, 2006), but they are too few to cover the scope of this issue nor the pace at which change is happening. In particular, for the more detailed R&D and critical, firm-level of analysis that is needed, analysts today must continue to look to individual researchers whose work necessarily relies on accumulated experience in the Chinese market and relationships with key actors in China's scientific, academic, government and business communities. Theory is only beginning to catch up and is mainly concentrated on management-related issues. As a result, research and analysis on the impact foreign R&D investment is having on China's technological aspirations often provide little more than a snapshot of China's present situation. If U.S. and foreign scholars alike are to fully understand what dynamics are at play in the globalization of R&D to developing economies, particularly China, then a more systematic approach will be needed. In the meantime, however, analysts must rely on traditional indicators of S&T advancement, independent research, periodic surveys and anecdotal indicators of how this trend is playing out on the Mainland. One aspect of the R&D trend in China that is apparent, however, is the fact that the type of R&D being conducted is changing.

■ China R&D Rising

MNCs have invested in commercial-oriented R&D on the Mainland for over a decade. Even over this short period of time, however, the trend has evolved through several distinct stages, each a response to changes in foreign and domestic (PRC) interests and incentives. Emerging slowly at first, foreign R&D investment in China began to explode in the mid-1990s, but then contracted somewhat by the late 1990s/early 2000s as companies began to consolidate their R&D assets in China following the market downturn in the information technology industry (Walsh, 2003 a). Since then, there appears to be another period of expansion under way. One reason is that the trend has gone mainstream. As foreign R&D investment in China has become more conventional, additional overseas investors have sought to get in the game, while many already in the market are expanding their R&D presence on the Mainland. A follow-the-leader dynamic remains strong in the Chinese market. Yet, in addition to fashion, there are a number of reasons to believe the present expansionary trend will continue for some time.

Several key factors are helping to spur the current expansion in overseas R&D in China and are likely to extend this trend into the foreseeable future. The first is a shift in the dominant rationale arguing for R&D investment in China from one emphasizing the need to meet PRC demands for technology transfer in the form of R&D programmes (to promote the company's long-term interest by maintaining a good relationship with PRC officials and partners) to one stressing internal corporate interests. In other words, MNCs at some point dating around the turn of the century began to seek R&D investment opportunities in China premised primarily on the need to implement a global business model. This made an R&D presence in China imperative rather than optional. Though subtle, this shift in perspective has resulted in tangible differences in the way MNCs approach R&D efforts in China. For example, rather than set up additional "show R&D" facilities as many MNCs had done in the 1990s to meet formal or informal technology transfer mandates, most foreign-invested R&D centres in China today conduct genuine research and development projects, most focusing on applied research as well as on design and development projects.[1]

Once foreign firms in China began to conduct true commercial research in China, this led to other changes that transformed the conduct of foreign

---

1 The World Investment Report 2005 parses applied research into three forms termed "adaptive R&D", "innovative R&D" and "technology monitoring" to describe the type of R&D being conducted in developing economies (see UNCTAD, 2005a, p. xxvii).

R&D in China. For example, R&D centres began instituting much stricter security measures and taking additional steps to safeguard intellectual property rights (for example, instituting and attempting to enforce non-disclosure agreements for in-house researchers). Following China's entry into the WTO, MNCs also took advantage of the opportunity to transform and consolidate their R&D centres into wholly foreign owned enterprises, alleviating the need for Chinese partners and the related, often-complicating factors that arise in conducting joint R&D at home or abroad. Moreover, having transitioned to more substantive R&D, and in many cases also integrating China-based R&D operations into their global R&D network, MNCs in China today are unlikely, barring major political or regional security upheavals, to quickly reverse course or terminate these efforts.

In addition, companies conducting R&D in China today have extended their outlook and their research work to focus on longer-term efforts. Intel's China R&D staff, for instance, is working on research projects expected to bear fruit only in three to five years' time. Similarly, Microsoft's Beijing R&D centre, along with other companies, are working on next-generation technologies that will not come to market for five to ten years, similar to Nokia's China researchers who are reportedly developing and designing products on a five-year timeframe (Wei, 2005; UNCTAD, 2005a).[1] This, again, suggests that multinationals are in it for the long term and are willing to expend considerable time, talent, training and treasure for rewards that will be realized only in later years.

A further reason to believe the R&D trend in China will continue for some time is that the rise and substantive shift in foreign R&D investments in China has, in turn, stimulated a parallel increase in domestic firms' spending on R&D. While still modest in relative terms, Chinese firms such as Huawei, Lenovo, ZTE (Zhongxing Telecommunication Equipment), and others have begun to reinvest a higher percentage of their corporate profits

---

[1] See also Microsoft Research Asia: Backgrounder on the Microsoft website. Available at http://research.microsoft.com/aboutmsr/visitmsr/beijing/.

into R&D.[1] PRC officials and corporate leaders readily acknowledge this to be one of the key lessons learned as a result of the influx of foreign R&D and have incorporated this understanding into their development strategies and business plans. Another lesson learned is the need for Chinese researchers to spend additional time, energy, and expenditure on conducting basic scientific research. Given the rising levels of applied research taking place in both foreign and domestic enterprises in China, PRC officials are alert to the need to invest more in basic research activities in order to ensure China's own long-term technology development goals (Blaniped, 2004). At present, China ranks among the world's lowest spenders on basic R&D (NSB, 2006). Thus, increased funding and attention to basic research is highlighted as part of China's 11th Five-Year Plan (FYP) for 2006–2010 (FBIS, 2006c).

Moreover, as the last example suggests, PRC officials have made a strategic decision to base the country's long-term economic development on advances in S&T (Xin, 2005). An integral part of this strategy (Kejiao Xingguo or "Revitalizing the Country through Science, Technology, and Education") is China's acceptance, to a degree unprecedented elsewhere, of the need to rely on foreign R&D investment and other forms of international scientific cooperation and technology transfer. Both China's latest 11th FYP as proposed and the recently released National Guideline on China's Long-and Medium-Term Plan for Science and Technology Development (2006–2020) call for continued openness to foreign technology investments as a means to improve China's own scientific and technological capabilities. As part of this effort, China plans to "encourage transnational companies to establish R&D bodies in China", as outlined recently in a speech by Chinese President Hu Jintao (FBIS, 2006b). It should be noted, however, that although these plans and other policy statements often emphasize Beijing's intention to develop indigenous technology capabilities and national technical standards, this approach is often mis-characterized as an effort

---

1 Chinese companies are estimated, on average, to spend only 1 percent of sales on R&D. On increased corporate R&D spending, see Roberts (2004); ZTE: focusing attentions on the future to gain the advantage in the development of 3G and NGN, China Information Industry website (30 October 2003). Available at http://www.cnii.com.cn/20030915/ca199582.htm.

solely to eliminate the nation's dependence on foreign technology. Rather, China's concept appears to be to seek enhanced access to, and assimilation of, foreign technology inputs as a continuous (if, in relative terms, reduced) means of developing indigenous technologies. As described in a recent *People's Daily* report, the recently released National Guideline on stressing independent innovation doesn't mean to resist introduction of advanced technologies. With the trend of economic globalization and further opening-up, China should make full use of both domestic and foreign resources to push forward the independent innovation at a higher footing (*People's Daily*, 2006).

Medium-and Long-Term Plan for Science and Technology Development calls for a reduction to 30 percent of China's reliance on foreign technology in 15 years' time, down from the present estimated dependence rate of over 50 percent.[1]

In the past, a development strategy so reliant on foreign technology transfer would have been viewed as an admission of a serious weakness in China's indigenous technological capacity. To the extent that China's innovative institutions and practices remain comparatively immature, this is true. However, in an increasingly globalized economy, China's approach may be better viewed as a strength than as a weakness. In fact, in this regard China can be considered ahead of many in understanding, as the latest *World Investment Report* concludes, that "...no country can rely entirely on knowledge within its borders" (UNCTAD, 2005a). If so, this too argues for a long-term trend in foreign R&D dollars and assets directed at the Chinese market.

Finally, the competitive dynamic that has led to increased R&D spending on the part of domestic firms in China will, in turn, influence foreign R&D investors, who are likely to further enhance their R&D activities and investments on the Mainland in order to remain competitive in this critical market. This is likely to be also a key driver for the increased levels of foreign venture capital that is flooding into China's metropolitan

---

1 This 15-year "blueprint" was announced 9 February 2006. See China to strengthen basic research to meet major strategic demands, *Xinhua News Agency* (9 February 2006); Wu Chong, China unveils plans for science-based development, SciDev. Net, 10 February 2006. Available at http://www.scidev.net/news.

areas. As a result, a potentially beneficial cycle of increased research inputs resulting in technological advances or innovations could develop within China's territorial confines, as PRC policy makers clearly hope will happen. Yet, this possibility also raises new concerns, particularly in the economic competitiveness and security realms, which could further complicate China's relations with the United States, its neighbours in Asia, the European Union and others around the globe.

■ Implications

There are four important indicators of how the rise in foreign R&D to China will affect the PRC's own technological development and its economic, political and security relations with other powers: how China chooses to leverage foreign R&D inputs, how transparent it is in these efforts, how successful these efforts prove and how quickly these achievements are realized and perceived.

As noted earlier, China's current near-and long-term strategies for scientific and technological development depend heavily on continued foreign investment in R&D. If realized, this will provide China with enormous potential for technology transfer opportunities and tens, if not hundreds, of billions of additional R&D dollars added to China's already large annual R&D expenditures. In fact, some analysts suggest that China is nearing a critical technology "take-off" point based on Beijing's current pace of national R&D spending (Jefferson, 2004). The added billions of foreign R&D dollars and related assets, if effectively absorbed and applied in ways beneficial to China's technology development efforts, could hasten the realization of this technological turning point. Moreover, if a take-off is imminent, what impact would this, in turn, have on MNEs and their home-base economies? The follow-on dynamics to a more technologically advanced and innovative China have yet to be fully explored, though the need for expanded research into the potential two-way effects of foreign R&D investment in China and other developing economies is clear and has been articulated in the literature (Ramamurti, 2004).

Though important from a commercial and trade perspective, the potential technological take-off by China, fuelled in part by foreign R&D investments, could have even more serious implications for the military and security interests of the United States and other regional powers, a possible repercussion already being debated. In particular, the extent to which China seeks, and is able to, leverage commercial, dual-use technologies for its ongoing military modernization campaign would become an even greater concern than it has been to date. A reflection of this concern is contained in the Pentagon's recently released Quadrennial Defense Review (QDR), which notes that "Of the major and emerging powers, China has the greatest potential to compete militarily with the United States and field disruptive military technologies that could over time offset traditional U.S. military advantages absent U.S. counter strategies" (USDoD, 2006, p.29). In fact, there are strong indications that China's present defence-industrial strategy is, indeed, premised on an ability to convert commercial technology to military use (Cheung, 2004; FBIS, 2006a). However, the uncertainties surrounding this effort could promote greater caution by MNCs (and their respective governments) in expanding R&D collaborations and investments in China. Thus, the more transparent China can be with regard to its intentions and efforts to adapt commercial technology to military applications, the more likely western economies will be willing to allow investment in advanced R&D in China; the less transparent, the more circumspect and cautious investors and foreign legislators will become, thereby undermining China's overall efforts, perhaps to mutual disadvantage. It is, therefore, largely in Beijing's hands whether the trend toward increased and more advanced foreign R&D investment can, in political terms, continue over the long term and provide a win-win opportunity for both domestic and foreign investors.

A third indicator of how foreign R&D in China will impact technology development on the Mainland is the degree to which China can effectively absorb foreign technology, research, and know-how and apply it to China's own scientific and technology development efforts. To effectively leverage foreign R&D, however, China must foster greater interaction between foreign and domestic research enterprises and institutions, which recent studies show remains surprisingly low. China must also enhance the horizontal connections between its own research communities, bridge the gap that still exists between researchers and domestic industry on the Mainland, and provide enhanced training and financial incentives to state and private-sector researchers. Increased support for entrepreneurs, greater freedom of expression, and mandated merit-based promotions would also help spur innovation and disseminate more broadly professional standards, skills and practices. Success breeds success, but only when lessons are shared. Conversely, if China is unable to effectively leverage foreign R&D inputs, its own technology development will suffer, as it has repeatedly in the past. This scenario could exacerbate latent fears of a zero-sum outcome where MNE R&D investments are perceived as unfairly exploiting China's human, tangible and intangible resources.

Finally, if China is successful in its efforts to leverage foreign R&D investment for its own S&T goals, the extent and pace of this success will matter. In this case, faster may not be better. China's rapid ascent as a leading recipient among developing countries of foreign R&D investment has surprised and unnerved some observers. In part, this reflects concern over the effects of globalization and the response (or lack thereof) by national policy makers to address new and unexpected challenges posed by a global economy. In addition, those concerned with China's military modernization efforts are particularly wary of the rate at which the PRC might improve its science and technological capabilities as a result of increased foreign R&D investment. Thus, an oft-heard question among China analysts is whether foreign R&D centres in China are actually producing anything innovative at all. The subtext of this question is: "when do we need to worry?"

Following a decade of foreign R&D investments in China, evidence of adaptive and innovative results is only starting to emerge. Recent examples include Intel's processor-based Open Research compiler chip designed by Intel China researchers in conjunction with colleagues at the Chinese Academy of Sciences. Researchers at Nokia's China-based R&D centre are also reported to have independently developed a new model (3620) cell phone, which is being sold around the world (UNCTAD, 2005a). In another heralded example, Microsoft's research arm in Beijing contributed the "digital ink" pen used in the company's new Tablet PC. Though still modest by western standards, the emergence of innovations generated in China-based research laboratories represents important progress in China's ability to absorb foreign technology transfers for domestic application. Moreover, researchers in China are likely to be innovative in unexpected ways, not only in developing new technologies but in adapting and applying existing technologies in heretofore unprecedented ways. China's potential is clear and the building blocks for technological advancement appear to be in place (at least along China's eastern cities and provinces). Recognizing these innovative essentials, the UNCTAD cites China as one of only a few developing countries that holds the potential to realize "cumulative learning processes" that will foster technological advancement through global technology networking (UNCTAD, 2005a).

Yet it is also possible that the overall extent of achievements such as those just described could be underestimated or even hidden from view. One reason is that MNCs conducting R&D in China may not necessarily wish to highlight the technological advances these centres produce (except to a Chinese audience) for fear this would cause a backlash at home, where concerns over outsourcing and offshoring have grown as high-and low-tech jobs and opportunities in many areas have visibly diminished. Another reason to suspect we may not be seeing the entire innovative picture in terms of foreign R&D in China is that the contributions made to research and product development by a China-based team might constitute only a small fraction of a new product or innovation. This is, in fact, often the case in high-tech, global industries where R&D is increasingly structured to allow cross-country, 24/7 R&D collaboration. Thus, the piece of the puzzle contributed by a China-based R&D team might be effectively hidden as one component of a larger product, as software code is to electronics. Both dynamics, if they occur to any large degree, could mask significant advances in foreign R&D efforts in China and possibly also rising Chinese capabilities, thereby surprising many outside observers once these advances become more widely known. Ultimately, however, this sort of surprise would serve neither China's nor foreign investors' interests. If both China and its investment partners are to avoid the latter danger, a concerted and collaborative effort is needed to better understand the dynamics at play in the China market and the innovative impact they are having on both domestic and foreign economies. In other words, it will be increasingly important for both countries to demonstrate how these investments aid each side's long-term R&D and innovation goals. Without such assurances and concrete examples, scepticism will grow as R&D investment expands.

These challenges, however, are not restricted to China alone. The rapid emergence of foreign R&D in China is changing the Asia-Pacific landscape as well, in particular, China's relations with Japan, Taiwan region and South Korea. The rapid increase in foreign R&D in China has, in some ways, adversely affected neighbouring economies. For example, MNCs deciding where in Asia to locate new R&D centres are frequently choosing the Chinese Mainland over or before other nearby, more traditional locales. Already, too, the rush to China has affected perceptions within Asia, with the highest percentage of respondents to a recent survey listing only Japan above China as the "country considered as [the] centre of North Asia's research and development" (FBIS, 2006d).

Regional concerns over China's ability to draw rising levels of foreign R&D investment have led to new efforts to enhance bilateral and even trilateral (China-Japan-Korea) commercial R&D collaboration. Bilateral R&D collaborations between China and Japan are expanding, as they are between South Korea and the Mainland (InfoWorld, 2003; Yang-Taek, 2004; Gu, 2005). Triangular arrangements are also emerging. For instance, Chinese and Japanese firms have agreed to work together to develop Linux-based software for the Asia region, and in one case have pulled a Korean company into these efforts as well.[1] In addition, despite persistent

---

1 See joint news release, Official signing Redflag Software, Miracle Linux and Haansoft for co-development of "Asianux", 6 October 2004. Available at, https://www.miraclelinux.com/english/press/2004/102601.html. Another notable project announced in 2005 between China's Sun Wah Linux Limited and VA Linux System Japan K.K. seeks to "jointly develop a universal Debian GNU/Linux infrastructure and actively promote the adoption of Debian-based systems in both Japan and China" (see "Linux developers from China, Japan to cooperate", *People's Daily*, 3 March 2005).

political sensitivities, China, Japan and South Korea are working together via a trilateral arrangement to coordinate and co-develop next-generation information technologies (Maeda et al., 2005). Formation of these types of regional partnerships in part reflect nervousness on the part of China's neighbours—they fear being left behind in China's wake as the Mainland draws and develops more advanced technologies—as well as an effort to leverage this potential. South Korea, in particular, is alert to China's rapid closing of the gap in key industry sectors such as information technology. Thus, recent efforts to cooperate more closely with China on industrial R&D and technology standard projects appear to represent initial steps toward accommodating China's rise as a technological as well as economic power.

If this latter trend develops more fully, it could have important political and economic ripple effects throughout the region. While there may be apparent and emerging economic and technological complementarities today among three of North East Asia's leading economies (Japan, South Korea and the PRC), it is unclear what enhanced integration and interdependence among these three states might lead to over time. Will closer economic relations enhance or exacerbate political (and persistent historical) concerns among these three Asian powers? What do closer trilateral relations suggest for Taiwan region's future economic and political concerns? And will these potentially mutually advantageous economic complementarities last, or will they be fleeting opportunities as Mainland Chinese enterprises, industries and innovative institutions mature? Other issues worth consideration include the impact that China's emerging high-tech economy is having on South East Asian economies, which remain wary of China's political-military aspirations and gun-shy about overextending regional economic and financial interdependencies stemming from still-vivid memories of the 1997 Asian financial crisis. Due to these uncertainties and the lack of a clear understanding of how the influx of foreign direct investment (FDI) and MNE R&D investments in China is influencing the PRC's own economic, technological, and political-security ambitions, the notion of increasing higher-end industrial and technological collaboration with the Mainland is perceived in the region as both potentially risky as well as a vitally important opportunity for all of Asia's economies wishing not to be left behind in China's economic wake.

Even such nascent considerations of China-centric economic regionalism have promoted speculation over whether or not an Asian economic bloc, akin to the European Union, is feasible among Asia-Pacific nations. Conventional wisdom holds that this is not a likely outcome in the near term, yet it remains an idea appealing to Asia's leading industrial and high-tech economies as a potential means toward enhancing their collective global competitiveness, with China serving as the economic engine for this new economic arrangement. While not likely to come about in the short term, efforts ongoing among China, Japan and South Korea to develop Asia-wide technologies and technical standards could be a first step in this direction.

■ Conclusions

China's rise as an emerging international R&D hub is beginning to garner the attention and study it deserves, for China potentially lies at the forefront of what the U.S. National Academy of Sciences has termed a "new industrial order" in which:

The big winners in the increasingly fierce global scramble for supremacy will not be those who simply make commodities faster and cheaper than the competition. They will be those who develop talent, techniques, and tools so advanced that there is no competition.[1]

What is clear is that the rapid rise in foreign R&D investments in China is due to a convergence of factors. Chief among these are China's openness to foreign direct investment, effective leveraging of market demand, continuous efforts to specifically attract foreign R&D and its enormous investment in modern infrastructure (financed in large part by years of unprecedented levels of FDI), all of which are occurring in the midst of a new wave of global economic interaction. In short, China is in the right

---

1 This statement was contained in a letter sent by the National Science Foundation in a letter to the President's Council of Advisors on Science and Technology. Cited in National Academy of Sciences, Rising above the Gathering Storm, pp. 1-3. Available at http://fermat.nap.edu/books/C309100399/html/19.html.

place at the right time. Whether the decision making that led China to this point has been fully deliberate, somewhat desperate, serendipitous, or a combination of all three, Chinese officials today clearly understand what is needed to develop a modern, high-tech, and competitive market in the context of a globalizing or, as some would say, flattened world economy. This puts the PRC, ironically enough, on the economic-industrial technological frontier. The key question will be whether China can effectively exploit this rare opportunity, or whether it will fall prey to the systemic weaknesses that have undermined China's technological development efforts in the past. In the meantime, investors are likely to continue to look to the PRC for new R&D opportunities, with the potential for rapid and perhaps revolutionary results.

References

Assimakopoulos, D. and Yan, J. (2006), "Sources of knowledge acquisition for Chinese software engineers", *R&D Management*, 36(1), 97-106.

BCG & KW (Boston Consulting Group & Knowledge at Wharton) (2004), "China and the new rules for global business", *China Report: Studies in Operations and Strategy*, 26 May.

Blaniped, W. A. (ed.) (2004), "Proceedings of the Sino-U.S. forum on basic sciences for the next fifteen years", held at February 2004, Beijing, Arlington, VA: George Mason University, 16-17.

Cheung, T. M. (2004), "Harnessing the dragon: Civil-military integration and China's defence modernisation", in R. H. Yang (ed.), *CAPS Papers*, No. 36, January, Taipei: Chinese Council of Advanced Policy Studies.

China Daily (2005), "Overseas investment on the up, excerpts from the Chinese Academy of Foreign Trade and Economic Cooperation (CAFTEC), 2005 Report of Transnational Corporations in China", *China Daily*, 1 February.

Chong, W. (2006), "China unveils plans for science-based development", scidev.net, 10 February, available at: http://www.scidev.net/content/news/eng/china-unveils-plan-for-science-based-development.cfm.

EIU (Economist Intelligence Unit) (2004), "China is #1 for R&D investments", *Economist Intelligence Unit*, October.

Fan, E. X. (2003), "Technological spillovers from foreign direct investment-a survey", *Asian Development Review*, 20(1), 34-56.

FBIS (2006a), "China to improve capability to supply new, advanced weapons and equipments during the Eleventh Five-Year-Plan period", accessed through the Foreign Broadcast Information Service (FBIS) [CPP20060105029020], *Beijing Zhongguo Xinwen She*, in Chinese, 5 January.

FBIS (2006b), Adhere to the path with Chinese characteristics leading to independent innovation, and work hard to build an innovation-oriented Country, accessed via FBIS. Text of Hu Jintao Speech on Innovation at National S&T Conference on 9 January [CPP20060109412003], *Beijing Xinhua Domestic*

Service in Chinese, 9 January.

FBIS (2006c), "China to improve capability to supply new, advanced weapons and equipments during the Eleventh Five-Year-Plan period", accessed via [CPP20060105029020], *Beijing Zhongguo Xinwen She*, in Chinese, 5 January 06.

FBIS (2006d), Report by Kwo'n Hyo'k-chu, Hong Chu-yo'n, Korea losing bid to become research hub, accessed via FBIS [KPP20060115971049], *Seoul JoongAng Ilbo*, in English, 15 January.

Gilboy, G. (2004), "The myth behind China's miracle", *Foreign Affairs*, 83(4), July/August.

Gu, G. Z. (2005), "Japan & China: What's really at stake?", Financial Sense Online, 25 April, available at http://www.financialsense.com/fsu/editorials/ 2005/0425b. html. Accessed 25 May 2005.

Hu, A. (2005), "Technology parks and regional economic growth in China", *Research Policy*, 36(1), 76-87.

Info World (2003), "Major Asian IT groups to collaborate on open source", *Info World*, 14 November.

Jian, G. and Jefferson, G. H. (2004), "Science and technology take-off in China?: Theoretical and empirical perspectives", Workshop on Global R&D in China, Nanjing, 27-29 May, 2005.

Li, J. and Yue, D. (2005), "Managing global research and development in China: Patterns of R&D configuration and evolution", *Technology Analysis & Strategic Management*, 17(3), 317-338.

Maeda, Y., Nakatsuka, M. and Iwata, H. (2005), "Global standardization activities: CJK (China-Japan-Korea) meeting on information and telecommunications standards", *NTT Technical Review*, May, 62-64.

Meyer, K. E. (2004), "Perspectives on multinational enterprises in emerging economies", *Journal of International Business Studies*, 35, 259-276.

Moris, F. (2004), "U.S.-China R&D linkages: Direct investment and industrial alliances in the 1990s", *Info Brief* (NSF 04-306), February, National Science Foundation, Washington, DC.

NAS (National Academy of Sciences) (2006), "Rising above the Gathering Storm: Energizing and employing America for a brighter economic future", Report by the Committee on Science, Engineering, and Public Policy (COSEPUP), Washington, DC: National Academies Press.

National Science Board (NSB) (2004), Science & Engineering Indicators—2004, Arlington, VA: National Science Foundation.

National Science Board (NSB) (2006), Research and development funds and technology linkages, Arlington, VA: National Science Foundation.

OECD (2005), Science, Technology and Industry Scoreboard 2005, Paris: OECD.

People's Daily (2006), "Try to build an innovation-oriented nation", People's Daily Online, 10 January, available at http://english.people.com.cn/200601/10/eng2006 0110_234334.html (accessed 9 February 2006).

Pillsbury, M. (2005), "China's progress in technological competitiveness: The need for a new assessment", A report prepared for the U.S.-China Economic and Security Review Commission, 21 April.

Ramamurti, R. (2004), "Developing countries and MNEs: Extending and enriching the research agenda", *Journal of International Business Studies*, 35, 277-283.

Roberts, D. (2004), "China's power brands", *Business Week International*, 3907, 45, 8 November, 77, available at http://www.businessweek.com/magazine/content/04_45/ b3907003.htm.

Sun, Y. (2002), "Sources of innovation in China's manufacturing sector: Imported or in-house developed?", *Environment and Planning A*, 34(6), 1059-1107.

UNCTAD (United Nations Conference on Trade and Development) (2005a), "Drivers and determinants", *World Investment Report*, Chapter V, Geneva: United Nations, 167-172.

UNCTAD (2005b), "Figure IV. 11: Most attractive prospective R&D locations in the UNCTAD survey, 2005-2009", *World Investment Report*, Chapter IV, Geneva: United Nations, 153, 185, 196.

USDoD (U.S. Department of Defence) (2006),"Quadrennial Defense Review Report", 6 February, Office of the Secretary of Defence, 2006, Quadrennial Defense Review, available at: http://www.defenselink.mil/qdr/report/report20060203.pdf.

Von Zedtwitz, M. (2004), "Managing foreign R&D laboratories in China", R&D Management, 34(4), 439-452.

Walsh, K. (2003a), "High-Tech R&D investment in China: Outlining rewards and risks", Presentation prepared for the Industrial Research Institute, 15 July.

Walsh, K. (2003b), Foreign high-tech R&D in China: Risks, rewards, and implications for U.S-China relations, Washington, DC: Henry L. Stimson Centre.

Walsh, K. (2005), Testimony before the U.S.-China economic & security review commission hearing on China's high-technology development, 21 April, Palo Alto, California, USA.

Weber, L. (2005), Statement before the U.S.-China economic and security review commission hearing on China's high technology development, 21-22 April, Palo Alto, California, USA.

Wei, R. (2005), "Building R&D potential", *China International Business*, 1 December.

Xin, F. (2005), "From imitation to innovation: A strategic adjustment in China's s&t development", Presentation before the Seminar on Latin American, Caribbean, and Asian Strategies for Science, Technology, and Competitiveness, 17 April, Okinawa, Japan.

Xinhua News Agency (2006a), "Foreign investors select China as research and development base", Xinhua, 9 February.

Xinhua News Agency (2006b), "China to strengthen basic research to meet major strategic demands", Xinhua News Agency, 9 February.

Xue, L. and Wang, S. (2001), "Globalization of R&D by multinational corporations in China: An empirical analysis", Paper presented at the Sino-U.S. Conference on Technological Innovation, 24-26 April 2001, Beijing.

Yang-Taek, L. (2004), "Towards a dynamic wave: IT cooperation of China-Korea-Japan", *East Asian Review*, 16(3), 41-74.

Yuan, Z. (2005), R&D by TNCs in: China, Globalization of R&D and Developing Countries, Part II, Proceedings of the Expert Meeting, Geneva, 24-26 June, New York and Geneva: UNCTAD, 109-115.

The Energy Factor in China's Foreign Policy

Charles E. Ziegler[1]

■ Introduction

Rapid economic growth has made China dependent on the global economy for a range of raw materials, from iron ore and steel to cotton and wood. Of the various resources China needs to power its economic miracle, none is more important than oil. From 1992 to 2005 the People's Republic of China went from self-sufficiency in petroleum to dependence on imports for over one-third of total consumption. China is the world's second largest energy consumer, and in 2004 it surpassed Japan as the world's number two oil

---

1 Charles E. Ziegler is Professor and Chair of the Department of Political Science at the University of Louisville, and Director of the Institute for Democracy and Development. He is co-editor of and contributor to *Russia's Far East: A Region at Risk* (University of Washington Press, 2002), and author of *The History of Russia* (Greenwood, 1999), *Foreign Policy and East Asia* (Cambridge University Press, 1993), and *Environmental Policy in the USSR* (University of Massachusetts Press, 1987). His articles have appeared in *Problems of Post-Communism*, *Asian Survey*, *Pacific Affairs*, *Comparative Politics*, *Political Science Quarterly*, *British Journal of Political Science*, and many other journals and edited books. The author would like to thank Igor Danchenko for his able research assistance on this project.

importer. Petroleum imports are projected to continue to increase at a rapid pace. At the same time, China is evolving into a global power, with national interests beyond the East Asian region.

This conjunction of growing energy dependence and rising economic influence and military raises the following questions. How has China's foreign policy behavior changed during a period of growing energy dependence? Will China pursue energy security through strategies that result in conflict, as realist theory would predict, or will its energy vulnerability lead it toward cooperation with rival oil consuming nations through participation in multilateral organizations or other forums, in line with liberal explanations? Finally, to what extent might China's energy interests bring it into conflict with other major importing nations such as Japan and the United States?

The following section sets out the argument for the strategic nature of energy for major powers, with a specific focus on oil.[1] Then I present data in China's increasing energy dependence, setting it in comparative perspective with China's East Asian neighbors, and evaluate Beijing's efforts to shift China's energy balance. China's energy diplomacy with the Middle East, Russia and Central Asia, the Asia-Pacific, Africa and Latin America constitutes the subject of the next section. Beijing's efforts toward greater energy security through multilateral organizations are discussed, with particular attention to China's participation in the World Trade Organization and the Shanghai Cooperation Organization. The evidence suggests that energy demands have indeed accelerated China's rise to global prominence and, at least in the short term, appears to reinforce the cooperative aspects of Chinese foreign policy. The liberal argument that economically interdependent states tend to avoid costly conflicts appears more persuasive than does realism in conceptualizing China's foreign policy in its search for energy security.

---

1 While this paper will discuss China's imports of oil and natural gas as they relate to Chinese foreign policy, the chief focus here will be on oil. As noted in the section on China's energy dependence, the share of natural gas in the country's energy balance is growing, but remains relatively small. China is self-sufficient in coal, and its imports of electricity are negligible.

■ Oil and Foreign Policy

Øystein Noreng has argued that for governments, energy is a politicized commodity, critical to economic and military strength and therefore vital to national security. The significance of energy as a component of foreign trade far outweighs its proportion of the total value of turnover. Simply put, political leaders view oil in a different category than footwear, electronics, or automobiles.[1] Energy, and in particular oil, is too important to be left to market forces alone.[2]

Considerable attention has been paid in the international relations literature to the link between economic interdependence and conflict. Liberalists in the field, going back to Kant, argue that greater economic interdependence moderates the prospects for conflict, while realists contend that economic ties exacerbate conflict by increasing a state's vulnerability in an anarchic environment.[3] Surprisingly few academic studies have focused on oil in foreign policy despite the strategic nature of this commodity. Logically, support for either realist or liberal theories from a study of energy interdependence should be particularly persuasive, given the vital importance of oil for national security. For example, oil dependence heightens uncertainty, and there is evidence that major powers in the past have gone to great lengths, including war, to ensure oil supplies. If the world's major rising power is employing cooperative strategies rather than using military means to ensure energy supplies, that choice may have significant theoretical and policy implications.

The vulnerability of oil consuming states depends on whether they have alternative forms of energy available either domestically or in the

---

1 Richard Rosecrance argues just the opposite, that importing energy is no different than importing fashions or automobiles. *The rise of the trading state: Commerce and conquest in the modern world*, New York, Basic Books, 1986, 233-236.

2 Øystein Noreng (2002), *Crude Power*, London: I.B. Tauris, 42.

3 Edward D. Mansfield and Brian M. Pollins (2001), "The study of interdependence and conflict: Recent advances, open questions, and directions for future research", *Journal of Conflict Resolution*, 45, December, 834-859; Katherine D. Barbieri (1996), "Economic interdependence: A path to peace or a source of interstate conflict?", *Journal of Peace Research*, 33, 29-49; Dale C. Copeland (1996), "Economic interdependence and war: A theory of trade expectations", *International Security*, 20, Spring, 5-41.

international environment. Consumer states can reduce dependence on oil through various strategies, with resort to war as only the most extreme measure. Domestically, states can provide incentives for exploration and enhanced production, assuming that sufficient reserves exist or are suspected to exist, to make such efforts worthwhile. Governments can also adopt conservation policies to reduce consumption. A third strategy to reduce strategic dependence is to shift from imported oil to alternate fuels—coal, natural gas, nuclear power, wind or solar energy—wherever possible. Finally, states may establish strategic reserves to dampen the shock of unexpected supply interruptions or to even out severe price fluctuation.

Internationally, consumer states may improve their energy security by diversifying imports, obtaining oil from as many suppliers as possible. Second, they may form or join multilateral organizations in order to bargain more effectively with supply cartels or with major producers. Third, states may encourage oil majors within the country to acquire oil properties abroad, to control upstream production. States that do not have nationalized oil companies may enter into corporatist arrangements with private companies, since the interests of the government and those of private energy companies overlap significantly. Finally, the states that are sufficiently powerful may use military force to ensure the flow of oil.

For modern industrial and industrializing states, oil is a vital component in economic growth. Oil prices are closely tied to inflation and economic growth rates. For example, the Energy Information Administration estimates that doubling the price of oil 1999–2000, from $11 to $22 per barrel, resulted in 50% increase in inflation in the United States in 1999, and 75% increase in 2000. The same price increase resulted in 50% decline in GDP for growth 1999, and a full 1.0% decline in GDP in 2000. The surge in world oil prices to over $65 per barrel in 2005 has further constrained growth and fueled inflation. Given the strong emphasis China's leaders place on social stability and continued rates of high economic growth, steep price increases and shortages threaten domestic order.

Since oil is so important to the economic health of nations, policy makers will accord high priority to ensuring secure supplies at relatively stable prices. Small, militarily weak oil importers can do little to affect the global market. Membership in consumer organizations and stockpiling oil in strategic reserves may dampen the impact of fluctuation in the oil markets, but for the most part these states are highly vulnerable. If an oil importing state is relatively small and militarily weak, then it will tend to rely on multilateral cooperation and stockpiling.

Large, militarily powerful states, however, have more options. First, large consumer states like China or the U.S. are more likely to be home to one or more major energy companies. Even in neo-liberal capitalist systems such as the United States, the interests of these companies and the state overlap to a large degree. By importing and distributing large volumes of foreign oil, preferably at fairly consistent prices, energy companies earn huge profits and preserve market share. Political leaders, of course, have as a major goal strong economic growth and modest inflation, each linked to stable oil imports. Oil companies, then, become an integral component of state energy policy, in a corporatist relationship. This relationship is quite different from that posited in the pluralist model, where large powerful corporations pressure a reactive government.

Most large states also have relatively powerful military forces, which can be used to protect supply routes, or employed in times of crisis to secure oil supplies, either individually or, more likely, in tandem with other large oil importing powers. Certainly this describes the United States as the world's current hegemon, but one could also include Japan, Germany, Britain and France in the past, and China and India as significant emerging oil consumers in the present.

■ China's Oil Dependence

Concurrent with increasing oil dependence, China has come to be viewed as a great power, not merely a regional actor.[1] China's quarter-century of rapid economic growth and its relative openness to the outside world have forced

[1] See Evan S. Medeiros and M. Taylor Fravel (2003), "China's new diplomacy", *Foreign Affairs*, November-December, 22-35.

others to take it seriously. Relatively neglected in the assessment of China's rising global influence is how the country's rapidly growing demand for energy might affect China's foreign policy.[1] In 1971 China's share in the world's primary energy demand was a mere five percent (with 23 percent of the world's population); in 1995 China's share of the world's population slipped to twenty-one percent, while its share of energy demand more than doubled to eleven percent. China's consumption of oil surpassed its domestic production in 1993, and imports have grown rapidly in recent years. In 2003 China's imports of crude oil increased by 31 percent over 2002, and demand for crude rose by 35 percent in 2004.[2]

Unless China's economy experiences a dramatic meltdown, the country will continue to consume increasing amounts of energy. The International Energy Agency estimates that by 2020 China's share of primary energy demand will increase to sixteen percent, while its share of population shrinks to nineteen percent.[3] Beijing is promoting the exploration of new oil and gas fields within the PRC, but specialists agree that imports will constitute an increasing share of the country's energy consumption. China's energy needs may heighten the potential for competition and conflict with other oil importing nations, most notably the United States and Japan. Conversely, China's vulnerability as an energy importer could lead toward greater cooperation and integration within multilateral institutions.

In this paper I suggest that: a. China's rapidly growing energy demands mesh closely with broader foreign policy goals of promoting a stable international environment conducive to economic development. Cooperative approaches will therefore prove more likely than competitive ones, at least in the near future; b. The major actors in China's energy policy are largely in accord on the goal of developing reliable sources of imported oil, although

---

1 Two of the best studies are Philip Andrews-Speed, Xuanli Lia and Roland Dannreuther (2002), The strategic implications of China's energy needs, Adelphi Paper #346, London: IISS, July; Bernard D. Cole (2003), "Oil for the lamps of China" —Beijing's 21st-century search for energy, Washington, DC: National Defense University.

2 *The Financial Times* (21 January 2004); *People's Daily Online* (14 January 2004); *China Economic Net* (9 June 2005).

3 *International Energy Agency* (2000), "China's Worldwide Quest for Energy Security", 14.

differences of emphasis between domestic development and foreign imports can be discerned; c. The principle of non-interference in other countries' internal affairs confers an advantage in China search for reliable energy suppliers, while Western industrial democracies, most notably the U.S., often find their stated policies at odds with authoritarian, repressive oil producers.

■ China's Energy Balance

China's oil strategy for the 21st century calls for diversifying oil imports, cooperation on developing oil and gas wells in other countries (the "going abroad" plan), establishing a national oil reserve, increased efficiency in oil and coal consumption, reforming the National Energy Commission and tasking it with responsibility for oil security, creating a national oil foundation to develop oil finances and futures, and reducing the volume of oil imports carried by foreign tankers from 90 to 50 percent. Increasingly, Chinese publications are referring to securing oil supplies as a vital component of the country's national security.[1]

China is the largest producer, and the largest consumer of coal, in the world. The country holds 33 percent of the world's coal reserves, and currently produces more coal than it consumes, but as demands for electricity continue to increase coal exports have been reduced. While Chinese consumption of coal is expected to increase along with other sources of energy, much of China's reserves are sulfur-rich brown coal. Extensive use of coal contributes to extraordinarily high levels of pollution—China's largest cities are among the most polluted in the world, especially in levels of sulfur dioxide and particulates. In order to combat air pollution, China's energy strategy calls for decreasing the share of coal in the energy balance from 77.9 percent in 1995 to between 60.8 and 63.3 percent by 2015.[2]

---

1 *People's Daily* (14 November 2002), http://english.people.com.cn/200211/14/eng20021114_106819.shtml; *People's Daily* (9 January 2004), http://english.peopledaily.com.cn/200401/09/eng20040109_132208.shtml.

2 Gao Shixian (2000), "China", in Paul B. Stares (ed.), *Rethinking Energy Security in East Asia*, Tokyo: Japan Center for International Exchange, 48.

Oil and natural gas consumption are expected to rise dramatically in the future, along with nuclear and hydroelectric power projects such as the Three Gorges dam. But China's domestic deposits of oil and gas are limited. China has less than two percent of the world's total oil reserves, and only about one percent of proven natural gas reserves. The older oil fields in northern and eastern China face declining output, while newly discovered fields in Xinjiang are remote from population centers, relatively small, and expensive to develop. Consequently, China's oil companies since 1997 have embarked on an aggressive campaign to secure properties and rights to oil and gas around the world, in Russia, Kazakhstan, Sudan, Azerbaijan, Indonesia, Iraq, Iran, Venezuela, and elsewhere.

In recent years, between 50 and 60 percent of China's oil imports have come from the Persian Gulf states, making that volatile region vitally important to China. In addition to being overly dependent on one region, China has no strategic oil reserves, and it is vulnerable to fluctuations in price and supply resulting from crises around the world. Like the United States, China is seeking to reduce its dependence on Middle Eastern oil. America's strategic domination of the Middle East constitutes an additional vulnerability for China. Beijing's frequent calls for a more multi-polar world order are understandable in the context of the country's vulnerable energy situation.

Although China is trying to enhance its energy security through expanded domestic production, it simply does not have the oil reserves to meet growing demand. In 2001 China produced 3.2 million barrels per day (bpd) of oil, and imported no less than 1.4 million bpd. In 2003–2004 China experienced phenomenal growth in both oil consumption (from 5.56 million bpd to 6.53 million bpd) and imports (from 2.02 million bpd to 2.91 million bpd). In just one year, the percentage of oil imported increased from 36 to 45 percent.[1] A rapidly growing reliance on imported oil has thrust China into the role of a major actor in world oil markets.

---

[1] Energy Information Administration, Department of Energy, Country Analysis Brief for China, 2005, http://www.eia.doe.gov/emeu/cabs/china.html.

Table 1 Energy production and imports in northeast Asia, 2003–2004

	China	Japan	South Korea
Oil consumption, million barrels per day	6.53 mln bbl/day	5.57 mln bbl/day	2.1 mln bbl/day
Net oil imports, million barrels per day	2.91 mln bbl/d	5.45 mln bbl/day	2.1 mln bbl/day
Percent of oil imported	45%	97.8%	100%
Natural gas production, trillion cubic feet	1.21 tcf	0.09 tcf	0
Net gas imports, trillion cubic feet	0	2.57 tcf	.816 tcf (all LNG)
Percent of natural gas imported	0%	96.3%	100%
Coal production, million short tons	1630 mmst	3.5 mmst	3.7 mmst
Net coal imports, million short tons	0	175.8 mmst	76 mmst
Percent of coal Imported	0	98%	95%

Source: U.S. Department of Energy, "Energy Information Administration Country Analysis Briefs", China (2005), Japan (2004) and South Korea (2005), at www. eia. doe. gov.

As is clear from Table 1, China is much better off in terms of energy resources than the other major countries of Northeast Asia. However, Japan's energy demand is stagnant, while China's is growing rapidly. And unlike its neighbors Japan and South Korea, who have strategic reserves of 100 days or more of oil, China has no more than a week's worth of domestic consumption held in state-owned facilities. Spurred by uncertainties in the international market, the Chinese government in 2003 announced plans to improve its energy security by building a national oil reserve. Scheduled for inauguration in 2005 and completion by 2010, the strategic reserve would provide China with 70–75 days' worth of oil at the current level of consumption.[1]

---

[1] Michael Mackey (2004), "China setting up a strategic oil reserve", *Asia Times*, 7 February, http://www.atimes.com/atimes/China/FB07Ad02.html.

Oil consumption in China, as in most countries, is closely linked to the transportation sector. Much of the growth in oil consumption over the next decade will be the result of increasingly affluent Chinese consumers purchasing automobiles. In 1999 China had only 5.34 million private automobiles, or about one for every 250 Chinese. By comparison, in the U.S. in 2000 there were about 210 million private vehicles (automobiles and light trucks), or 72 for every 100 Americans.[1] But the automotive industry in China is growing rapidly; projections anticipate 140 million vehicles on the road by 2020. Car sales in 2004 alone were five million, making China the third largest car market, after the United States and Japan.[2] The government has encouraged automobile consumption as a means of stimulating the economy, to restore growth rates that weakened following the 1997 Asian crisis. Beijing's policy makers are clearly more concerned with keeping the population quiescent in the short term, than with the long-term energy and environmental consequences of promoting private transportation.

Demand for natural gas is increasing rapidly in China, as it is in much of developed and developing world. Gas is much cleaner in generating electricity than either coal or oil, releasing far less carbon monoxide, carbon dioxide, sulfur dioxide and particulates. China has extremely high levels of sulfur dioxide and particulates in its urban areas, resulting from heavy reliance on coal, which accounts for about three-fourths of China's current energy balance. The share of natural gas in China's energy balance is projected to grow from about 3 percent in 2002 to about 8–9 percent by 2010, as the share of coal decreases.

China inaugurated the domestic West to East Pipeline in July 2002 as one of several major projects that Beijing is promoting to increase the supply of natural gas flowing to power generation plants in the more populated and developed coastal areas. Originating in the Tarim basin of the Xinjiang-Uighur autonomous republic, the pipeline will cover some 4200

---

1 People's Daily (6 October 2001); US. Department of Transportation, Office of Highway Policy Information, http://www.fhwa.dot.gov/ohim/onh00/onh2p3.htm.

2 *Financial Times* (24 March 2004); *Asia Pulse* (5 August 2004); *The Economist* (5 June 2005).

kilometers en route to Shanghai, and is designed to deliver 12 billion cubic meters of natural gas per annum. Total estimated cost is over $18 billion, including $12 billion for exploration and development of fields and retail chains, and $5.6 billion for the pipeline. The eastern 1500 kilometer segment of the pipeline was completed and gas started flowing to Shanghai in late 2003. China's state company PetroChina had initially formed a consortium with Russia's Gazprom, Royal Dutch/Shell, and Exxon Mobil, but the deal foundered on pricing issues and domestic political support for the project. By August 2004 PetroChina had terminated its agreements with all three foreign partners.[1]

To summarize, China's energy strategy calls for decreasing the proportion of coal in the energy balance, increasing the share of natural gas, and developing nuclear and hydroelectric power to deal with frequent shortages of electricity brought about by rapid economic growth. To maintain social stability the government is actively promoting automobile ownership, so demand for oil has soared. Domestic exploration and production are a priority, but limited reserves of both oil and gas are making China increasingly dependent on imports. Energy needs have integrated the China into the global economy. To cope with China's energy demands, the government and state oil and gas companies have partnered their diplomatic efforts.

■ Energy and Diplomacy

China's limited supplies of oil and natural gas have played an important role in broadening that country's interests beyond the East Asian region.[2] China's state-run oil companies, supported by the government, have pursued a strategy of buying energy properties around the world in an attempt to

---

1 Premier Zhu Rongji, who stepped down from his position in 2003, had been an enthusiastic supporter of foreign participation in the project. *Financial Times* (4 August 2004); *Russian Oil and Gas Report* (4 August 2004).

2 The US Department of Defense Annual Report to Congress, The Military Power of the People's Republic of China 2005, refers to resource demands, particularly energy, as a "driver" of Chinese strategic behavior. Accessed at http://www.dod.gov/news/Jul2005/d20050719 china pdf.

secure oil and gas supplies. Chinese foreign policy has focused on developing bilateral ties with important selected countries, but it is increasingly willing to work through multilateral institutions with other oil consuming nations. As a major energy consumer and importer, China shares America's goals of ensuring reliable energy supplies at moderate supplies. Of course, Beijing is competing with the United States and other energy importers for these finite resources. Moreover, China's pursuit of energy security frequently clashes with U.S. national security interests, as Beijing courts oil-rich countries regarded as pariahs by Washington, such as Sudan, Venezuela, Burma, and Iran.

Liberal theories of international relations would predict that growing interdependence should motivate Chinese leaders to eschew military instruments of statecraft in favor of diplomacy, markets, and participation in international organizations. The realist perspective would place more emphasis on how China's growing energy dependence generates insecurity. Realism would predict an inclination to develop military forces capable of defending the vital sea lanes of communication, particularly the Strait of Malacca, through which 80 percent of the country's oil imports transit. Other evidence supporting the realist approach would include a demonstrated willingness to intervene militarily in oil supplying countries. However, China as yet has shown little inclination to task its modernizing military with ensuring energy supplies. This may be simply a nod to reality, since the PRC is far from being able to challenge the United States globally, or it may be a rational calculus that non-military means are more cost-effective and present a greater likelihood of success than using armed forces. Evidence from Chinese activities around the world suggests that Beijing is utilizing political, diplomatic and economic levers to secure long-term energy supplies from a wide range of sources.

■ The Middle East

As noted earlier, China is heavily dependent on the Middle East for oil imports, with Oman, Yemen, Iran and Saudi Arabia as the largest suppliers.[1] At the present time virtually all of China's imported oil comes via ocean going tankers, and supply routes could be interdicted either at the source (the Strait of Hormuz) or in transit, at the Straits of Malacca.[2] China faces uncertainties—deliveries could be disrupted and prices affected by conflicts or instability in the Middle East, as in 2003 and 2004. Security experts have raised the possibility of terrorist actions against tankers transiting the Straits of Malacca, or against ports adjacent to the narrow waterway. Even with its recent growth in military spending and the development of its navy, China still must rely on the United States to protect these vital sea lanes.

Beijing's planners are considering many alternative sources of energy. For China, the Middle East will remain in first place as a supplier of crude oil for the indefinite future. This region has about two thirds of the world's reserves, combined with low production costs. Chinese domestic oil costs about 25 percent more per barrel to produce than the average production costs of the world's large petroleum companies.[3] The strategy of Chinese oil companies has been to invest in upstream and downstream of Middle Eastern production (especially in Iran, Iraq, and Kuwait) to reduce possible disruption of oil supplies. China's foreign policy seeks to strengthen political relations with the Middle Eastern oil-producing states, while courting additional suppliers who would not impose the Asian premium of $1–2 per barrel.

China's energy needs, combined with the Persian Gulf countries' demand for technology and consumer goods, have elevated the region in China's foreign policy priorities. Former President Jiang Zemin visited Saudi Arabia in 1999 and signed an oil cooperation agreement providing for

---

1 Steven W. Lewis (2002), China's oil diplomacy and relations with the middle east, Rice University: James A. Baker III Institute of Public Policy, September, 7.

2 Sergei Troush (1999), "China's changing oil strategy and its foreign policy implications", CNAPS Working Paper, Fall.

3 Comprehensive production costs (production plus discovery) for a barrel of oil lifted by Chinese corporations was $12.30 at the end of the 1990s, compared with $9.40 per barrel for non-Chinese oil majors. Shi Zulin and Xu Yugao (2002), The impacts of China's accession to the World Trade Organization (WTO) on China's energy sector, Berkeley, CA: Nautilus Institute, 13.

Saudi participation in Chinese refining in exchange for the kingdom opening its markets to Chinese investment. The Saudis, however, have restricted foreign participation in oil exploration and development. Jiang visited the Middle East again in April 2000, and in November 2002 Beijing sent a Mideast peace envoy to Israel, Syria and Palestine to demonstrate China's commitment to stability in the region, and a small flotilla completed China's first naval tour of the Arabian Sea since the 16th century. In August 2002 the Chinese National Petroleum Corporation (CNPC) announced a $230 million contract to build twin 500 kilometer oil and gas pipelines in Libya, and in 2004 Syria concluded a joint venture with CNPC, forming a Syrian-Chinese oil company (Kobab) to develop the Kbibah oil field in northeast Syria.[1]

Chinese companies have also sought entree to Iraq's oil fields, which account for ten percent of the world's reserves. In 1997 China signed a deal with Iraq to develop the Al Ahdab oilfield in central Iraq, and in 1998 began negotiations for the Al Halfayah field, in the expectation that they would be well-positioned once the sanctions were lifted.[2] The U.S. occupation of Iraq and the ensuing instability placed these expectations on hold. In February 2004 Zhongxing Telecom won China's first postwar contract in Iraq, a $5 million deal to supply telecommunications equipment, reportedly in the face of resistance from the Coalition Provisional Authority.[3] As of late 2004 China had not concluded any energy deals in Iraq, but the Chairman of China Petrochemical Corporation had indicated his company's readiness to take advantage of any business opportunities there.[4] Poor relations between Iran and the United States have provided an opening to Chinese companies. President Hu Jintao has praised Iran and indicated China's readiness to work with Iran to purchase LNG and develop the upstream sector of Iran's oil industry. Iran is China's second largest supplier of oil, after Saudi Arabia, and the two countries have concluded oil and gas deals worth $70 billion. In

---

1 Ed Blanche, "Chinese Oil Diplomacy Focuses on Middle East", Lebanonwire, 27 November 2002, http://www.lebanonwire.com/0211/02112716DS.asp; MENA Business Reports (27 July 2004).

2 *Global News Wire* (26 September 2003).

3 *AFP* (10 February 2004).

4 *China Post* (2 August 2004).

addition to cooperating on oil and gas, Chinese firms are working on mine projects, port and airport construction, electricity and dam building, cement, steel, and railway industries in Iran, and the two countries are promoting tourism. Hu has emphasized Beijing's willingness to cooperate with Iran on building regional stability and dealing with the situations in Afghanistan and Iraq, and Iran's Ambassador to China has described political relations as "excellent".[1]

China's energy dependence on Iran has made relations with that country a matter of significant national interest. The energy relationship has made Beijing less willing to support American efforts in the United Nations to pressure Teheran to compromise on its nuclear weapons program. China has rejected U.S. proposals to refer Iran to the UN Security Council for possible sanctions, expressing instead a preference for resolving the issue within the UN's International Atomic Energy Agency.[2] Beijing would apparently prefer not to be forced to choose whether or not to exercise its veto in the Security Council, an action that would be sure to strain ties with Washington.

Given the complementarity of Chinese and Gulf state economies, trade, investment, tourism, and other forms of economic cooperation will continue to grow, as will Chinese political influence in the region. However, it is unlikely that China will seriously challenge America's dominant position in the Middle East any time soon.

■ Russia, Central Asia, and the Caucasus

Russian and Central Asian energy resources could help China reduce its dependence on Middle Eastern oil, and thus enhance its security. Pipelines, after all, are generally a more reliable form of transportation than tankers. Central Asian and Russian oil occupy the second tier in Chinese priorities. These regions have substantial deposits of oil and natural gas, and China

---

1 IRNA (9 April 2004; 24 March 2004).

2 Statement by Zhang Yan, China's permanent representative to the UN: "China Calls for Resolving Iranian Nuclear Issue within IAEA", *People's Daily Online*, http://english.peopledaily.com.cn/200409/19/eng20040919_157555.html.

views the development of these resources as key to its energy security, a "strategic backup" to other sources. However, the costs of extraction and transportation of oil are considerably higher than Middle Eastern crude. More importantly, Russia and the Caspian states combined account for less than ten percent of the world's reserves, compared with the Middle East's two-thirds.

Russia and Central Asia do have a key advantage in natural gas, though, since their reserves, at 37 percent of the global total, far exceed those of the Persian Gulf states. At present gas accounts for only a small fraction of China's energy needs, but as the energy balance changes and pipelines come on stream this will change. Russia will likely provide an increasing share of China's energy needs. But in the more distant future, China is also looking to import gas from Turkmenistan, Kazakhstan and Uzbekistan. As Russian and Central Asian gas becomes available via pipelines, it could displace more expensive liquid natural gas (LNG) imported from Indonesia and Australia.[1]

In 2001 Russian's President Vladimir Putin and China's former President Jiang Zemin agreed to build a 2300 kilometer oil pipeline that would run from Angarsk, north of Irkutsk, along the south of Lake Baikal and then skirt Mongolia, dropping southward to terminate at Daqing, northeast China. The Yukos oil firm was to provide most of the oil, which would supply idle refineries in the northeast Daqing region. The pipeline was expected to supply 20 to 30 million tons of crude per year, nearly one-third of China's imports at 2004 rates.

In 2003 several events conspired to undermine the original plan. Japan challenged the Daqing route, proposing the pipeline terminate at Nakhodka on the Pacific coast. This route would prove more costly, but it would have the advantage of giving Russia several buyers (Japan, South Korea, China, Taiwan region and the United States) in place of a single customer. To

---

[1] Shell Vice President F.K. Lung calculates that pipeline gas is generally cheaper if the distances involved are less than 3000 kilometers. Between 3000 and 9000 kilometers LNG and gas offer similar prices, depending on construction costs, and beyond 9000 kilometers LNG is cheaper than piped gas. F.K. Lung, "Clean Fossil Energy—Roles for Natural Gas and Coal", http://apec-egcfe.fossil.energy.gov/7thtech/p206.pdf.

sweeten the deal, Japan offered to invest as much as $7 billion to underwrite construction costs. Second, the Nakhodka route would benefit the economically depressed Russian Far East, through construction of the pipeline, refurbished terminals, and transport tariffs, and so fit more closely with President Putin's goals of raising living standards in Russia's poorer regions. Finally, the government's attack on Yukos and its founder and CEO Mikhail Khodorkovsky in 2003–2004 effectively quashed that company's ability to carry out the project, leaving the state-owned monopoly Transneft to construct the pipeline.

Political competition between China and Japan may be nearly as important as economic incentives in securing Russian oil. Chinese-Japanese tensions are on the increase as growing Chinese influence in the Asia-Pacific confronts rising Japanese nationalism. China is intensely suspicious of Japan's intentions, and has criticized the Japanese government for sending Self-Defense Forces to Iraq to assist the American campaign. The Xinhua News Agency accused Japan of seeking to become a military power, and to secure its oil interest in the Gulf.[1]

The controversy suggests that while economic considerations dominate energy planning in Putin's Russia, Chinese energy diplomacy is more a mix of politics and economics. Chinese officials were reportedly furious when Moscow revisited the 2001 agreement, seeing it as a violation of the spirit of their proclaimed "strategic partnership". Curiously, Japan's maneuvering also seems influenced by politics. Japan can certainly use the oil, and would prefer to diversity its supplies (about 80 percent of its imports now come from the Middle East), but domestic Japanese demand has been stagnant for some years now. In any case, Japan will receive increasing amounts of Russian oil and gas from the Sakhalin I and II projects as they reach maturity over the next three decades.

Central Asia may prove a more attractive energy source than Russia. China has concluded projects of varying sizes with the various Central Asian states and Azerbaijan in recent years. In May 2003 China Petroleum and

1 *Japan Economic Newswire* (9 December 2003).

Chemical Corporation (Sinopec) and China's National Offshore Oil Company (CNOOC) bid to acquire a 16.67 percent share in the North Caspian Sea PSA. The deal foundered when five of the six partners—Shell, Exxon-Mobil, TotalFinaElf, Conoco Phillips and Italy's ENI—exercised their pre-emption rights and purchased the share from British Gas. Had the Chinese companies succeeded in their bid, they would have acquired a significant share in one of the world's largest fields, which includes the huge Kashagan oil field in addition to several others. The Kazakh government had enthusiastically supported China's involvement in the project and, when this did not work out, claimed a sovereign right to purchase the BG share.[1]

Chinese interest in Central Asian oil stems from a desire to promote overall economic regional integration, and to build a land bridge between Central Asia and Russia that would be more reliable than Persian Gulf crude. CNPC initially made headlines in 1997 with a deal with Kazakhstan in which China was expected to invest $9.7 billion to update the Uzen oil field and construct a 3200-kilometer pipeline from the western province of Aktobe into western China. However, the Kazakh fields held reserves that failed to justify such investment, and CNPC put the project on hold in 1999. The issue was raised again during Nazarbaev's December 2002 visit to Beijing, when the Chinese proposed that Kazakhstan supply them with up to one million barrels per day of oil. Kazakh energy minister Vladimir Shkolnik has said that construction of a pipeline system that could eventually supply China was continuing.[2] Record oil prices have made the project more feasible. In addition, China has the option to pump the oil through the Caspian pipeline to Novorossiysk via a swap arrangement.

China's strategic interests in the Central Asian region—maintaining stability, preventing terrorism, separatism and religious extremism, and

---

1 Dan Roberts (2003), "Western oil majors flex their muscles", Financial Times, 10 May; Lina Saigol (2003), "Battle lines drawn for caspian oil", Financial Times, 8 May; AFX European Focus (7 May and 12 May, 2003). Ibragim Alibekov, "Kazakhstan Asserts State Interests in Kashagan Oil", Eurasianet. org, http://www.eurasianet.org/departments/business/articles/eav070904.shtml. The sixth partner in the joint venture, Japan's Inpex, declined to increase its stake.

2 Interfax-Kazakhstan, in Global News Wire-Asia Africa Intelligence Wire (29 January 2003). The perception that a Kazakhstan to China pipeline would eventually be constructed was reinforced by a series of interviews conducted by the author in Kazakhstan in June 2003.

controlling narcotics trafficking—coincide with those of Russian and Central Asian leaders. Neither Russian nor Central Asia can meet all of China's growing oil needs, so competition is muted. For China, closer economic integration with the Central Asian states in the form of rail, road and air links, oil and gas pipelines, and electrical grids, is an important element in Beijing's strategy to diversify energy supplies, while neutralizing the potential for instability in Xinjiang.[1]

The Asia-Pacific Region

As Table 1 demonstrates, Japan and South Korea are energy-dependent countries, and so are competitors with China for scarce energy resources. In addition to the rather bitter competition between Japan and China to determine the route of Russia's Siberian pipelines, the two nations have also clashed over plans to exploit a natural gas field which straddles their exclusive economic zones in the East China Sea.[2] However, China, Japan and South Korea have through the Committee on Northeast Asian Cooperative Initiative discussed the possibility of coordinating purchases of oil from the Middle East to eliminate the Asian premium.[3] With South Korea, energy ties have to this point been more cooperative than competitive, as evidence by plans to extend Russian gas pipelines through China to South Korea via an underwater spur. India, with its high recent growth rates and limited energy supplies, is another competitor for oil and gas.

Southeast Asian oil and gas have played an important role in China's energy balance, but exports to China have declined significantly in recent years as Indonesian and Malaysian reserves become depleted. In 1996 the Asia Pacific accounted for 36.3 percent of China's imported oil; by 1999 the

---

1 On Xinjiang's links to the Central Asian region, see Sean R. Roberts (2004), "A 'Land of borderlands': Implications of Xinjiang's Trans-border Interactions", in S. Frederick Starr (ed.), Xinjiang: China's Muslim Borderland, Armonk, NY: M.E. Sharpe.

2 Mariko Sanchanta (2004), "Gas provokes Japanese clash", *Financial Times*, 7 July

3 Karen Teo (2004), "Big three to fight 'Asian premium' on Saudi sales", The Standard (Hong Kong), 25 November, accessed at the Energy Bulletin, http://www.energy-bulletin.net/3349.html.

share had dropped to 18.7 percent.[1] Nonetheless, China remains one of Indonesia's top four markets for crude, and Chinese firms are eager to cooperate on energy projects. In 2002 the China National Offshore Oil Corporation (CNOOC) purchased most of the Spanish firm Repsol-YPF's assets in Indonesia for $585 million, making it the largest offshore oil producer in Indonesia. However, Indonesia's oil production is declining and domestic demand is growing, so the potential for growth in energy imports in limited. Estimates are that by 2010 Indonesia will become a net oil importer. Planning ahead, Jakarta is seeking to diversity its export base away from oil products.

Prospects are more favorable for natural gas. In 2002 Beijing and Jakarta concluded several memoranda of understanding that enhanced energy cooperation, and Indonesia bid on a multi-billion dollar contract to supply Guangdong province with LNG over a twenty-five year period. Australia won the bid, but China and Indonesia subsequently signed a contract valued at $8.5 billion to supply liquid natural gas to Fujian province, starting in 2007. Energy cooperation is a factor dampening decades of hostility between the two Asian giants, granting China new opportunities to develop political and military relations. For example, Indonesia is considering purchasing arms from China, which is eager to sell military equipment. Beijing's diplomatic approach to Jakarta in recent years has been skillful.

The U.S. approach toward Indonesia, by contrast, is often contradictory, and has earned it considerable resentment. Congress, which had restricted military assistance in 1992, severed all forms of contact with the Indonesian military in 1999, after troops engaged in human rights abuses in East Timor. At the same time, the U.S. is pressuring Indonesia to cooperate in the war on terror. Chinese leaders are not troubled by human rights issues, nor do they exert pressure toward democratization. In Southeast Asia China is increasingly viewed as a positive force, a status quo power, rather than a revolutionary troublemaker as in past years.

---

[1] Wang Yanjia (2003), "Oil security in China", Institute of Energy Economics, Japan Symposium on Pacific Energy Cooperation.

The huge LNG contract Australia landed with China in August 2002 was billed as Australia's single largest trade deal. North West Shelf Venture agreed to supply over three million tons per year of LNG to Guangdong province for 25 years, generating export earnings of approximately one billion dollars annually. Although considerable smaller than Australian LNG exports to Japan ($2.6 billion annually), the sales would increase total exports to China by about 15 percent.[1] However, leadership changes in Beijing, the SARS outbreak, revisions to China's energy strategy, and delays by the Guangdong local government on approving the receiver terminal hindered progress on the agreement.[2] In addition, China will be competing with the west coast of the United States for Australian LNG. Starting in 2007, Chevron Texaco is planning to import LNG from Australia's Gorgon project to a terminal in Mexico, and then pipe the gas north to California.[3]

China has also worked with the Association of Southeast Asian Nation (ASEAN) to ensure stable energy supplies by creating regional oil stockpiles. In July 2003 China joined the ASEAN nations, Japan and South Korea to set up an ASEAN Plus Three Energy Partnership, a governing group to explore ways to ensure stable energy supplies for the region, including coordinating on oil stockpiling. Japan and the Republic of Korea were to fund the group's research programs. The first formal meeting of the Energy Partnership was held in June 2004, where members discussed how to improve energy security, enhance exploration, share information, and develop stockpiling.[4]

Common energy needs may lead China's foreign policy to be more accommodating in East Asia. One example is in the six-nation dispute over the Spratly and Paracel islands in the South China Sea, where a militant Chinese posture has led to repeated armed clashes in the past. China does not plan to give up its extensive claims to the oil and gas-rich waters of the

---

1 "China LNG delivers Australia's largest ever trade deal", Australian Trade Commission, 8 August 2002, http://www. austrade. gov. au/corporate/layout/0,,0_S1-1_-2_-3_PWB1655449-4_-5_- 6_-7_,00. html.

2 Nigel Wilson (2004), "LNG on a slow boat to China", *The Australian*, 18 March.

3 Nick Muessig, "LNG: Where Will it Go?" Neftegaz. ru, http://neftegaz. ru/english/analit/comments. php?one=1&id=1250.

4 Pacific Forum CSIS 3rd quarter 2003, http://www. csis. org/pacfor/cc/0303Qchina_asean. html; Alexander's Oil & Gas Connections (29 June 2004), http://www. gasandoil. com/goc/news/nts42644. htm.

South China Sea, but Beijing's leaders appear to be substituting a policy of engagement for confrontation. In late August 2003 the Chairman of the National People's Congress, Wu Bangguo, who was in Manila for an Association of Asian Parliaments for Peace conference on economic development and terrorism, proposed that China, the Philippines, and other claimants to the Spratlys engage in joint oil exploration and development. In March 2005 national oil companies of China, Vietnam and the Philippines signed an agreement to conduct a joint survey of oil deposits in the South China Sea. Political and corporate officials hailed the accord as an historic event that would contribute to peace and stability in the region.[1]

While Chinese leaders are increasingly willing to grant major state oil firms economic autonomy, their activities are expected to mesh with Beijing's foreign policy strategy. When China's oil companies seek to acquire holdings in oil-rich states around the world, these acquisitions serve the twin goals of strategic energy diversification and expanding political presence. Government and corporate interests are not identical in China, but there is considerable overlap. China's political officials are well aware that their country needs increasing supplies of raw materials, above all energy, to continue to maintain high economic growth rates, and they are using statecraft to help China's energy companies acquire properties across the globe.

■ Africa and the Americas

With the Middle East in turmoil, and Russian pipelines uncertain, Chinese companies have increasingly sought out business opportunities with African and Latin American oil producing states. The share of China's crude oil imports from Africa increased from 8.5 percent to 28 percent from 1996 to 1999.[2] East Asian imports of crude from West Africa for the first three months of 2004 were 1.3 to 1.4 million bpd, considerably higher than the one million bpd average in 2003. Most of this was driven by China's surging

---

1 *Radio Free Asia* (14 March 2005), http://www. rfa. org/english/news/business/2005/03/14/china_vietnam_spratlys/.

2 Wang, "Oil security in China".

demand for sweet crude.[1]

China's interest in Africa during the Cold War was to present an alternative to the superpower rivalry of the United States and the Soviet Union. Competition then was for ideological influence with the developing world, through such projects as the Tanzania-Zambia railway and aid to Mozambique, in which China presented itself as a defender of the poorest Third World states. This ideologically driven approach declined after Deng's pragmatic market reforms were begun, and policy toward the African continent now is driven more by a blend of political and economic interests.

The political side of China's recent attention to Africa is a response to Taiwan region's efforts to spread largesse in exchange for diplomatic recognition from smaller nations on the continent.[2] China's search for new energy supplies also accounts for a significant part of Beijing's Africa policy. In 2002 China provided $1.8 billion in development assistance to African countries, while China's trade with the continent reached $12.4 billion.[3] China can help Africa's energy exporting states by providing direct investment and technology. In turn, China receives much-needed oil and other raw materials, in addition to a more visible presence on the continent.

In February 2004 President Hu Jintao visited Algeria, Egypt and Gabon, all major oil producers. In Algeria, Hu and Algerian President Abdelaziz Bouteflika signed a framework energy agreement and accords on technological cooperation and educational exchanges, and China extended a preferential loan worth $48 million. Major Chinese projects in Algeria include a CNPC refining agreement worth $350 million, a $525 million contract with Sinopec to develop the Zarzaitine oil field in the Sahara, and a contract for China National Oil and Gas Exploration and Development Company to build an oil refinery near Adrar. Chinese firms are involved in the

---

1 "China Boosts Asian Demand for African Crude" Reuters (9 April 2004), http://www. gulf news. com/Articles/Business2. asp?ArticleID=117383.

2 Richard J. Payne and Cassandra R. Veney (1998), "China's post-cold war African policy", *Asian Survey*, 38, September, 867-879.

3 Carter Dougherty (2009), "China, seeking oil and foothold, brings funds for Africa's riches", *The Boston Globe*, 22 February.

construction of an air terminal at Hourari Boumedienne airport, a teaching hospital in Oran, and some 55,000 apartments. Algeria is eager to increase its output from the current one million bpd to 1.5 million bpd, and China is a willing customer.[1]

Gabon has far less oil than Algeria (current production, at 270,000 bpd, is down more than a third from the peak year 1997), but it is still important given China's status as a latecomer to the ranks of oil importing nations. During Hu's 2004 visit Total Gabon and China's Unipec (a subsidiary of Sinopec) signed the first contract for the delivery of Gabon crude, and Sinopec has exploration plans for the West African nation.[2]

Sudan is a key energy producing state for China in Africa. Government-sponsored massacres in the western region of Darfur have resulted in U.S. economic sanctions, and most major oil companies have reduced their presence in this troubled country. China resists criticism that its energy investments in Sudan have funded the brutal Janjaweed militias, arguing that China and Sudan have normal business relations. Sudan has received the bulk of Chinese investment in Africa, but Beijing argues this is simply normal business relations. China's National Petroleum Corporation has developed a plan to invest $1 billion in upgrading Sudan's refineries and pipelines. Approximately $700 million of this would go toward constructing a 750-km pipeline from the Kordofan field to the coast, while the remainder would be used to increase capacity at the Khartoum refinery.[3] Sudan only supplies a small fraction of China's oil imports, but it is crucial as a base for energy development in Africa.

The African oil producing states have relatively backward energy technologies and need foreign investment to modernize their facilities. In some cases, such as Sudan, U.S.-imposed sanctions and pressures from human rights organizations have led Western oil firms to pull out, giving Chinese companies a chance to establish a foothold. The Chinese government

---

1 AFP Algiers Petroleumworld. com (4 February 2004), http://www. petroleumworld. com/story3469. htm.

2 AFP Algiers Petroleumworld.com (3 February 2004), http://www.petroleumworld.com/story3461.htm.

3 *BBC News* (19 May 2003).

provides foreign assistance to complement the investment from its oil companies. For example, the Chinese have financed administrative offices in Gabon and the Ivory Coast, an airport terminal in Algeria, and communications networks in Ethiopia.[1]

Chinese involvement in Latin America is small but growing, and much of the interest can be attributed to the continent's raw materials, including oil and gas. Beijing has requested permanent observer status in the Organization of American States. In 2004 the Brazilian oil major Petrobras invited Sinopec to bid on an offshore bloc, to conduct oil exploration. Petrobras' plan is to contribute technology, while the Sinopec Group would provide funding for the joint exploration venture. China is reported willing to contribute one billion dollars to refurbish Brazilian ports, in exchange for oil and raw materials. Brazil's President Luiz Inacio Lula de Silva provided political support for the project during his May 2004 visit to Beijing.[2] China is Brazil's third largest trading partner, after the United States and Argentina.

Venezuela is South America's largest producer of crude, and PetroChina has identified Venezuela as one of the top four countries from which it expects to obtain oil over the next seven years. Venezuela under President Hugo Chavez is highly critical of the United States, although the country continues to supply well over one million barrels of oil per day to the U.S. In 2000 Venezuela signed an agreement to export 6.5 million tons per year of orimulsion, a coal substitute, for use in China's thermal power plants and steel mills. The deal was touted as greatly expanding Venezuela's exports of this unique form of energy. However, the Venezuelan Energy Ministry suspended orimulsion production in mid-2004 as unprofitable.[3] In June 2004, China's ambassador to Caracas has public reiterated his country's goal of developing large-scale energy projects with Venezuela. But this country,

---

1 *BBC News* (19 May 2003).

2 *AFX News* (3 August 2004); *Financial Times Information* (23 July 2004). Energy cooperation was just one component of the meeting, to which da Silva took 400 officials and nine ministers. The Brazilians also pledged to expand agricultural and mineral exports, and concluded deals on aircraft, steel, and automobiles. U.P.I. 28 May 2004.

3 *Inter Press Service* (30 June 2004). China agreed to provide two-thirds of the financing needed to modernize the emulsion plant in Venezuela.

like Middle Eastern oil producers, is volatile, with major labor unrest cutting oil production sharply in 2002 and 2003.

Chinese oil companies have even sought to acquire major holdings in North America, the most notable of which was the 2005 attempt by China's National Offshore Oil Company (CNOOC) to purchase the American oil company Unocal. The CNOOC bid, valued at $18.5 billion, resulted in a firestorm of criticism from the U.S. Congress amid fears that U.S. energy security would be compromised. CNOOC's chairman Fu Chengyu insisted his company's attempt to outbid Chevron was purely commercial, but the process collapsed amid charges that the Chinese government was subsidizing the purchase to enhance its leverage over oil and gas producers in Central and Southeast Asia.[1] Chevron lobbied Washington far more effectively than did CNOOC, and acquired Unocal for nearly two billion dollars less than the Chinese offered. Clearly, politics and security issues shaped the behavior of leaders in both countries.

Chinese companies will continue a long-term strategy of acquiring energy assets around the world. The Unocal experience may lead China to focus on the more unstable or politically unsavory oil and gas producers. China's arrangements with individual producers—Iran, Saudi Arabia, Russia, Kazakhstan, Indonesia, Azerbaijan, Sudan, Brazil and Venezuela—are promising, but each of these countries faces serious domestic or international problems. The uncertainty of bilateral energy ties has contributed to a new appreciation for multilateral organizations in Beijing's international energy policy.

■ China, Energy, and Multilateral Organizations

China's growing involvement in the global economy, and its more active diplomacy, provide Beijing's leaders with a new perspective on participation in multilateral institutions. The organizations that are of greatest relevance to

---

[1] Unocal's holdings include production and operations in Thailand, Indonesia, Burma, Bangladesh, The Netherlands, Congo and Azerbaijan. The company is conducting exploration in Vietnam, and has a significant interest in the Baku-Tblisi-Ceyhan pipeline.

China's energy strategy are the World Trade Organization (WTO), the Shanghai Cooperation Organization (SCO), and the International Energy Agency (IEA).

Securing membership in the World Trade Organization has been an important component of Chinese foreign policy, although it is a mixed blessing for Chinese businesses and the Chinese people. The open market provisions of the WTO will pay the greatest dividends in areas where China has a comparative advantage—textiles, clothing, processed foods and leather goods. China's agricultural sector will be hit hard, as will much of China's energy industry. Expectations are that output of all energy sectors will be reduced, with the greatest impact falling on downstream industries. Many of China's inefficient refineries, which rely on outmoded technology, will be forced to close or will be forced to join with foreign partners. Retail sales outlets will be taken over by the larger multinationals as non-tariff barriers fall. The impact will be lower on upstream oil and gas, including exploration and development.[1]

Tariff cuts under the WTO mean that Chinese companies will have to reduce production costs in order to compete with imports. Under WTO China was required to phase out its trade barriers to the import of oil products by the end of 2004. In addition, restrictions on distribution will be lifted, allowing U.S. and other foreign firms the right to sell gasoline and other oil products in the Chinese market. Royal Dutch Shell, Exxon Mobil and BP are now retail marketing in China; these companies own some 300 of China's 75,000 gasoline stations. The number of retail gasoline stations will increase as car ownership continues to grow.

By lowering import barriers and tariffs WTO membership will encourage gasoline consumption in China. In 2003, China had some 96.5 million motor vehicles on the road, of which about 80 percent were publicly owned. But China's affluent middle class is purchasing automobiles at a furious pace—car sales increased by 75 percent in 2003, and production for 2004 is

---

1 Shi Zulin and Xu Yugao (2002), The impacts of China's Accession to the World Trade Organization (WTO) on China's energy Sector, Berkeley, CA: Nautilus Institute.

expected to be 40 percent higher than the previous year.[1] Imports are also expected to increase as WTO regulations force price reductions. Imported cars had been taxed at 80-100 percent tariff rates, which allowed domestic manufacturers to keep automobile and parts prices high. Shortly after joining the WTO, prices on Chinese-made cars dropped as much as 20 percent. Tariffs on imported cars are projected to decline to 25 percent by 2006, and tariffs on spare parts will drop to 10 percent.[2] Lower prices, together with the government's policy of promoting private automobile ownership, virtually guarantees continued growth in demand for oil.

Energy cooperation through the Shanghai Cooperation Organization has recently gained in importance for China. Originally formed to deal with territorial issues arising from the breakup of the Soviet Union, the SCO, whose members also include Russia, Kazakhstan, Uzbekistan, Kyrgyzstan, and Tajikistan, has in recent years focused more on problems of terrorism, religious extremism, and narcotics smuggling. China and Russia have used the organization to gain Central Asian support in their campaigns against separatism in Xinjiang and Chechnya, and both Moscow and Beijing view the organization as a possible counterweight to American influence in the region.

China's new focus on SCO energy cooperation derives from its concern over instability in the Middle East, and the goal of securing both Russian and Kazakh oil and gas.[3] Within the SCO Russia, Kazakhstan and China appear to be forming an energy and security triangle. Kazakh oil is currently exported through the Caspian Pipeline Consortium, which runs through southern Russia and terminates at Novorossiysk, and there are plans to ship Kazakh oil through the Baltic pipeline when it is finished. Russia's state natural gas monopoly Gazprom has secured rights within Kazakhstan, as it has within all five of the Central Asian states. Russia's Unified Energy Systems, the electricity monopoly, has tied Kazakhstan and its neighbors

---

1 *People's Daily* (8 February 2004).

2 "WTO fulfills the Chinese people's dream of a family car", *China Today* (30 March 2002), http://www.china. org. cn/english/2002/Mar/29796. htm.

3 Sergei Blagov, *Asia Times Online* (27 February 2004), http://www. atimes. com/atimes/Central_Asia/FB27Ag01. html.

into an electrical power grid.[1] Kazakhstan continues to negotiate with China on an oil pipeline eastward, while the government suppresses Uighur separatists and leases agricultural land to ethnic Chinese.[2] Trade among the three continues to grow. Government officials and political observers in Kazakhstan are increasingly worried that economic and political pressures are forcing Astana to tailor its policies to suit Moscow and Beijing.[3]

Emphasis on energy cooperation within the SCO could lead to conflict with the United States, since American oil companies have been actively developing Kazakhstan's oil sector for over a decade. Kazakhstan's western fields already pipe about 300,000 bpd through the Caspian Pipeline Consortium, in which Chevron has a leading interest, and the Kazakh government plans to export up to ten million tons of crude oil per year through the Baku-Tblisi-Ceyhan pipeline. Washington adamantly supported the BTC pipeline's route through the Caucasus, in part because it skirts Russian territory.[4] And the U.S. has worked hard to consolidate support among its new Central Asian allies in the war on terror. Defense Secretary Donald Rumsfeld visited Kazakhstan and Uzbekistan in February 2004 to discuss expanding military relations and ensuring security in the oil-rich Caspian region.

China is not a member of the International Energy Agency, but it (along with Russia and India), has signed a memorandum of policy understanding to strengthen cooperation with the agency. The IEA, created after the 1973–1974 oil crisis, seeks to develop rational energy policies, and to help its members cope with supply and price disruptions and with environmental issues relating to energy use. Based in Paris, the IEA is linked to the OECD

1 See Gregory Gleason (2003), "Russia and the politics of the central Asian electric grid", *Problems of Post-Communism*, 50, May-June, 42-52.

2 Robert M. Cutler (2004), "Emerging triangles: Russia-Kazakhstan-China", *Asia Times Online*, 15 January, http://www. atimes. com/atimes/Central_Asia/FA15Ag03. html.

3 This perception came up repeatedly in interviews conducted by the author in Almaty, Atyrau, and Karaganda in June 2003.

4 Another reason cited is the powerful U.S. business and legal interests that are profiting from the pipeline, including BP, ConocoPhillips, Unocal, and the Baker Botts law firm, the family firm of former Secretary of State James Baker III, which is representing the consortium.

and its members are the OECD countries. China's goals mesh closely with those of the IEA, including security of supply, more efficient use of energy, technological advances, regulatory reform of the energy sector, environmental sustainability, and producer-consumer dialogue. The IEA works with China and countries in Eastern Europe, Latin America and Africa through its Committee on Non-Member Countries.[1] The IEA has held conferences on natural gas use in China, seminars on energy efficiency standards, energy modeling and statistics, and developing emergency oil stocks.

■ Conclusion

The evidence presented in this article suggests that China's foreign policy on energy security is accurately described by the liberal perspective on international relations. China, at least at this point in time, has pursued a cooperative path in the energy field. Beijing is critical of the United States over its Middle East policies, but Chinese leaders appear willing to work together to keep energy producing regions quiet and stable. And China is actively cooperating with other importing nations through various multilateral forums. In line with liberal theory, energy dependence appears to have exerted a moderating influence on Chinese foreign policy, leading Beijing toward cooperative strategies. This does not preclude the possibility that military force could become a viable option in securing energy supplies. But at present, the Chinese military does not have the projection capabilities that would allow it to intervene militarily in oil producing states, or to protect the vital shipping routes in the South Pacific.

Securing reliable and diversified energy supplies is central to China's security today, and the need will become even more pressing in coming decades. As a net energy importer, China has a stake in the stability of neighboring oil and gas producing regions, which China's leaders perceive as linked to domestic economic growth rates and societal quiescence. As a

---

1 See the IEA website, at www. iea. org.

major oil consuming nation, China has shared interests with other major oil and gas importing nations, such as the United States, Japan, South Korea, and members of the European Union. These include securing stable and diversified supplies, maintaining stable and moderate prices, and protecting the transportation routes through which oil and natural gas flow.

The driving elements in China's foreign policy since the Deng era have been continued modernization and development of the economy, a focus on the regions bordering China, and promoting nationalism as the leading ideological current.[1] China's foreign policy is concerned above all with preserving national sovereignty and national security.[2] Economic development and maintaining domestic stability are a high priority of the regime, and readily available supplies of energy are critical to keep economic growth rates at their recent high levels, as well as to provide the capabilities needed to strengthen China's international role and preserve the country's historic boundaries (that is, to prevent Taiwan region's independence). The country's national interests are increasingly difficult to protect, as China's growing dependence on imported oil and gas make it more vulnerable to the vagaries of the international energy market and global instability.

China's energy requirements constitute one significant factor driving Beijing to move beyond regionalism; China is indeed becoming a global power. This study suggests that energy demands have caused China's business elites and government officials to move beyond a regional focus on the Asia-Pacific, developing joint ventures and acquiring properties in Central Asia, Africa and Latin America. Politics and economics are still mixed in China's unique brand of capitalism, so it is difficult to separate the interests of China's petroleum firms from those of the Chinese state. In many instances, as in Western capitalist countries, government officials have close ties to the oil industry, and their goals mesh closely with those of business.

---

1 Zhao Quansheng (2004), "Chinese foreign policy in the post-cold war era", in Liu Guili (ed.), *Chinese Foreign Policy in Transition*, New York: Walter de Gruyter, 295-322.

2 See Deng Yong (1998), "The Chinese conception of national interests in international relations", *The China Quarterly*, 154, June, 308-329.

China's emergence as a global energy actor has had a major impact on the world economy, and will continue to do so in the foreseeable future. Energy policy in China, as in the United States, is focused on increasing supply rather than curtailing demand through conservation, mass transportation, and alternative technologies. China's foreign energy policy is critically important to economic development, and sustained economic growth is vital to maintain social stability. Chinese officials are positioning their country, economically and politically, to meet its rapidly growing energy needs in the coming decades. Energy dependence, in turn, constitutes a powerful incentive for a constructive, cooperative Chinese foreign policy.

Knowledge and Innovation in China: Historical Legacies and Emerging Institutions

Erik Baark[1]

■ Introduction

If we are to believe the Chinese Communist Party (CCP) Central Committee and the State Council, "innovation is the soul of a nation's economic progress" and Chinese enterprises should develop capacities to absorb and develop new technology (Zhongguo Jishu Chuangxin Zhengce, 2000, p.1). Chinese President Hu Jintao outlined major strategic tasks for building an innovation-oriented country at a national conference on science and technology (S&T) in January 2006 envisaging that the People's Republic of

1 Erik Baark, teaches in Division of Social Science, Hong Kong University of S&T.

China (hereafter simply China) will embark on a new path of innovation with Chinese characteristics, the core of which is allegedly to adhere to innovation, seeking to leapfrog development in key areas, and make breakthroughs in key technologies (*Xinhua News Agency*, 2006). A new emphasis on knowledge creation and diffusion in policy debates in China articulates these ambitions for promoting innovation. Information and communication technology are seen as a key area of focus in the drive to modernize the economy and to create new industrial and service sectors in China—epitomized in the ambition to develop a new knowledge-based economy (Dahlman & Aubert, 2001; Grewal et al., 2002).

But what do these ideas mean in a Chinese context? What sort of institutional framework exists in China for innovative activities and knowledge generation, and how do historical legacies and contemporary values shape the practice of innovation in China? Regardless of how challenging these broad questions appear to be, they need to be recognized by any business organization—domestic as well as foreign—engaged in innovation in China. Even if it is difficult to provide precise answers, it is important that managers possess an awareness of the cultural and institutional context that has emerged through processes that have unfolded over many centuries. One may seek inspiration from the study of Chinese philosophical thought, which has become an important element of comparative philosophy (for example, Bahm, 1977; Fleming, 2003). But the social context of Chinese knowledge creation and diffusion received more extensive treatment in works on historical research on traditional Chinese science and technology (for example, Needham, 1954–2004; Needham, 1969; Sivin, 1995). Scholars have thus examined the dynamics of Chinese discoveries and the development of systematic treatments of knowledge about natural phenomena in China, providing a sort of internal history of the development of Chinese scientific knowledge. In addition, some researchers have examined political, economic and cultural factors and their relationship to the growth and stagnation of scientific and technological activity in China (Qian, 1985; Bodde, 1991). In particular, a vigorous debate has persisted with regard to the factors underlying different paths of economic and technological development in China and Europe (Graham, 1973; Sivin, 1984; Pomeranz, 2000).

To my knowledge, however, few attempts have been made in the academic literature to look into the recent experience of Chinese innovation from a perspective grounded in long-term historical and cultural trajectories. Perhaps the best example of this approach is the article published by Baum (1982), which sought to identify significant traits of traditional Chinese culture that were seen to impede scientific progress in China. Although the traits may appear to be discussed by Baum in a particularly critical mode, his work shares with the present study the basic rationale that understanding a dynamic China must involve both insight into the new phenomena—many of which have been imported, or inspired, from overseas—and an awareness of the old legacies that have evolved over millennia. The complexity of the environment for innovation in China is precisely the dynamic tension between new and old, between foreign and indigenous, between values and practice.

This study accordingly seeks to throw light on conditions for Chinese innovation by means of an examination of the epistemological and social dimensions of traditional Chinese concepts of knowledge and innovation. Based on the identification of these legacies, I shall analyse how such concepts have shaped emerging institutions governing knowledge accumulation and innovative activities in China today. The institutions are emerging in the sense that they are being transformed by policy reforms initiated to support China's technological and economic development; but many institutions in China are also emerging in the sense that they govern activities that are new or previously insignificant in the Chinese economy (such as venture capital investment). In other words, this essay argues that emerging institutional fabric governing innovation in Chinese society represents an evolving synthesis of values and routines that have been formed over centuries on the one hand, and new principles introduced as part of ongoing political and economic change on the other hand.

Space does not allow a full-fledged discussion of all the legacies that may have a potential influence on the institutional fabric governing knowledge and innovation in China. Therefore, I shall focus on three key legacies. Firstly, I shall examine the Chinese perception of scientific knowledge in terms of its social or political utility and legitimacy. Secondly, the study explores the tension between the exploitation of existing knowledge and the exploration of new knowledge in the process of learning and innovation. Thirdly, the essay discusses the cultural prestige accorded to creativity, innovation and entrepreneurship and the potential conflict with the social/political constraints rooted in the search for harmony and social stability.

Each of these legacies has, I argue, shaped contemporary social and cultural values related to innovation in China. The study will illustrate this influence with respect to the following emerging institutions that I propose are significant in regulating innovative activities. Firstly, the social standing of knowledge in China still has some bearing on the dominant way of thinking about the utility of knowledge and its legitimate bounds. Secondly, a preoccupation with exploitation rather than exploration of new knowledge has impacted mind-sets concerned with diffusion and/or invention together with the emerging institutions governing intellectual property rights. Thirdly, the precarious nature of knowledge exploration and creative entrepreneurship in the innovative process continues to shape institutions regulating linkages between innovators and producers.

The methodology of this study is qualitative. It is an exploratory development of theoretical ideas grounded in a rereading of literature concerning traditional Chinese science and technology, combined with observations of the formation of the emergent institutional fabric for innovative activities in China. For this purpose, I take a cue from the social epistemology approach to identify the social and political context of key perceptions of knowledge in traditional China. I then trace the significance of these key perceptions for the values and tensions characterizing emerging institutions that provide the socio-political context of innovation in China today. No simple causality is implied, since the process of formation of such institutions is a process of coevolution of changing cultural values, policy-induced principles or regulation, and routines developing in response to changing economic and political conditions.

The point of departure for this study is that the emerging institutional framework for innovation in China can largely be traced to the interaction of the traditional Chinese social epistemology of knowledge and attitudes to innovation on the one hand, and the contemporary influence of policies adopted for science and technology by the Chinese Communist Party on the other hand. The Party's S&T policies have swung from a Soviet-inspired, centrally planned and authoritarian approach to a market based, entrepreneurial approach inspired by the model of capitalist economies; at the same time, it has swung from celebration of eminent scientists and engineers to the anti-intellectual criticism of the Cultural Revolution. Nevertheless, the Chinese leadership has continued to forcefully regulate and direct knowledge creation and innovation, at times with a significant influence from foreign ideologies, in order to achieve its goal of transforming China.

■ Theoretical Background: Social Epistemology and Institutional Change

In the following section, I present a brief discussion of the theoretical approaches that inform my examination of legacies and institutional fabric in China. On the one hand, I am adapting a broadened study of epistemology to a cross-cultural context in order to investigate the position of Chinese traditional perceptions of knowledge claims. The point of departure is the relatively recent ideas related to social epistemology; but this is a contested area of research and for the purposes of this study, I adapt these ideas to come closer to what may be called cultural epistemology. On the other hand, I shall follow an increasing body of scholarship in recognizing the central role of institutions in economic development, and will briefly place my interpretation of the character and usefulness of institutions in the shaping of knowledge and innovation activities.

Social epistemology

The roots of Chinese concepts of knowledge stretch far back into the rich history of Chinese philosophy, and there are indeed many important ways in which the epistemological or metaphysical character of Chinese thinking about knowledge can be analysed (for example, Lenk & Paul, 1993). In a cross-cultural comparison, the distinctiveness of Chinese philosophers' argumentation about "truth" and verification may be examined in terms of linguistic characteristics (Hansen, 1985), or more generally as styles of reasoning that reflected the circumstances in which the investigators operated (Lloyd, 2004).

For the purposes of the present study, however, the issue is not merely whether a different epistemology exists in Chinese thought. Examining variation in knowledge systems this is the main area of concern for a cultural epistemology, and this exercise tends to focus on philosophical, linguistic, or anthropological issues. The key questions under investigation in the present work extend beyond what people see as constituting valid and truthful knowledge and knowing; they enter the territory of social epistemology—namely, the study of how the products of cognitive pursuits are affected by changing the social relations in which the knowledge producers stand to each other (Fuller, 1988).

The term "social epistemology" is itself contested, however. In the words of Goldman (1999), social epistemology focuses on social paths or routes to knowledge, examining the spread of information or misinformation across a group's membership. Goldman's approach helps us see beyond the conventional Kantian epistemological issues of the knowledge pursuit of individuals, and thus considers collective or corporate entities as potential knowing agents. However, he maintains that social epistemology should be veritistic in the sense that it has a normative purpose of evaluating social practices in terms of their respective knowledge consequences, that is, whether they serve to reveal truth. Therefore, his approach is too limited to address the wider questions of how various social or cultural interests can develop a consensus on alternative knowledge claims and epistemic practices. Such questions are far more central in social constructivist or post-modern studies of science, which Goldman dismisses as proponents of "Veriphobia"—the utter repudiation of truth as a viable criterion for studying epistemic phenomena (Goldman, 1999, pp.7-9).

Probably one of the most celebrated postmodern studies of the context of the formation of knowledge was the "archaeology" proposed by Foucault (1972). His archaeological approach outlines a method of analysis of discursive practices that reveals how they give rise to a corpus of knowledge, and how this in turn assumes the status and role of the science. It explores the discursive practices "as a body of anonymous, historical rules, always determined in the time and space that have defined a given period, and for a given social, economic, geographical and linguistic area, the conditions of operation of the enunciative function" (Foucault, 1972, p.131). This leads to the important idea that power and knowledge are mutually generated in the discursive practices, forming a set of rules that defines disciplines of science or social control. The power-knowledge system is thus seen as a ubiquitous framework of government disciplining the population. Ultimately, the idea gave rise to Foucault's later concept of "governmentality", which includes

> the ensemble formed by the institutions, procedures, analyses and reflections, the calculations and tactics that allow the exercise of this very specific albeit complex form of power, which has as its target population, as its principal form of knowledge political economy, and as its essential technical means apparatuses of security (Burchell et al., 1991, p.102).

The key contribution of Foucault's theoretical ideas to a study of knowledge in its social and cultural setting is thus the creation of an awareness of a symbiotic power-knowledge relationship developed in discursive practices. However, the complexity and esoteric character of Foucault's analysis renders it unwieldy and futile as a concrete methodology for the purposes of the present study.

The perspective that appears more useful for my purposes is one that is concerned with the way that knowledge is created and communicated in a society, and how social norms and cultural values influence such activities. Thus there is a need to adopt a theoretical framework that explores the cultural or cross-cultural aspects of social epistemology. In a discussion of practices in Thai culture which prefers continuity to truth in its epistemic dealings, for instance, Hongladarom (2002) argues that recognition of a variety of cross-cultural epistemic practices is desirable. To assume that all cultures aim at truth as the goal of their epistemic practices—as Goldman (1999) does—could result in a homogenization that would render all epistemology monocultural. Hongladarom suggests that it is necessary to acknowledge that some other, pragmatic considerations may get into the picture as the primary goal of justifying beliefs rather than truth. With this argument, the normative stance of western epistemology is called into question and the contingency of both western and eastern epistemic practices become apparent. More importantly, this contingency becomes an area of scholarly concern and empirical research.

The dimensions of social epistemic practices that I shall investigate below include goals, power and utility. The particular purpose of gaining knowledge typically involves a higher level of understanding, which may aim at "finding truth" as well as maintaining cultural or social order. The social context also defines the ways that power is expressed in knowledge, and knowledge contributes to maintaining or upsetting power relationships. Associated with both of the above dimensions is the social definition of the utility of knowledge, that is, what knowledge can—or should—be used for. All three overlapping dimensions contribute to the overall social definition of epistemic practices.

Institutions

It is crucial to recognize that there are several strands of institutional analysis, with different focus (law, property rights, contracts, and so on) and a variety of disciplinary backgrounds (economics, sociology, and so on) that occasionally share little more than the label of institutional theory. Therefore, Nelson (2005, p.151, emphasis in original) argues that "the term institutions in any particular use need to be carefully tailored to the questions under consideration, and to the broad theory being employed to probe at those questions". An analysis of institutions governing knowledge accumulation and innovative activities in China should thus seek an appropriate scope. The perspective adopted in this study is based on a concept of institutions inspired by Douglas North (1990), who included both formal and informal social norms and other constraints imposed by a society's beliefs and values. This perspective seeks to understand the ways in which institutional change provides incentives or constraints for the production and utilization of knowledge. Informal constraints shape the activities of researchers, innovators and entrepreneurs, and thus constitute a culture-specific framework for the generation and exploitation of knowledge. In a society where many transactions are taking place in contexts that are not significantly affected by legislation or regulation, the informal rules help to provide a stable environment for many transactions in the market. At the same time, these informal constraints also influence the behaviour of many actors and provide particular incentives—or disincentives—for such transactions. Informal institutional constraints include long-standing perceptions of the value of technological knowledge and the conditions for its transfer. The social and political support for an intellectual property regime or the protection of trade secrets likewise constitute informal conditions that influence the ability of various actors to exploit technological knowledge as a competitive asset.

On the other hand, formalization of the institutional fabric has been a natural extension of the increased complexity of modern societies. Formal constraints such as political or judicial rules, economic rules, or contracts help to create a reliable environment for principal-agent relationships and thus to regulate economic activities and bring down transaction costs. The formal rules that make up the property rights regime are essential to the operation of a modern economy. North argues

> The formal rules descend from politics to property rights to individual contracts. Contracts will reflect the incentive-disincentive structure imbedded in the property right structure (and the enforcement characteristics); thus the opportunity set of the players and the forms of organization they devise in specific contracts will be derived from the property rights structure (North, 1990, p.52).

However, the existence of formal rules is characteristically only one component of the institutional framework outlined by North. Formal rules are embedded in the structure of enforcement of regulation and rights, which provides a framework for individuals to assess the costs of enforcing contracts.

Moreover, institutions are shaped by the legacies of the past, and may be undergoing either incremental or sudden change. Ge'rald Roland (2004) has argued that it is useful to distinguish between fast-moving and slow-moving institutions. Cultural values typically change slowly, incrementally and continuously, while political institutions can experience rapid, discontinuous change. In China during reform, one finds a similar mix of slow-moving institutions largely shaped by legacies of the past and fast-moving institutions that are linked to the ambitions of leadership as well as the ubiquitous influence of globalization. In other words, institutional change is linked to both historical legacies and contemporary influences; the cultural values that shape the institutions governing knowledge and innovation are not fixed.

It is by recognizing the dynamic nature of institutional change and its embeddedness in social and cultural contexts that are similarly undergoing change that one may arrive at an understanding of the institutional conditions for knowledge-based activities in China today. Thus the institutions that I shall discuss in this study are emerging in the sense that they reflect tensions between values based on traditional legacies and contemporary impacts from policy as well as the rapidly changing social and economic structures in the country.

■ Legacies of Traditional China

The following sections will briefly discuss a number of selected legacies with regard to knowledge and innovation in traditional China. Some aspects will be discussed in explicitly comparative terms through contrasting Chinese and western developments, but most will be explored more descriptively focusing on Chinese perspectives.

Knowledge: utility and legitimacy

Few civilizations have been as explicit and persistent in professed reverence for knowledge as the Chinese traditional culture. Confucius was deeply concerned with the importance of learning in cultivating superior men, and advocated "the silent treasuring up of knowledge; learning without satiety; and instructing others without being wearied" (Legge, 1900, p.78). Acquiring knowledge through the study of classic texts became the accepted route to upward social mobility and political prominence during the Han period, and official examinations providing assessment of candidates with regard to an ever-widening body of knowledge remained a key ingredient in Chinese approaches to government by means of civil service (Elman, 2000). Moreover, new scientific knowledge was generated and discussed among the educated elites and the officials at the Imperial court, and both scientific and technological knowledge were disseminated through extensive networks of printing, particularly with expansion of markets for encyclopedias during the Ming Dynasty (1368–1644). At the time, Chinese literati also sought knowledge from foreign sources, including the Jesuits who brought new mathematical and astronomical theories and methods to China (Elman, 2005).

Yet, the concept of scientific knowledge in China was noticeably different from those that came to dominate in the West. In their comparative study of Chinese and Greek sciences, Lloyd & Sivin (2002) argue that the fundamental concepts concerning the results of systematic investigations in China and in Greece were strikingly dissimilar. The Greeks focused on nature and on elements, seeking to explore what ultimately constitutes material objects and to identify the causes of various phenomena. The Chinese investigators were fundamentally concerned with a different set of concepts such as dao, qi, yin-yang, and the five phases wuxing using these to produce a synthesis of understanding in which heaven, earth, society and the human body all interacted to form a single resonant universe. This conception of a cosmic order had implications for not just astronomical studies of celestial bodies and natural balances in human bodies, but also for social harmony and orderly behaviour of rulers. Such differences in cosmology reflected not only intellectual traditions, but also the pervasive influence of social contexts on the search for—and application of—knowledge. In other words, the social epistemology of ancient Greece and ancient China manifested differences in its focus, investigative approach, perspective on the utility of knowledge, and mode of debate, as briefly summarized in Table 1.

In ancient Greece, the scholars sought knowledge for fame and livelihood as teachers and prominent members of the Greek schools that contended in endless debates for popularity among pupils. Practical application of this knowledge became a secondary concern, as few philosophers had opportunities for influence through employment or patronage at the courts of Greek rulers. In contrast, the accumulation of knowledge for Chinese intellectuals often provided opportunities for employment in administration or as advisers to the ruling elite. Practical application of mathematical astronomy in China aimed at the production of an accurate calendar that would help predict regular occurrences and thus help identify unpredictable events that needed to be interpreted as deviations from cosmic harmony. Other important applications of mathematics appeared in the calculation of taxes, determination of volumes, and surveying. Indeed, Harbsmeier (1993) argues that there was little room in traditional Chinese culture for knowledge for its own sake. For the ancient Chinese it was action that was primary, personal action and political action. Insight was valued in so far as it led to successful action.

Table 1 Contrasting social epistemology in ancient Greece and ancient China

	Ancient Greece	Ancient China
Object of analysis	Focus on nature and elements of nature	Focus on cosmic order and principles of behaviour (dao)
Investigative approach	Exploring material objects and causes of phenomena	Examine heaven, earth, society and human body as a resonant universe
Utility of knowledge	Philosophers sought knowledge for fame and livelihood as teachers	Chinese intellectuals used knowledge as advisers to rulers
Mode of debate	Contending ideas debated	Consensus rather than divergence

The important point that derives from Lloyd and Sivin's analysis is that concepts of the aims of a search for knowledge, and its application, in the Chinese civilization has acquired characteristics which were shaped by the cultural and social context of the early philosophical thinkers and practitioners of science. The production of knowledge was embedded in a social and cultural context that relied on doctrines laid down in prehistoric times and refined for the purpose of government. These Chinese doctrines did not encourage pluralism and deviance—as Greek society had done. Lloyd and Sivin state that

> In a social system that valued civil service above every other career, philosophers who wanted to be politically engaged—or simply respectable—understood the danger of proposing alternatives to the current dispensation of power. Open divergence of view was generally limited to areas that did not threaten the political status quo. Such areas were few and far between, for the government usually treated outsiders with views opposed to any of its policies as disloyal and potentially rebellious (Lloyd & Sivin, 2002, p.245).

An extension of this social epistemology of knowledge is what Munro (1996) has termed the "imperial style of inquiry" in China. This approach to knowledge and inquiry is rooted in totalism: the Confucian belief that there is an ordered structure integrating everything that exists—that the same order runs through both the human and natural spheres. This belief justifies imperial authority by making the emperor responsible for the harmony of all the related parts. It centres on copying antecedent models, whose ultimate legitimacy comes from the emperor. The models ensure that any particular situation under study will be understood in terms of the officially recognized integrated totality (Munro, 1996, p.ix). Munro argues that the totalistic worldview included several strengths, including a stability derived from a mutual sense of obligation and responsibility between ruler and the population, and within a family. The prizing of education was another important strength of the totalistic worldview; education mobilized the principles of social obligation and shared values that fostered a kind of communitarian spirit that helped the literary elite to work together to solve problems of government. It also promoted a self-discipline based on role models that gave precedence to virtuous behaviour based on inner values.

Learning: transmission and exploitation

Knowledge and learning in traditional China tended to be associated with the accumulation, dissemination and refinement of existing knowledge. Indeed, excellence in the assimilation of the classical works of history and philosophy provided vital social status. One of the most powerful notions of social organization in traditional China was the concept of the four classes of people: scholars, farmers, artisans and merchants. These categories, which were seen as all embracing and indicating a descending order of prestige, became popular during the Han dynasty and have since maintained the position of a "Confucian scale of values" (see Bodde, 1991, pp.203-212). The scholars derived their social prestige from the system of examinations that became the point of entry into the administrative structure of the imperial government. In the crucial social transformations that took place during the Han dynasties, this group had replaced a declining nobility and warrior-class, and thus became the scholar-gentry and rural landlords that held ultimate economic and political power throughout most of Chinese imperial history. The Chinese model of generalized training in government was one of the most long-lasting institutions that the world has ever seen. It emphasized the acquisition of knowledge on the nature of moral studies and the organization of society—in particular, knowledge of the ideas transmitted by the classical Confucian works. It thus tended to discourage innovation, and most specialists in scientific or engineering fields who emerged in the course of Chinese history did so either on the basis of their professional duties or as a result of a sideline interest.

According to mainstream Chinese philosophical traditions, knowledge was defined by a cosmic order that ideally maintained harmony and hierarchical structures in human society and nature. Knowledge was derived from an understanding of these harmonies and hierarchies, and was circumscribed by the authority that a legitimate ruler was endowed with.

This conception provided a great impetus for the transmission of knowledge and for a reverence for elite education as the means to acquire and apply knowledge. But it also led to an amplification of the explicit role of power in relation to knowledge. The apex of political power, usually in the person of the emperor, was able to define the legitimacy of knowledge—in terms of what was appropriate and what would be proscribed. Important areas of scientific knowledge, such as astronomy, would thus be susceptible to the scrutiny of political "correctness" by the powers that be. For example, a study of Chinese astronomy shows how the generation and validation of knowledge about the heavens in Han dynasty, China related closely to developments in statecraft and politics (Cullen, 1996). We can recognize a sort of integrated power-knowledge system in Chinese traditional society that is reminiscent of the modern disciplines described by Foucault (1972).

There are various levels of sophistication related to learning capabilities according to the utilization of knowledge from existing sources or from new sources. At the most basic level, learning is the straightforward adoption of new knowledge, providing a skill that enables individuals to carry out predefined operating routines. For individuals this approach to gaining knowledge often takes the form of rote learning; for organizations it might involve copying a procedure from another organization. Simple or even complex routines permeate the direct—perhaps automatic—application of knowledge to a productive task (Nelson & Winter, 1982). In the terminology of March (1991), this level of learning may be characterized as "exploitation" of knowledge. At a more sophisticated level, learning aims at changing routines and generating new knowledge. This involves dynamic routines, or "a capacity to innovate routines". Such learning implies the questioning of the existing body of knowledge, the search for new or recombined knowledge and the extension of frontiers of knowledge. In other words, a more sophisticated strategy for learning will emphasize "exploration".

So far, Chinese approaches to knowledge have been predominantly "exploitative". This does not mean that China was devoid of creativity and inventions. Nevertheless, Munro (1996) argues that the critical weaknesses of the Chinese totalistic worldview and the imperial style of inquiry is its failure to recognize new kinds of knowledge. One problem is that humans and nature are seen as sharing traits such as purposive action towards certain goals, a hierarchy of elements, roles and relationships, and so on, and that such principles are considered innately part of the human mind. This establishes a primacy of mind over matter: the mind is endowed with knowledge of goals, hierarchical ranks and roles in such a way that a clarified mind will be able to restore order in nature and society (Munro, 1996, pp.6-8). The result is a Chinese position on the relationship between mind and matter that contrasts with the idea of a free search for objective truth that became the hallmark of the scientific method developed in the West. Following the approach informed by this attitude creates an emphasis on emulation of models representing intuitive clarity and enlightenment, diverting attention from the details of the current problem.

Knowledge can be embodied in many different forms. The first and foremost is of course people: wise men, teachers, advisers, judges, and so forth all embody knowledge that they can transmit or bring into play in a problem-solving situation. But knowledge is also codified in various media such as texts and pictures, which can further promote its diffusion in society. Chinese inventions such as paper and printing have certainly contributed a great deal to the systematic dissemination of information and knowledge. Finally, knowledge can be embodied in artefacts and equipment, providing another important avenue for its diffusion in society. However, the illustrious achievements of the Chinese civilization in dissemination of information have been shaped by two significant features: on the one hand, throughout much of China's history the rate of literacy in the population reduced the channels for diffusion of knowledge and effectively relegated communication and debate to a relatively small elite; on the other hand, the canonization of knowledge in books served to provide doctrines with a means of glorification that discouraged radical departures from the models of the past.

Innovation: the challenge of creativity

The definition of innovation—the act of introducing something new—implies not only the discovery of new things, but also a certain degree of entrepreneurship in terms of introducing them in society. For this reason, innovation often involves extensive risk and can generate opposition from conservative forces. In his essay on innovation Francis Bacon argued

> As the births of living creatures, at first, are ill-shapen: so are all innovations, which are the births of time. Yet notwithstanding, as those that first bring honour into their family, are commonly more worthy, than most that succeed: so the first precedent (if it is good) is seldom attained by imitation (Bacon, 1985, p.75, italics in original).

In modern times, innovation still proceeds on a dangerous course with many risks, and often involves what Joseph Schumpeter called the gale of creative destruction where

> the new technology, the new source of supply, the new type of organization (the largest-scale unit of control for instance) creates competition which commands a decisive cost or quality advantage and which strikes not at the margins of the profits and the outputs of the existing firms but at their foundations and their very lives (Schumpeter, 1975, p.82).

In other words, innovation almost invariably produces changes in the existing structures of production and economic activities, and often brings about crucial transformation in society. Consequently, there is a tension between the pursuit of innovation and the maintenance of economic structures or social stability.

Attitudes to innovation and creativity can be examined as a philosophical issue, or from a psychological and a cultural angle (Weiner, 2000). However, philosophers in traditional China were ambiguous in their discussion of innovation and creativity (Puett, 2001). On the one hand, the influential thoughts of Confucius and his followers maintained that the key task of rulers and the population as a whole was to uphold—or restore—the virtues of government and social relationships practised by wise kings of the past. That attitude seemed to reflect a strong conservatism, harking back to earlier stages of natural conditions rather than welcoming new creation.

On the other hand, the creation of new political and social structures by creative acts, such as the unification of the Chinese empire under the Qin (221-206 BC) and Han (206 BC-AD 220) dynasties might be accepted in practice. The tension between the innovator as a villain, transgressing or breaking up existing practices, and the innovator as a hero, bringing in a new era of practical order, has been a leading theme in Chinese historiography (Puett, 2001).

The concepts of innovation used in contemporary Chinese debate are usually derived from translations of western words. The preoccupation with "newness" in the West has explicit intellectual roots in the Enlightenment. When new approaches were introduced into Chinese debates, they often encountered overriding priorities of respect for ancient sages and maintenance of social order. In other words, Chinese values emphasized innovation as a form of reinterpretation of the past. For example, Chinese artists would usually fully respect the traditions while striving to establish their own styles (Li, 1997).

China was of course the origin of a number of important new technologies, including the famed three innovations—printing, gunpowder and the magnet—that Francis Bacon identified as extremely significant for the development of modern European societies. In spite of the creation of such important inventions, however, China did not witness an accelerated pace of innovation as part of its economic development. Students of Chinese history and the history of science have therefore been fascinated with what Joseph Needham has called "one of the greatest problems in the history of culture and civilization—namely, the great problem of why modern science and technology developed in Europe and not in Asia" (Needham, 1969, p.154). In a major effort to redress the paucity of historical evidence available in western languages about science and technology in traditional China, Needham set out to identify the various social and intellectual constituents that induced the Chinese civilization to excel in scientific and technological achievements in medieval times (Needham, 1954-2004).

Mark Elvin found evidence of innovative development and diffusion of technology related to agriculture (for example, rotation and combination of crops) and hydraulic systems (mostly water pumps) in late imperial times, but the aim of innovation was primarily effective adaptation to the natural environment or an extension of the range of useful resources (Elvin, 1975). The Chinese in the Ming and Qing dynasties also appreciated labour-saving devices and practices, but this concern appears to have seldom urged Chinese engineers to press forward with mechanization on a sizeable scale. What inhibited the search for principles of mechanization were perhaps, Elvin surmises, the propensity to be overly practical and to divorce the process of innovation from pursuit of imagination, scientific curiosity and experimentation. He quotes a Chinese scholar Cheng Tingzuo, who criticized Europeans for their "excessive ingenuity", implying that there should be a limit to the endeavours to identify the "laws of nature" and the substitution of labour with mechanical devices. It was with the advent of western science and technology after the Opium War that the Chinese were forced to deal with the effects of such "excessive ingenuity".

The political syntax of the traditional Chinese imperial order carried strong connotations of a fixed division of labour between the powerful ruling classes of scholar-officials who were trained in classical administrative philosophies and various actors engaged in the application of technologies for defence, production and commerce. This imperial order left little space for creativity and innovation, even if it remained favourable to the rapid adoption of techniques developed elsewhere. In order to maintain stability and unity in the Chinese empire, the dominant values were intolerant of "creative destruction" and its attendant principles of free competition. The elitist centres of knowledge accumulation were oriented towards transmission of authoritative and legitimate literature with an emphasis on practical aspects of ethical and political principles, and hardly engaged with the popular streams of technological ingenuity that played an important supplementary role in the economy.

■ Emerging Institutional Fabric for Knowledge and Innovation in China

This section will discuss the influence of the legacies on the institutional fabric for innovative activities in China. As mentioned earlier, the relationship between legacies and institutions should not be conceived of as a simple causal link. The legacies are not fixed elements of essential cultural traits, and the institutions are still in a fluid, formative stage. Therefore it is rather preferable to understand the institutional fabric as an evolving complex of more or less formalized values, where tensions between traditional and contemporary influences are played out. The pragmatic concern with the utility of knowledge meshes with the pervasive power-knowledge complex in defining the dimensions along which a "knowledge economy" in China could emerge. A preoccupation with exploitation rather than exploration of new knowledge tends to favour diffusion over invention, and to shape new institutions governing intellectual property rights. Finally, the tensions inherent in creative entrepreneurship tend to shape institutions regulating linkages between innovators and practitioners.

The emerging institutions that are examined here derive their characteristics from both the traditional legacies discussed above and from the pervasive influence of the political and organizational texture created by the Chinese Communist Party during more than five decades of transforming China. To a large extent, the policies and organizational framework for scientific and technological activities in China during these decades were derived from the model pursued in the Soviet Union. The influence of Marxist ideology, as put into practice by the Soviet authorities, has remained very powerful in shaping attitudes to knowledge and innovation. Therefore, the emerging institutions for innovation in contemporary China can be usefully seen as having co-evolved on the basis of both traditional attitudes and contemporary models inspired by foreign approaches and attitudes.

Knowledge vs. power: legitimacy and utility

The first characteristic that emerges is the importance of the confluence of knowledge and power relations, which have placed the search for knowledge in the services of the dominant social forces. This has constrained the scope of "legitimate" knowledge and reduced the pluralism that is a core element of innovation. In contemporary China the dominant forces of course include the political control vested in the leadership of the Chinese Communist Party, but power is also exerted by very strong nationalist values and principles that appear to be shared by the vast majority of the population. Thus there is a overriding sense of utility of knowledge that can serve the interest of China, in the form of, for instance, expanding the knowledge economy or high technology development to provide improved competitiveness to Chinese industries, improve the defence of Chinese sovereignty, or ensure social and political stability and avoid the chaos so dreaded by most Chinese. The institutional urge to ensure utility of knowledge for nationalist priorities can also be witnessed in achievements that seem to have value in terms of prestige rather than economic value, such as the launch of manned space flights.

Nevertheless, new knowledge will always potentially be seen as undermining political power. Control of information and knowledge among the population of China constituted a major concern of imperial government (Kuhn, 1990; Spence, 2001) and remains so today. Even under reform, there exist limitations to the search for new knowledge and explicit political control of the dissemination of information. Thus dissidents in the Chinese scientific community were constrained in their search for knowledge beyond their specialty in natural science, especially when they extended the professional norms of open scientific discourse and academic freedom to challenge political authority with demands for democracy (Miller, 1996).

But contradictions related to knowledge production and utility have also surfaced in concrete cases where those who present alternative and new knowledge, not approved by the powers that be, are ignored or persecuted. In the case of the huge and controversial Three Gorges Dam project at the Yangtze River, both environmental critique and doubts about the actual economic viability of the project were suppressed in the decision-making process leading up to the final approval of the project in 1992. In the case of the SARS pandemic in 2003, the containment or outright suppression of accurate information and knowledge about the origin and extent of the epidemic in China hampered efforts to reduce the spread of SARS both inside and outside the country. It was only through the courageous exposure of truthful information that Dr Jiang Yanyong was able to cut through political repression of vital knowledge and alert both the top Chinese leadership and the rest of the world about the serious situation with SARS infections in Beijing. Although these are extreme examples, they indicate the continued tension between official and alternative knowledge that is caused by the confluence of knowledge and power in China.

Exploitation vs. exploration: invention, imitation and diffusion

Chinese organizations adhere to the pursuit of access to an existing repository of knowledge in order to develop the economy. The application of knowledge already available from various sources has been the most important priority for Chinese organizations, and this priority has persisted to the present. It informs much of the planning and policies for development of science and technology that has been focused on "catching up" with advanced technologies available overseas. This priority thus basically shapes the Chinese approaches to innovation. While this has traditionally served China well in terms of diffusion of existing knowledge, it may reduce the propensity for people to engage in truly innovative activities. In spite of the fact that the Chinese government has created more extensive means of support for basic science such as the National Natural Science Foundation of China, the vast majority of projects in China are applied research. And a very large part of public funding for research and development (R&D) is directed by the overriding priority of emulating scientific and technological achievements of more advanced industrialized countries.

An indicator of the balance between exploration and exploitation can be seen in the proportion of invention and utility model patents filed by domestic applicants for obtaining patent rights in China. Chinese applicants have mostly applied for utility model patents, which have much lower requirements of usefulness, novelty and non-obviousness than invention patents, and are often called "petty patents" since they represent marginally incremental improvement of technology. Invention patents are generally recognized as involving much more creative and novel design, not found in prior art; in this sense they definitely represent explorative efforts. In 2004, for instance, invention patent applications by domestic applicants in China were 25 percent of total domestic applications. In contrast, the vast majority of foreign applications in China are for invention patents.

The predominance of exploitation of existing knowledge sources has also existed in other countries in East Asia. For instance, Kim (1997) shows how Korean organizations have moved from a duplicative imitation stage to a creative imitation stage, with a few firms finally reaching the innovation stage. It is in the innovation stage that a high intensity of effort aimed at generating new knowledge will be achieved, and where learning thus predominantly involves "exploration". Exploration through dynamic routines has been seen as closely associated with innovation (Cohen & Levinthal, 1989). Investments in innovation will facilitate learning via absorption of external sources of knowledge (Cohen & Levinthal, 1990). Increasingly, learning and innovation are seen as part and parcel of a firm's competitive strategies, resulting in dynamic positioning in increasingly competitive markets. Chinese enterprises under the influence of market forces generated by economic reforms are thus becoming extremely conscious of the need to protect strategic knowledge: they clearly want to keep essential knowledge tightly secured. At the same time, few of the leading Chinese firms are keen to occupy the very forefront of research frontiers; indeed, most firms will engage in a variety of linkages with foreign firms or organizations in order to access existing technologies. Even when a research effort is undertaken independently, the precedents of innovations introduced by others usually still define its objectives and scope.

Entrepreneurship and creativity

The innovative process constitutes actions that lead to the successful creation and deployment of new knowledge in a particular social context. In general, the process of technological innovation centres on knowledge transformations, including transformations involving the expansion of knowledge frontiers, the recombination of existing knowledge, or the embodiment of knowledge in machinery or software. Usually the process requires both the creation of knowledge and its effective application in a production process or a product. Nevertheless, it is also important to see creativity and innovation as processes embedded in social and cultural contexts, emphasizing the importance of cognitive, social and motivational influences on creative performance (Amabile, 1996). An overview of Chinese concepts of innovation indicates that some of the crucial aspects of creativity that have been highly appreciated in the West, such as its contribution to "creative destruction", are less strongly emphasized in China. Both creative and innovative activities are constrained by the urge to maintain stability and to protect existing industries.

Entrepreneurship is a vital element of the ambition to integrate research and production, since the fostering of an entrepreneurial spirit and creativity in organizations and the linkage of creative work in innovative networks are key competitive assets. The integration of research and production has formed an overriding concern of policy makers during the attempts to reform China's S&T system in the 1980s and 1990s. The legacy of the institutional characteristics underlying the policies may, however, create serious constraints on the future ability to mobilize domestic resources in the innovation process. Entrepreneurs will often lack an appreciation of the contributions that creative research and development might make to the competitiveness of the business, and it is also evident that a certain apprehension exists on the part of such entrepreneurs regarding cooperation with other firms or research institutes. The result is that the pursuit of R&D tends to become a more insular activity in China, at the same time that knowledge-based firms in industrialized countries are starting to realize the potential value of more open approaches to innovation.

The national innovation system in China has been through a transition from central planning to a market-based system (Liu & White, 2001). The current transitional innovation system in China is characterized by greater involvement of all actors in innovative activities, marking a departure from the strict division of labour associated with the central planning system. This has enabled more actors to play a dynamic role in the innovation process. Still, the authors conclude that some crucial activities such as education and linkages remain very weak, and that the legacies of the earlier phase of central planning continue to reduce the effectiveness of the Chinese innovation system. This has led some Chinese researchers to call for the remodelling of the principal elements of the innovation system, creating a better legal environment for innovation, strengthening horizontal linkages and undertaking a strategic readjustment of research institutes operated by the government departments (for example, Feng, 2000, pp.199-207).

The innovative entrepreneur still tends to be a lonely figure in China, celebrated for achievements that benefit society and key political interests, but also arousing suspicion from powerful incumbents and segments of the population that have vested interests in stability. Creative entrepreneurs challenge established ideas about a hierarchical division of labour in innovation as well as the economy. They tend to be operating in an environment that offers only limited support for the extraordinary effort required to break through conventional norms and launch new ways of doing things. In this sense, innovation in China remains a task of immense significance, but also of arduous persistence.

■ Conclusions

The purpose of the present study has been to sketch the role of knowledge and innovation in traditional Chinese society, and on this basis to draw up a tentative inventory of emerging institutions that shape China's current strategies for scientific and technological development. Space has not allowed for a full-fledged empirical investigation of the potential linkages between tradition and contemporary values. Thus, this exercise remains exploratory; I am outlining characteristics and relationships that I have found significant but cannot prove their significance at present. However, in conclusion I would like to present some theoretical conjectures that I believe arise from the examination presented above. The conjectures discussed below outline the various legacies examined, the evolving institutional fabric which partly arises from the influence of these legacies and the tendencies that I feel reflect the current status of the institutional fabric for knowledge and innovation in China.

One legacy that emerges most clearly from the social epistemology for traditional Chinese knowledge accumulation is the close symbiosis of knowledge and power. This aspect has provided Chinese intellectuals with a concern for the utility and practical value of knowledge that has allowed them to help the ruling power govern China; but has also tied their inquiries to a totalistic conception of the universe that linked human and natural worlds in a way which aimed to ensure stability and consensus—not disruptive or innovative questioning of existing models. In contemporary institutions of knowledge generation and research, this legacy may lead to an exaggerated focus on nationalist priorities in R&D, or in the repression of knowledge that does not accord with the views of the powerful.

Closely associated with the legacy of symbiotic relationship between knowledge and power is the Chinese tradition of learning, which has stressed the transmission, assimilation and refinement of existing knowledge—particularly knowledge imparted by the great masters of the past. This legacy has affected the tension between exploitation and exploration of knowledge in contemporary institutions, which still encourages imitation more than invention. Although such a bias towards rapid diffusion through imitation and incremental improvements can help China during a "catch-up" phase, it may become a problem when the country's organizations move closer to knowledge frontiers and when competition based on intellectual property becomes fierce.

The legacies of traditional China have included an ambivalent attitude to creativity and innovation. In particular, the destructive aspect of innovation, challenging social stability and economic structures, has been regarded in a negative light—even if some of the innovations that were the result of breaking down the old order, such as the governance reforms of the First Emperor of the Qin Dynasty (221-206 BC), were embraced by subsequent rulers. It is perhaps not popular to say that current institutions contain a similar ambivalence to the creative and innovative entrepreneur, especially since a flood of political statements and literature appear to support innovation to the fullest extent. But the predicament of innovators today may still be difficult, swimming as they do in a sea of acidic attitudes towards the new and untried, with precious little effective support from peers, officials, or the population at large.

References

Amabile, T. M. (1996), Creativity in context, Boulder, CO: Westview.

Bacon, F. (1960), The new organon and related writings, *Library of Liberal Arts*, 97, New York: Liberal Arts Press.

Bacon, F. (1985), *Of innovations, the essays or counsels, civil and moral*, Cambridge, MA: Harvard University Press, 75-76.

Bahm, A. J. (1977), *Comparative philosophy: Western, Indian, and Chinese philosophies compared*, Albuquerque, NM: World Books.

Baum, R. (1982), "Science and culture in contemporary China: The roots of retarded modernization", *Asian Survey*, XXII(12), 1166-1186.

Bodde, D. (1991), *Chinese thought, society, and science*, Honolulu, HI: University of Hawaii Press.

Burchell, G., Gordon, C. and Miller, P. (1991), *The foucault effect: Studies in governmentality*, Chicago, IL: The University of Chicago Press.

Cohen, W. M. and Levinthal, D. A. (1989), "Innovation and learning: The two faces of R&D", *The Economic Journal*, 99, 569-596.

Cohen, W. M. and Levinthal, D. A. (1990), "Absorptive capacity: A new perspective on learning and innovation", *Administrative Science Quarterly*, 35, 128-152.

Cullen, C. (1996), *Astronomy and mathematics in ancient China*, Cambridge: Cambridge University Press.

Dahlman, C. J. and Aubert, J. E. (2001), *China and the knowledge economy: Seizing the 21st century*, Washington, DC: The World Bank.

Elman, B. A. (2000), *A cultural history of civil examinations in late imperial China*, Berkeley, CA: University of California Press.

Elman, B. A. (2005), *On their own terms: Science in China*, 1550-1900, Cambridge, MA: Harvard University Press.

Elvin, M. (1975), "Skills and resources in late traditional China", in D. H. Perkins (ed.), *China's Modern Economy in Historical Perspective*, Stanford, CA: Stanford University Press, 85-113.

Feng, Z. (ed.) (2000), *Guojia chuangxin xitong yanjiu gangyao* (A Compendium of Research on the National Innovation System), Jinan: Shandong jiaoyu chubanshe.

Fleming, J. (2003), "Comparative philosophy: Its aims and methods", *Journal of Chinese Philosophy*, 30(2), 259-270.

Foucault, M. (1972), *The archaeology of knowledge*, London and New York: Routledge Classics.

Fuller, S. (1988), *Social epistemology*, Bloomington and Indianapolis, IN: Indiana University Press.

Graham, A.C. (1973), "China, Europe, and the origins of modern science: Needham's the grand titration", in S. Nakayama and N. Sivin (eds.), *Chinese science: Explorations of an ancient tradition*, Cambridge, MA: The MIT Press.

Goldman, A. I. (1999), *Knowledge in a social world*, Oxford: Clarendon Press.

Grewal, B., Xue, L., Sheehan, P. and Sun, F. (2002), *China's future in the knowledge economy: Engaging the new world*, Melbourne and Beijing: Centre for Strategic Economic Studies, Victoria University and Tsinghua University Press.

Hansen, C. (1985), "Chinese language, Chinese philosophy, and 'truth'", *The Journal of Asian Studies*, 44(3), 491-519.

Harbsmeier, C. (1993), "Conceptions of knowledge in ancient China", in H. Lenk and G. Paul (eds.), *Epistemological issues in classical Chinese philosophy*, Albany, NY: State University of New York Press.

Hongladarom, S. (2002), "Cross-cultural epistemic practices", *Social Epistemology*, 16(1), 83-92.

Kim, L. (1997), *Imitation to innovation: The dynamics of Korea's technological learning*, Boston, MA: Harvard Business School Press.

Kuhn, P. A. (1990), *Soulstealers: The Chinese sorcery scare of 1768*, Cambridge, MA: Harvard University Press.

Legge, J. (1900), *The four books*, China: The Commercial Press.

Lenk, H. and Paul, G. (eds.) (1993), *Epistemological issues in classical Chinese philosophy*, Albany, NY: State University of New York Press.

Li, J. (1997), "Creativity in horizontal and vertical domains", *Creativity Research Journal*, 10, 107-132.

Liu, X. and White, S. (2001), "Comparing innovation systems: A framework and application to China's transitional context", *Research Policy*, 20, 1091-1114.

Lloyd, G. E. R. (2004), *Ancient worlds, modern reflections: Philosophical perspectives on Greek and Chinese science and culture*, Oxford: Clarendon Press.

Lloyd, G. and Sivin, N. (2002), *The way and the word: Science and medicine in early China and Greece*, New Haven, CT and London: Yale University Press.

March, J. G. (1991), "Exploration and exploitation in organizational learning", *Organization Science*, 2(1), 71-87.

Miller, H. L. (1996), *Science and dissent in post-mao China: The politics of knowledge*, Seattle, WA and London: University of Washington Press.

Munro, D. J. (1996), *The imperial style of inquiry in twentieth-century China*, Ann Arbor, MI: Centre for Chinese Studies.

Needham, J. (1954-2004), *Science and civilization in China*, Vols. 1-7, Cambridge: Cambridge University Press.

Needham, J. (1969), *The Grand Tritration: Science and society in east and west*, London: George Allen and Unwin.

Nelson, R. R. (2005), *Technology, institutions, and economic growth*, Cambridge, MA: Harvard University Press.

Nelson, R. R. and Winter, S. G. (1982), *An evolutionary theory of economic change*, Cambridge, MA: Belknap Press.

North, D. C. (1990), *Institutions, institutional change, and economic performance*, Cambridge: Cambridge University Press.

Pomeranz, K. (2000), *The great divergence: Europe, China, and the making of the modern world economy*, Princeton, NJ: Princeton University Press.

Puett, M. (2001), *The ambivalence of creation: Debates concerning innovation and artifice in early China*, Stanford, CA: Stanford University Press.

Qian, W. (1985), *The great inertia: Scientific stagnation in traditional China*, London: Croom Helm.

Roland, G. (2004), "Understanding institutional change: Fast-moving and slow-moving institutions", *Studies in Comparative International Development*, 38(4), 109-131.

Schumpeter, J. (1975), *Capitalism, socialism and democracy*, New York: Harper.

Sivin, N. (1984), "Why the scientific revolution did not take place in China—or didn't it?", in E. Mendelsohn (ed.), *Transformation and tradition in the sciences*, New York: Cambridge University Press.

Sivin, N. (1995), *Science in ancient China: Researches and reflections*, Aldershot: Variorum.

Spence, J. (2001), *Treason by the book*, New York: Viking.

Weiner, R. P. (2000), *Creativity & beyond: cultures, values, and change, Albany*, NY: State University of New York Press.

Xinhua News Agency (2006), "Hu outlines strategic tasks for S&T innovation", Xinhua News Agency, available at http://news3. xinhuanet. com/english/2006-01/09/content_4036110. htm. Accessed 24 May 2007.

Zhongguo jishu chuangxin zhengce (Policies on Technology Innovation in China) (2000), Beijing: Kexue jishu wenxian chubanshe.

Index